blues TRAVELING

The Holy Sites of Delta Blues

SECOND EDITION

Steve Cheseborough

University Press of Mississippi
Jackson

www.upress.state.ms.us

Copyright © 2004 by Steve Cheseborough
All rights reserved
Manufactured in the United States of America
"Annie Mae's Café" written by George Jackson and Larry Addison
p 1986 Malaco Music Co. Used by permission. International
copyright secured.
Photographs by author

09 08 07 06 05 04   4 3 2 1
∞
Library of Congress Cataloging-in-Publication Data

Cheseborough, Steve.
    Blues traveling : the holy sites of delta blues /
Steve Cheseborough.—2nd ed.
        p.   cm.
    Includes bibliographical references (p.), discography (p.), and
index.
    ISBN 1-57806-650-6 (pbk. : alk. paper)
    1. Blues (Music)—History and criticism. 2. Blues musicians—
Homes and haunts—Guidebooks. 3. Musical landmarks—
Mississippi—Guidebooks. 4. Musical landmarks—Tennessee—
Memphis—Guidebooks. 5. Musical landmarks—Arkansas—
Helena—Guidebooks. 6. Mississippi—Guidebooks. 7. Memphis
(Tenn.)—Guidebooks. 8. Helena (Ark.)—Guidebooks. I. Title:
Blues traveling. II. Title.

    ML3521 .C53   2004
    781.643'09762—dc22

                                                          2004043023

British Library Cataloging-in-Publication Data available

To my mom

CONTENTS

ACKNOWLEDGMENTS

I thank the friends who accompanied me on some of my blues travels: J. P. Caldwell, Julia Cannon, Susan McClamroch, Katharine Mitchell, Milly Moorhead, Maria Otamendi, Jed Pauker, Butch Ruth, Ashley Tinsley, Ursula Vesala, and Marcia Weaver.

I thank my editor, JoAnne Prichard, for her patience, coolness, and intelligence on this project. I thank David Evans and Melissa McGuire, who gave recommendations and insights.

I thank these people for information, directions, and smiles along the path: Cristen Barnard, Tutwiler; Robert Birdsong, Sr., Robert Birdsong, Jr., James Butler, and John Ruskey, Clarksdale; Brett Bonner, Dick Waterman, and Edward Komara, Rashida Hakeem and the rest of the staff at the University of Mississippi Blues Archive, Oxford; Sam Carr, Lula; Ellis Darby and Bobby Leatherman, Robinsonville; Charlie Doherty and Patty Crosby, Port Gibson; Miss Annie Eggerson, White Station; Barbara Evans, Sardis; Marvin Flemmons, Drew; Joe Garrison and Dr. Joe Stephens, West Point; Morris and Jean Gist, Sonny Payne, and Bubba Sullivan, Helena; Sammy Greer and Aikei Pro, Holly Springs; J. K. Gurner and Jack Gurner, Water Valley; Jimmy

Holmes and Sonny Reedus, Bentonia; Billy Johnson, Leland; Kinney Kimbrough, Chulahoma; Steve LaVere and Pat LeBlanc, Greenwood; Gene Lee, Chellie B. Lewis, and everybody at Malaco Records, Jackson; Cheryl Line, Cleveland; Leo McGee and Eddie Sharkey, Rosedale; Yvette Patacsil, Perry Payton, and Malcolm Walls, Greenville; Little Poochie, Natchez; Sid Selvidge and Howard Stovall, Memphis; Mary Shepard, Indianola; Othar Turner, Gravel Springs.

And I thank all the bluesmen and blueswomen of Mississippi, living and dead, for inspiring and comforting me every day with their beautiful music.

chapter 1

LOOKING FOR THE BLUES

Blues Traveling through History

Perhaps the first "blues traveler" in Mississippi was the Harvard archaeologist Charles Peabody, who dug up an Indian mound near Clarksdale in 1901–1902. He looked up from the ground and took careful note of the local black workers' songs.

As Peabody reported in an article he wrote for a folklore journal, the workers sang almost constantly during the day and as they relaxed in the evening. They sang hymns, ragtime pieces, and (what most interested Peabody) "improvisations in rhythm more or less phrased, sung to an intoning more or less approaching melody." The lyrics of those songs were "'hard luck' tales (very often), love themes, suggestions anticipative and reminiscent of favorite occupations and amusements." If that wasn't the blues, it certainly was close. Among the verses he recorded in his notes are some that have become familiar blues lines:

> They had me arrested for murder
> And I never harmed a man

> The reason I loves my baby so
> 'Cause when she gets five dollars she give me fo'.

Some have not entered the blues lexicon:

> *Old Dan Tucker he got drunk,*
> *Fell in de fire and kicked up a chunk*
>
> *Oh we'll live on pork and kisses*
> *If you'll only be my missus.*

According to Peabody's description, the guitar accompaniment also sounded like the blues—"mostly 'ragtime' with the instrument seldom venturing beyond the inversions of the three chords of a few major and minor keys."

In 1903, W. C. Handy, an Alabama-born, African American band musician who had been touring the country for years, settled in Clarksdale to lead an orchestra of black musicians. Handy's first exposure to the blues happened soon after that, while he was waiting for a long-overdue train in the Tutwiler depot:

A lean, loose-jointed Negro had commenced plunking a guitar beside me while I slept. His clothes were rags; his feet peeped out of his shoes. His face had on it some of the sadness of the ages. As he played, he pressed a knife on the strings in a manner popularized by Hawaiian guitarists who used steel bars. The effect was unforgettable. His song, too, struck me instantly.

Goin' where the Southern cross' the Dog.

The singer repeated the line three times, accompanying himself on the guitar with the weirdest music I had ever heard. The tune stayed in my mind.

It certainly did. A few years later, Handy would publish "The Yellow Dog Rag" (which he would rename "The Yellow Dog Blues"), incorporating that line. And he would become known as the Father of the Blues for pieces like that one and "The St. Louis Blues" and "The Memphis Blues"—songs written in standard notation, arranged for bands, and published nationally as sheet music, based on what Handy heard from anonymous guitar-plunking Mississippians like the man in the train station.

Handy's compositions spurred the first blues craze. The word "blues" became nationally known and identified with the twelve-bar, AAB (sing line, repeat line, answer with rhyming line) format—a format that does not apply, by the way, to much of the very real blues of Charley Patton, Skip James, Fred McDowell,

R. L. Burnside, and dozens of other genuine down-home blues artists, past and present. But even today, if you ask a rock, pop, or jazz musician to play the blues, that standardized format is what you will get.

The next blues craze began in 1920, when bandleader-composer Perry Bradford persuaded the Okeh record company in New York to make the first recording of a black blues singer. That first recorded singer was not a scraggly, self-taught, guitar-toting southern man of the sort Handy had heard in Tutwiler, though. It was Mamie Smith, a well-dressed woman with a professionally trained voice, singing before a full orchestra. Smith's voice is smooth, lacking what we now consider bluesy effects. Still, blacks who were hearing such a sound on records for the first time were thrilled. It was a huge hit. Smith's recording would be followed by those of other sophisticated blueswomen, or "Classic blues" singers, as they are known, eventually including the great, rougher-voiced Ma Rainey and Bessie Smith.

It wasn't until the mid-twenties that the companies would record the kind of person Handy had seen in Tutwiler and whom we still consider the quintessential blues singer: a self-accompanied male singer. Among the earliest were the banjo-playing (and not scruffy at all) Papa Charlie Jackson of New Orleans, the southeastern guitar virtuoso Blind Blake, and the most popular and influential of them all, the Dallas street singer Blind Lemon Jefferson. Jefferson traveled widely, recorded prolifically, and became the first superstar of the country blues. He showed record companies that there was lots of money to be made in recording male, rural, southern, self-accompanied blues singer-guitarists. So the companies combed the South, auditioning everyone of that description they could find and giving the promising ones tickets to recording studios in the North. Soon they hastened the process by sending the recording equipment south and setting up temporary studios in hotel rooms.

They found the richest mine of bluesmen—and a few blueswomen—in or near the flat, fertile cotton lands of the Mississippi Delta: Charley Patton, Son House, Willie Brown, Louise Johnson, Skip James, Tommy Johnson, George "Bullet" Williams, Rubin Lacy, Memphis Minnie, Kansas Joe McCoy, the Mississippi Sheiks, Kid Bailey, Bukka White, Robert Johnson, Mattie Delaney,

Geechie Wiley, Ishmon Bracey, Mississippi John Hurt, William Harris, Eugene "Sonny Boy Nelson" Powell, and many others. These musicians went to Memphis or all the way up to Chicago or Grafton, Wisconsin, to sing and play for a few bucks and the chance to become immortal. As producer Frank Walker said of those sessions: "You might come out with two selections or you might come out with six or eight, but you did it at that time. You said goodbye. They went back home. They had made a phonograph record, and that was the next thing to being president of the United States in their mind."

Commercial country-blues field recording peaked in the late 1920s. By the thirties the record companies, hurt by the Depression, were releasing records only by proven artists, most of whom were southerners transplanted to Chicago, such as Big Bill Broonzy, Memphis Minnie, and Tampa Red. But down in Mississippi, people continued to play the down-home blues in jook joints and on street corners, even if they weren't making it onto record as often.

The blues just might have been born in Mississippi. On the other hand, it might not have. The first blues may have been played somewhere else in the rural South. There are early reports of blues in east Texas, Alabama, Louisiana, and even Missouri.

What is clear is that the blues, since its beginnings, has always found a home here. Mississippians have always made up a large proportion of all blues singers and an overwhelming proportion of the finest blues singers. That includes the whole Chicago blues scene from the 1930s to the present—nearly all its stars have been Mississippi-born. And that is true of both the prewar acoustic period and the later electric period, when Mississippians like Muddy Waters, Elmore James, B. B. King, and Little Milton set the standard.

Mississippi was more rural and agricultural, with a greater concentration of cotton planting, than other states. And it had a large, poor, strictly segregated black population, which was overwhelmingly rural and working in agriculture. In other words, Mississippi has long been more southern than the rest of the South, and that goes double for the Mississippi Delta, which has been dubbed "the most southern place on earth." So the conditions that fostered the blues throughout the South were intensified in Mississippi, especially in the Delta.

When people speak of the delta of a river, they usually mean the area where it washes into the sea or a lake. But the Mississippi Delta is hundreds of miles upstream, in northwest Mississippi (it has a mirror image in northeast Arkansas, but "the Delta" usually refers just to the Mississippi side, and that's how we'll use it here). It's a flat, leaf-shaped expanse of seven thousand square miles, with the Mississippi and Yazoo rivers on its curved sides and Memphis and Vicksburg at its tips.

Thousands of years of Mississippi River floods left the Delta with a thick, dark layer of fertile topsoil. In its natural state, the Delta was a jungly place full of swamps, large trees, vines, and animals. Nineteenth-century settlers quickly perceived its economic value, however. The area was cleared, and it became first a huge lumber camp and then a huge cotton plantation. Both the lumber and the cotton operations were labor intensive, as was the building of levees to protect the settlers and their farms from the regular, gargantuan floods. So tens of thousands of blacks were brought in to work the Delta—first as slaves and later as levee gangs, sharecroppers, tenant farmers, or transient day laborers from the hill country.

Today, the Delta is a sparsely populated, generally quiet place. But back in the twenties and thirties, before the mechanization of agriculture, its fields and now-sleepy towns were alive with people. The crowds and the money attracted musicians (many Delta blues artists were actually born in the hills) who interacted, competed, and innovated. As ethnomusicologist David Evans has explained, the Delta, despite its rural nature, functioned like an urban area, pulling in people from widespread places with diverse musical traditions. In this environment, the famed Delta blues developed.

Outside the Delta, Mississippians also played the blues. The North Mississippi hill country is home to a droning, hypnotic variety of blues exemplified by Mississippi Fred McDowell, Junior Kimbrough, and R. L. Burnside, among others, as well as to related traditions including African American fife-and-drum bands. The state capital, Jackson, has long been an important recording center, with plenty of live music as well. There and in nearby towns, Bo Carter, the Mississippi Sheiks, and others practiced their smoother blues styles. Bentonia is the birthplace of Skip James and Jack Owens, two artists with styles so similar to each other's yet distinctive from anyone else's that some scholars consider the town a unique blues "school." Jimmie Rodgers, the white singing brakeman whose yodeling versions of black blues songs were the start of country music, came from Meridian, in east-central Mississippi. And Memphis, Tennessee, has always attracted Mississippians, among them musicians who played on Beale Street and heavily influenced that city's sounds.

Mississippi blues reemerged as a national phenomenon in the 1940s, after the young Mississippian Muddy Waters caught the train north, bringing his slide-guitar-driven music style with him. His collaborators and competitors who also made the trip included fellow Mississippians Howlin' Wolf, John Lee Hooker, Jimmy Rogers, Big Walter Horton, Elmore James, Jimmy Reed, and Otis Spann.

The image of Muddy Waters leaving Mississippi and taking the blues with him is a powerful one, but it is not quite true. For one thing, when he arrived in Chicago, the blues was already there—although he did usher in a harder, electric version of it. And, for another thing, Mississippians didn't stop singing the blues after Muddy left.

Popular attention focused again on Mississippi blues—not just on its Chicago outpost—in the folk and blues revival of the 1960s. Young white northerners went south to scout out the old blues records of the twenties and thirties and, in some cases, the old people who had made them. Son House, Skip James, and Mississippi John Hurt were among those found alive and well enough to enjoy new performing and recording careers late in life.

That blues boom faded out soon enough. But there would be yet another in the nineties, kicked off by the rerelease of Robert Johnson's complete output as a double-CD box set that turned out to be a smash hit. That set was the first, and is still the only, million-seller by an original country-blues artist. A few years later, the Robert Mugge film *Deep Blues* showed that there still were down-home Mississippi blues artists in real life, not just on old records. Other fairly recent developments include *Living Blues* magazine moving its offices from Chicago to Oxford; Rooster Blues and Fat Possum record companies opening in Clarksdale and Oxford, respectively, to record a new generation of the state's bluesmen; several major Mississippi blues festivals beginning or picking up steam; and blues museums opening in Clarksdale and Robinsonville. Finally, Mississippi blues was enjoying a renaissance that extended even into Mississippi.

But that doesn't mean the Mississippi blues is the *same* as it was in 1929—or 1969. For one thing, you just don't hear much of the complex, solo, acoustic-guitar style that characterized Mississippi blues of the prewar period, except maybe in the hands of a young revivalist in Memphis or Oxford. But then you might hear such a revivalist in Seattle or New York, too. Don't expect to hear a Charley Patton, Robert Johnson, or Memphis Minnie playing on a corner or in a jook joint in Mississippi.

Yes, blues in Mississippi, as elsewhere, generally means electric blues. But even electric blues, sadly, is not easy to find. The best way to get your fill of live music is to schedule your visit around a blues festival. Besides the music at the festival, many local clubs, which otherwise use jukeboxes or deejays, will schedule live performances. When it's not festival time, look for live blues at clubs in the bigger towns and at concerts. Many of the old country jooks have closed or converted to recorded music only.

The physical remains of the old-time blues, such as ever existed at all, also are precarious things. Blues singers were mostly rambling sorts who didn't leave behind much in the way of estates, memoirs, letters, or other personal papers or belongings. They left their music, fortunately, and some sketchy details of the particulars of their lives. So you might not find the house where your favorite blues artist grew up or the joint where he first played your favorite song.

On the other hand, looking at things in a different way, there is much to see. The blues world hasn't changed as rapidly as the rest of the country—in fact, in many ways it hasn't changed a whole lot in the hundred years since the blues began. There are still cottonfields, shacks, and barbecue spots. There are courthouses and jails where defendants—many of them poor and black—receive some kind of justice. There are the roads, narrow, twisting, dark, and poorly marked, leading through fields, woods, and more fields, past cotton gins and over creeks. There are trains. And there is always the river—the Big River, the continent's Main Drain, with its boats, birds, fish, fishermen, levees, and bridges, its precious silt, its threat of flood.

There are old storefronts and depots, in front of which the crowds gathered on Saturday afternoons to listen to Charley Patton, Robert Johnson, or another of the hundreds of blues singers, most of them unrecorded and now unknown, who sang their hearts out as they passed through. And there are places where people still laugh, dance, drink, and listen to the blues.

This book will help you find what *is* left in the Mississippi blues world. And it will help you remember and visualize what is gone and to pick up clues from the songs, the landscape, and literature. Let's go.

Planning Your Blues Tour

Unfortunately, the days of local train service to little Mississippi towns are long past. You will need an automobile to get to most of the places in this book.

Chapters 2 through 10 form a rough circle beginning and ending in Memphis. So if you want to see it all, just follow the chapters in numerical order (or reverse numerical order).

If you are flying in from out of state to see Mississippi blues sites, you probably will arrive in Memphis, where you can rent a car and begin the tour. Note that Memphis—*not* New Orleans—is the most convenient major city from which to begin a Mississippi blues tour. The Mississippi Delta and most other areas of interest to blues lovers are in the *northern* half of Mississippi.

But if you happen to be in New Orleans and want to tour Mississippi blues sites, that's okay, too. Just be sure to figure in the extra driving time of about three hours from New Orleans to Jackson, where you would begin this tour (or you could take the train to Jackson and rent a car there). Start with chapter 8 and then follow the circle in either direction, looping from 10 back to 2 or vice versa. Other starting points work just as well. Jackson has an international airport, and there are regional airports in Tupelo, Greenville, and Meridian.

Of course, you don't have to do the whole tour. The places described in this book are close enough to one another that you can get from any spot to any other in four hours or less (in many cases, much less). So you might want to read through the book before starting your trip, and draw your own route. Whatever you choose—take your time, keep your patience and sense of humor handy, and have fun!

TRAINS

There is still one passenger line that might be of interest to blues travelers: Amtrak's City of New Orleans. It runs daily from New Orleans, with stops in Hammond, Louisiana, McComb, Brookhaven, Hazlehurst, Jackson, Yazoo City, and Greenwood in Mississippi, and then Memphis. It continues north to Chicago. Call Amtrak (800-USA-RAIL) for schedules, reservations, and more information.

Sonny Boy Williamson II and Willie Love rode the line from Jackson to New Orleans in April 1953, on their way to Houston for a recording session. On the train, the bluesmen danced, sang, and told jokes to the other passengers. When they got to Houston, one of the songs they recorded was Sonny Boy's "City of New Orleans" (different from the 1970s pop tune by Steve Goodman):

> *I heard the City of New Orleans gonna run today*
> *I got to find my baby before she get too far away.*

Bukka White's 1940 "Special Streamline" also celebrates this train line, re-creating the sounds and feelings of riding it out of Memphis, headed for New Orleans.

Amtrak gives passengers a good dose of New Orleans culture on the trip, with a jazz band playing in the lounge car and Cajun-inspired cooking in the dining car. The company has not yet offered live blues (or barbecue and moonshine) while the train passes through Mississippi, however.

Amtrak also plans to take over the Kansas City Southern as a passenger line. That train runs between Shreveport, Louisiana, and Meridian, Mississippi.

Guidelines for Good Times

Traveling the back roads of Mississippi, you might sometimes feel you've wandered into a foreign country or a different era. Here are some guidelines to help you get along and stay out of trouble.

FEELING THE RHYTHM

If Mr. Turner doesn't feel like playing right now, or if the goat is sold out, or the deejay won't play the kind of music you were expecting—relax or come back tomorrow or next year. And if you want to shoot pictures or video, ask permission and don't block others' views or dance-floor space.

This may be your dream vacation—perhaps you have planned and saved for years, and traveled many miles. But to the local people next to you, it may be a hard-earned night of fun before they head back to work in the morning. So don't expect them to defer to you or entertain you or pose for your picture.

Don't show up with the insulting attitude that this food and drink may be good enough for the locals, but not for you. Even if you eat steamed grains and organic vegetables at home, consider trying the barbecue if that's what's served—or at least don't turn your nose up at it. And even if you drink microbrews back home, have a regular old American mainstream beer. And enjoy it. You can resume your diet and your highfalutin tastes after your visit.

SITTING IN

If you are a decent blues musician and currently in practice, feel free to sit in at a jook joint or club performance. But if you haven't touched a guitar in twenty years, have never sung outside the shower, or have had way too much to drink, then resist the urge. And if you do sit in, remember that the idea is not to show off your flashy licks, but to keep the groove going and the people dancing. After one song, leave the bandstand unless the musicians and the crowd ask you to stay for another.

PHOTOGRAPHY AND RECORDING

Mississippi's stark natural beauty, the endless cottonfields, the colorfully decorated buildings, and the emotion-laden faces of blues musicians all appeal immensely to photographers of any level. But before you whip out your disposable sure-shot or your three-thousand-dollar Nikon, exercise some courtesy. Ask people for permission to photograph them or their businesses, homes, or children. It wouldn't hurt to just hang out for a while first, chatting, before you ask. If they say no, accept that answer. If they ask for money, don't get offended. Just pay up or put away the camera.

The situation is different at festivals and other public performances. There, you may freely shoot pictures of the performers, as long as you have the management's tacit or explicit permission. But at such events, make sure to be courteous to your fellow audience members. Just because you have a camera—no matter how big the lens is and even if you are shooting for a publication—it doesn't mean you have the right to push in front of other people, block their view, or disturb them by using a flash.

Overall, unless photography is your life, you'll find you enjoy the trip more when you pay attention to what's going on rather than to whether you're missing a photo opportunity. Plenty of books with fine photographs of blues musicians and Mississippi scenes are available.

These guidelines also apply to audio and video recording.

ACCOMMODATIONS

A rural, sparsely populated state, Mississippi has fewer hotels and motels than one would expect. A wide range of accommodations can be found in Memphis and in Jackson. You are also sure to find several of the usual motel chains, and perhaps an independent operator or two, represented in large towns (called "cities" here) such as Tupelo, Oxford, Clarksdale, Greenville, Vicksburg, Natchez, and Meridian. But even in those places, a room can be hard to come by if there is a big event going on—a blues festival or a college football game, for example. To be safe, make advance reservations. If you hope to stay in a smaller community, check ahead of time to find out if anything is available. Another option is the large casino hotels along the Mississippi River and on the Gulf Coast.

FOOD AND DRINK

Moonshine—"That's the soul of the blues," one musician says of moonshine. Generally called "corn liquor," "corn whiskey," or simply "corn," homemade spirits are fairly common in rural areas of Mississippi. At a jook joint, private party, or anywhere else, you might see people drinking a clear liquid out of pint bottles that once held factory-made booze—or, in situations where less discretion is necessary, out of a large jar.

Make no mistake, however—even if you're someplace where it seems to be openly tolerated, moonshine is illegal here, as it is everywhere else in the United States. As with other illegal drugs, one doesn't know the strength or quality of homemade corn. It varies by maker and by batch. Some folks say moonshine wreaks a nastier hangover than the legal stuff. Connoisseurs say precisely the opposite, however. They also prefer the taste of corn liquor to that of storebought—besides appreciating the fact that it is generally cheaper. No matter what you're drinking, use your own best judgment, and let someone else drive. As the Mississippi Sheiks sang in "Bootlegger Blues":

> *Bag of whiskey on my back and the sheriffs is on my track*
> *I'm going to make it to the woods if I can*
> *If you can, if you can*
> *You better make it to the woods if you can.*

Barbecue—If corn whiskey is the soul of the blues, barbecue is the heart. Slow-cooked pig meat has been a sacrament at blues performances at least since the days of Charley Patton, who reportedly used to ask for the most fat-laden pieces, which would insulate him against getting drunk. The tradition continues at blues festivals today, where the only problem is deciding among the fragrant smoke-filled booths. Outside of festivals, barbecue is usually better at barbecue joints than at sit-down restaurants. Ask around—or sniff around—for a good one.

If you're lucky, you might find a restaurant or stand serving such downhome delicacies as chitterlings (always pronounced and sometimes spelled "chitlins"), pig ears, or hog maws. All are delicious, especially with a big splash of hot sauce.

Fish—Fried fish is another food with a long connection to blues performances. "When the fish scent fill the air, we'll have snuff juice everywhere. We gon' pitch a wang wang doodle all night long," is how blues songwriter Willie Dixon put it. In recent decades, catfish has become one of Mississippi's prime agricultural products (the fish are raised in ponds) besides remaining a favorite dish. While it turns up in pâtés and other newfangled recipes these days, it's still impossible to beat a plate of plain old fried catfish with hushpuppies, fries, and coleslaw.

When "buffalo" appears on a menu, it does not refer to the meat of the big mammal or to a style of chicken wings but to a locally popular fish. Buffalo is fried like catfish but has a more delicate texture, stronger flavor, and bigger bones. Buffalo was a favorite fish in black communities through the 1950s. "People didn't like catfish then like they do now," says Greenville food writer Kathy Starr. Tony Hollins, who recorded "Fishin' Blues" in 1952, would probably agree:

> I'm goin' to get my hooks in the mornin', boys, I'm goin'
>   down on the bayou
> Lord, if I don't catch me a buffalo, I do hope I catch a trout.

Two festivals celebrating catfish and buffalofish are held on the same day in Belzoni.

Tamales—Hot tamales originated in Mexico but are also standard fare among blacks in the Mississippi Delta, and have been at least since the 1930s, when Robert Johnson sang "They're Red Hot" in celebration of this morsel, which were sold at "two for a nickel, four for a dime." The price has gone up since then, but they are still an inexpensive and tasty snack. Delta tamales are about the size of a cigar, much skinnier than the ones you may be familiar with in California or the Southwest. And the vegetarian varieties that have caught on in those places are unknown here.

Plate Lunches—Downhome eateries in Mississippi, as elsewhere in the South, usually offer a "plate lunch" or "meat plus two" in which you get the meat of the day and two choices from a list of vegetables; among these can be such southern specialties as collard greens, fried okra, and several types of peas and beans. A beverage, rolls or cornbread, and sometimes dessert are included. A vegetable plate, with three or four vegetables and without the meat entrée, is an option even if it's not listed on the menu. But strict vegetarians be warned: the vegetables often are cooked with hunks of meat for flavoring. If you order iced tea you'll be asked, "Sweet or unsweet?" Sweet tea, in which the sugar is added while the tea is still hot, so that it dissolves better, is a regional delicacy.

If you don't see a restaurant around—or even if you do—you can often find some excellent eating at the gas station/general stores along the state's two-lane highways. Where you live, food at such places might mean premade sandwiches or microwaveable fare. But in the South, good homecooked food is frequently available at these roadside stops (although not always, by any means). Fried chicken, fried catfish, barbecue, and smoked turkey legs may await you when you stop for gas. Vegetable side dishes might be offered as well. And there probably is a table where you can sit if you don't want to take it to go.

Legal Booze—Liquor laws are left up to individual counties. Some counties are dry, but, fortunately for thirsty blues fans, the Delta and the north Mississippi counties of most interest to them are wet. Some wet counties do not allow the sale of alcohol on Sundays, and a few do not allow the sale of cold beer in stores anytime. In wet counties, beer is available in supermarkets and convenience stores and wine and liquor in "package stores," which are usually small and inconspicuous. The microbrew craze that has swept the country in the past decade has pretty much bypassed Mississippi so far. It can be difficult to find anything but the mainstream brands in stores and bars.

CHURCH MUSIC

Most blues singers received early vocal training in church, and many return to church music toward the end of their lives. Some flip-flop back and forth between blues and gospel throughout their lives, believing that one must choose between the two styles, while others reconcile the two and even throw a church song into their blues performances.

The days of the bluesy, solo singing evangelists are over, however. You won't walk into a little church in Mississippi and hear singing accompanied by slide guitar à la Fred McDowell or Blind Willie Johnson (or, if you do, please notify this author immediately).

On the other hand, you still can hear a lot of powerful, soulful church singing with roots in old-time gospel and connections to the blues. Recommendations of individual churches are outside the scope of this book, but your best bets for such music are Missionary Baptist (look for "M. B." in the name) or Church of God In Christ (COGIC) churches. Services usually start at 10 A.M. Sunday, and often last two or three hours. If you go, dress nicely (no shorts or T-shirts, please) and donate generously when the plate is passed.

Another way to hear gospel music is at a gospel concert. These feature a succession of acts, mostly local but usually with one headliner from out of town, and have less preaching than church services. Still, the idea is to glorify the Lord, not just to dig on the music, so, again, dress and act respectfully. Look for posters advertising these concerts, ask at churches or record stores, or listen to gospel radio programs on Sundays.

The three major Delta blues festivals all include gospel performances. At the Mississippi Delta and King Biscuit festivals, gospel stages run concurrently with the blues events. At the Sunflower festival, the gospel singers take over on Sunday, after the blues performances on Friday and Saturday.

CASINOS

The state legislature legalized casino gambling in 1990, and old-fashioned, Bible Belt Mississippi quickly became the nation's third-biggest gambling mecca, after Las Vegas and Atlantic City. So as not to pollute the land with their evil enterprise, the casinos must be floating on water, or right next to it. There is a concentration of casinos on the Mississippi River near Tunica, capitalizing on the Memphis market. Another flotilla is around Biloxi on the Gulf of Mexico, attracting gamblers from New Orleans and those who fly in from other parts of the country. The cities of Greenville, Vicksburg, and Natchez also have river casinos, presumably to service their own citizens.

The casinos have had an immediate negative effect on the blues world: they took business away from jook joints, forcing nearby jooks to close or eliminate live music. People who used to pay a cover and then buy drinks in a jook now spend their entertainment dollars gambling at the casino, while drinking on the house and maybe listening to some music in the lounge.

The downhome acts that used to play the jooks are generally not the sort deemed suitable for the slick world of the casino lounges. On the other hand, some casinos present big-name soul-blues acts in concert in their theaters. Dorothy Moore, Bobby Rush, Little Milton, and Denise LaSalle are among the many artists who headline casino shows. Call the casinos for schedules or check the listings in the Memphis (for the Tunica area), Greenville, Vicksburg, Gulfport, or Biloxi newspapers.

One casino—the Horseshoe, near Robinsonville—has named its theater "Bluesville" and installed a blues museum. Curiously, Bluesville's music programming tends to be less blues-oriented than that of the other casinos.

Jook Joints

These places (sometimes spelled "juke joints") are not named after the jukeboxes found in them—rather, it's the other way around. Decades ago, Paul Oliver described jooks as "unappealing, decrepit, crumbling shacks, which never seem to have been built yesterday, but always thirty or forty years ago, and unpainted since."

Many of those shacks have crumbled since, and have not been replaced; others are in the process of falling down, and have still not been painted. The problem for today's blues travelers is that most of the remaining jook joints actually have become jukebox joints, without live music. The jukeboxes are likely to have blues on them, though, and you might get a feel for the kinds of places where Elmore James or Robert Johnson used to play. In many Delta towns, the black section—usually across the railroad tracks from downtown—is likely to have a place called a "cafe," or per-haps a building with no name at all but displaying a beer sign, where people are hanging out in front. Inside, people sit and drink and talk to their friends. Try Nelson Street in Greenville, South Third Street in Leland, or Church Street in Indianola, for example. The few jooks that regularly feature live music are included in this book, under the names of their communities. But ask around. (Note, however, that the term "jook joint" is not universal and may even have a negative, "country" connotation in cities and large towns. Just ask about "clubs" or where you might hear some blues.) Places open and close abruptly. You might find one we missed or one that just happens to have live music the weekend you're in town (and the one that usually has live music might not have it while you're there).

DANGER?

Walking into any bar where you are a stranger can be unnerving. And the apprehension can be magnified when you're far from home and don't dress or talk like the other people there, who all seem to know each other.

Don't, however, mistake your own discomfort for real danger. Chances are, the regulars at any Mississippi jook joint or nightclub will welcome you warmly, and you'll have many new friends by the end of the night. In any poor neighborhood, don't flaunt your cash, jewelry, camera, or other valuables—especially while you're outside the club. Inside, just be nice to everyone, especially the owner, and you'll have a great time.

Some visitors to the South have a fear of the police, worrying that they will be harassed, beaten, or jailed on a trumped-up charge. In reality, the worst problem you are likely to have with law enforcement is getting a speeding ticket—some towns and counties seem to love handing those out. Highway checkpoints for drunk drivers are also common, especially after college football games. So be careful, and mind the laws. If you really are speeding or driving drunk, and an officer cites you, that isn't harassment.

CONCLUSION

Your briefing on history and local customs is finished. With a car and this guidebook, you're ready to hit the highway!

Memphis & Beale Street

1. Beale Street & Walk of Fame
2. Center for Southern Folklore, Pembroke Square at Peabody Place, 119 S. Main Street
3. Graceland, 3734 Elvis Presley Boulevard
4. Stax Museum, 926 E. McLemore Avenue
5. Memphis Minnie's final residence, 1355 Adelaide Street
6. Furry Lewis's grave – Hollywood Cemetery, 2012 Hernando Road
7. Memphis Rock 'n' Soul Museum, 145 Lt. George W. Lee Avenue, in the Gibson Guitar Building
8. WDIA Radio Station, 112 Union Street
9. Sun Studio, 706 Union Avenue
10. Wild Bill's Lounge, 1580 Vollintine Avenue (at Avalon Street)
11. Albert King's grave – Paradise Gardens Cemetery

A. Blues City Cafe, 138 Beale Street
B. B. B. King's, 143 Beale Street
C. Black Diamond, 153 Beale Street
D. King's Palace Cafe, 162 Beale Street
E. A. Schwab, 163 Beale Street
F. Rum Boogie Cafe, 182 Beale Street
G. Former site of Mitchell's, Club Handy, and the Center for Southern Folklore, 209 Beale Street
H. Hard Rock Cafe (includes Pee Wee's site), 317 Beale Street
I. Palace Theater Lot, 326 Beale Street, just west of Legends Rhythm and Blues Club
J. Old Daisy Theater, 329 Beale Street
K. Monarch Club, 340 Beale Street
L. W. C. Handy Home, 352 Beale Street
M. Center for Southern Folklore – Pembroke Square at Peabody Place, 119 S. Main Street
N. Memphis Rock 'n' Soul Museum, 145 Lt. George W. Lee Avenue, in the Gibson Guitar Building
O. WDIA, 112 Union Street
Sun Studio, 706 Union Avenue (see Memphis area map)

chapter 2

MEMPHIS

The railroads, the highways, and the river all lead to Memphis—and bring the people and the music. Although it is in Tennessee, Memphis functions as the cultural and economic capital of North Mississippi.

Memphis has long been one of America's great music cities, where the blues, rock 'n' roll and soul all were nurtured, although it has never managed to polish up its music heritage and turn it into a major industry, the way Nashville has done with country-western.

Beale Street

To get there: From Memphis International Airport, follow the signs onto I-240 west, toward downtown. After 2 miles, switch to I-55 north and take that for 6 miles to Riverside Drive. Continue north on Riverside for about 1 1/4 miles, until you see the Beale Street sign. Turn right onto Beale and park wherever you can on or near the street.

For almost a century, Memphis's Beale Street was the focal point not only of the Mississippi Delta but of black America, eclipsing even Harlem in its crowds, excitement, and music. It left quite an impression on visitors:

You could used to walk down the street in days of 1900 and like that and you could find a man wit' throat cut from y'ear to ear. Also you could find people lyin' dead wit' not their throat cut, money took and everything in their pockets, took out of their pockets and thrown outside the house. Sometimes you find them with no clothes on and such as that. Sometimes you find them throwed out of winders and so forth, here on Beale Street. Sportin' class o' women runnin' up and down the street all night long.
—Will Shade, leader of the Memphis Jug Band

To me Beale Street was the most famous place in the South . . . and it was so much more than I had even envisioned. I don't know if I can explain it to this day—my eyes had to be very big, because I saw everything, from winos to people dressed up fit to kill, young, old, city slickers and people straight out of the cotton fields, somehow or other you could tell: *every damn one of them was glad to be there.*
—Sun Records producer Sam Phillips, who arrived from Alabama in 1945

Beale Street was the black man's haven. When you went to Beale Street and if you had problems or troubles or something away from there, once you got to Beale Street—no problem, no trouble. I told a white fellow once, "If you were black for one Saturday night and on Beale Street, never would you want to be white again."
—Deejay/performer Rufus Thomas

I didn't think of *Memphis* as Memphis. I thought of Beale Street as Memphis.
—B. B. King

A river port surrounded by vast agricultural lands, and the only real city between St. Louis and New Orleans, Memphis was the place to go for a good time. And Beale Street, just off the docks, was the specific destination.

It became the hub of black life for the entire region. And the crowds and the wide-open atmosphere attracted musicians of every stripe. In the late 1920s and early 1930s, Beale Street became home for blues singer-guitarists, mostly from North Mississippi and often in duos: Frank Stokes and Dan Sain, Memphis Minnie and Kansas Joe (who despite their nicknames were both Mississippians), Garfield Akers and Joe Callicott, along with solo acts Jim Jackson, Robert Wilkins, and Furry Lewis. All played on the street, in the park, at parties for whites who would venture onto Beale, on the touring medicine shows that would recruit there, and perhaps in the clubs occasionally, although the club gigs mostly went to pianists and jazz combos.

Jim Jackson's "Kansas City Blues," one of the biggest blues hits of the 1920s, is, despite its title, about Beale Street:

> *I's first on Main Street, started down Beale*
> *I's looking for that woman they call Lucille*

Jug bands also flourished on Beale. These groups, including the Memphis Jug Band, Cannon's Jug Stompers, and Jack Kelly and his South Memphis Jug Band, played the blues as well as waltzes, popular tunes, political jingles, or whatever was required.

The Depression and Boss Crump's reform movement chilled Beale's spirits in the 1930s. In the forties and fifties it sprung back, however, with the new styles of blues and jazz. WDIA had begun its history-making broadcasts of black music with black announcers, and the street swayed to the sounds of Rufus Thomas, Gatemouth Moore, B. B. King, and others.

In the 1960s, Beale hit another lull. Most of its businesses closed, except for a few pool halls and pawnshops. "Urban renewal" came in, demolishing many buildings on Beale and hundreds in the neighborhoods around it. Although Beale Street became a National Historic Area in 1966, it had ceased to exist as a community.

"There isn't much left to Beale Street now," blues writer Samuel Charters sadly observes in the opening line of his 1977 book *Sweet as the Showers of Rain*. Charters had appreciated the street's "looseness—its lack of fuss and pretense. It was a wide-open neighborhood with a lot of music in the clubs or on the street itself, a lot of casual drinking, and a lot of sex that didn't cost much money." He had no idea that it would again become home to blues-filled bars, nightclubs, and outdoor festivals.

Clubs began reopening on the street in 1982, although some of the original buildings are gone and others have been refurbished beyond recognition. The opening of B. B. King's club in 1991 helped make Beale a tourist destination.

The sad thing about Beale these days is that the neighborhoods around it have been torn down. It sits there, all lit up, surrounded by parking lots, office buildings, and construction sites. Still, there is some good music on Beale, especially during special events when stages are set up in the park and on the street, and usually in the clubs on any weekend.

- **B. B. King's**
  143 Beale St.
  (901) 524-5464

The name "B. B. King"—the name most identified with the blues—boosts the reputation and popularity of this club and, by extension, all of Beale Street. Strategically located, neon-bedecked, with outdoor speakers blaring the blues and its own gift shop next door, the club, which opened May 3, 1991, lets you know, loud and clear, that you're on Beale Street, land of the blues.

Don't walk in expecting to see B. B., though—he plays there only a few times a year, and those high-ticket shows generally sell out early. There is live music nightly, however, from Preston Shannon or another high-energy local blues act.

- **Other Clubs**

Other places that regularly present blues include the **Black Diamond**, 153 Beale St. (901-521-0800), the **Blues City Cafe**, 138 Beale St. (901-526-3637), and the **Rum Boogie Cafe**, 182 Beale St. (901-528-0150), which has part of the original Stax neon sign inside, as well as guitars signed by Son Seals, Ike Turner, Stevie Ray Vaughan, and many others.

- **King's Palace Cafe**
  162 Beale St.
  (901) 521-1851

The upstairs of this building once housed Hooks Brothers, a black-owned photography studio where Robert Johnson is believed to have posed for the 1935 pinstripe-suit photo that was on the cover of his 1990 *The Complete Recordings* boxed set—one of only two known photos of Johnson.

- **A. Schwab**
  163 Beale St.
  (901) 523-9782

Schwab's is open from 9 A.M. to 5 P.M. Mondays through Saturdays. An old-fashioned general store, this is the only remaining original business on Beale, a holdover from the street's glory days and before. Alsatian immigrant Abraham Schwab founded the store in 1876 at 142 Beale. It moved to 149 Beale in the 1890s and to its present location in 1911. The founder's grandson, Abe Schwab, runs the store today.

In the 1990 documentary *Deep Blues*, narrator Robert Palmer begins his exploration of the Mississippi Delta at Schwab's. Abe Schwab tells him that the store used to sell blues 78s (at three for a dollar) and people poured in, lured by the music playing on the speakers. When the store became overcrowded, the Schwabs would put on church music for a while to thin out the crowd.

The family learned that the people who bought blues records were also interested in voodoo. Schwab's began carrying bottled potions, candles, soaps, and other voodoo supplies, and still does. It also still carries music, on CDs and tapes instead of 78s. And it seems to have everything else—hardware, cleaning supplies, souvenirs, clothing. "If you can't find it at Schwab's, you're better off without it" is the slogan. The second-floor landing has an exhibit recreating the music and goods of the old days.

- **Former site of Mitchell's, Club Handy, and the Center for Southern Folklore**
  209 Beale St.

The building dates from 1896, and was originally a drugstore—one of the first twenty-four-hour drugstores in the country, providing around-the-clock emergency service on rough Beale Street. In the 1940s, the building housed Sunbeam Mitchell's third-floor hotel and second-floor lounge, famous for hospitality to poor or stranded musicians and for its chili. It later became the Club Handy, where jazz and blues musicians performed and jammed after hours.

Mitchell's and the Club Handy are fondly remembered in the Center for Southern Folklore's documentary *All Day and All Night: Memories From Beale Street Musicians,* which may be viewed at the center's new location. The Center for Southern Folklore occupied this building from 1996 to 1999, when it lost its lease and was kicked out to make way for Wet Willie's, a branch of the frozen-daiquiri bar chain.

• **Third and Beale**

This intersection is mentioned in many blues lyrics and was the heart of the community. Memphis Minnie and Little Son Joe lived in an apartment at this corner after moving from Chicago back to Memphis in the late 1950s.

• **Handy Park**
Between Third and Beale streets, Peabody Place, and Rufus Thomas Blvd.

The park once was the site of the Beale Street Markethouse and Cold Storage Plant, an indoor/outdoor market that was torn down in 1930. It became a park that year, and was dedicated to Handy on March 29, 1931. The statue of Handy went up in 1960, two years after his death. Mahalia Jackson sang at the statue dedication ceremony.

Cast in bronze and standing on a marble pedestal, Handy holds a trumpet and looks sternly across the park onto Beale Street. His wordy plaque reads:

FATHER OF THE BLUES
William Christopher Handy
Born November 16, 1873 Florence, Ala.
Died New York City, March 28, 1958
Enshrined forever in the hearts of the nation are his immortal songs, "Memphis Blues," "St. Louis Blues," "Beale Street Blues" and those who sow in tears shall reap in joy with his golden trumpet he gave everlasting voice to these and folk songs of his people in the south land. His music is known and beloved throughout the world as an inspiration to youth and as an enduring gift to America's treasury of songs. For more than thirty years he was a distinguished member of the American Society of Composers, Authors and Publishers (ASCAP) which proudly joins the citizens of Memphis in erecting this everlasting tribute to his memory.

You still can hear musicians playing for tips on the hallowed ground of Handy Park. It's generally an electric band these days; amplification is required if those playing are to be heard above the din of traffic and recorded music emanating from the street-facing speakers of nearby businesses. During festivals, there often are free performances by scheduled acts.

Handy Park has recently been closed for its $1.6 million transformation into a concert venue with a stage, restrooms, vending area, and ticket booth.

• Rufus Thomas Monument
Rufus Thomas Blvd. just north of Beale St.

Rufus Thomas, who died December 15, 2001 at age eighty-four, is perhaps the epitome of Memphis entertainers. A minstrel-show veteran, deejay, singer, dancer, comedian, bandleader, and wild-dressing World's Oldest Teenager, Thomas was best known nationally for his dance hits "Do the Funky Chicken" and "Walking the Dog." He is recognized in a state historic marker in front of the Palace Theater site and in this tall concrete monument, which describes him as follows:

> *Rufus Thomas*
> Ambassador of Soul
> The King of Rhythm and Blues
> The funkiest chicken of the South
> A star and veteran of service to this community
> A man whose talents have endured
> And whose performances have spanned generations
> Out spoken and outta sight

• Pee Wee's
317 Beale St.

Pee Wee's—or "P. Wee's," as the sign read—was the hangout and unofficial office of many musicians, because the staff would take messages for them. Pee Wee's is where Will Shade met Charlie Burse and asked him to join the Memphis Jug Band.

Legend has it that this is also where W. C. Handy wrote "Mr. Crump," which later became "Memphis Blues." Handy explains in his autobiography, however, that he "often used to use his cigar stand to write out copies of the following lyric for visiting bands." Note that he says "write out copies"—of a song that he had already written.

Of course, people did more than hang out and write music at Pee Wee's. It also was a rough gambling den, with the house joke "We can't close yet—no one has been killed." Handy used that as a slogan for the whole street in his "Beale Street Blues":

> *You'll meet honest men and pickpockets skilled,*
> *You'll find that business never closes till somebody gets*
> *killed.*

The building has been demolished, and its lot is underneath part of the Hard Rock Cafe, 315 Beale St. (901-529-0007). There is a historical marker about Pee Wee's on the sidewalk.

• Palace Theater Lot
326 Beale St., just west of Legends Rhythm and Blues Club

Once the largest black-entertainment venue in the South, the Palace was affiliated with the Theater Owners' Booking Association. The TOBA circuit provided national tours for black performers including Bessie Smith, Alberta Hunter (from Memphis), Butterbeans and Susie, and Ma Rainey. The Palace outlasted TOBA, and continued to bring in top touring jazz acts such as Duke Ellington, Count Basie, and Ella Fitzgerald.

Beginning in 1935, the Palace featured a weekly amateur night, at which Rufus Thomas worked first as the comic, then as emcee. Performers competed for small cash prizes, hoping not to be booed offstage. Later, the policy was changed so that every performer received one dollar.

Some of those contestants would later become famous. Others were already established performers, but they would come by anyway when times were hard. Frank Stokes, Bukka White, Robert Nighthawk, and Earl Hooker were among the contestants. To this day, B. B. King thanks Thomas for allowing him to compete every week, so that he could collect that dollar. On another night of the week was the "Midnight Ramble," when all-white audiences came to see black acts.

The Palace has been demolished. The covered patio of Legends Rhythm and Blues Club is on its lot. There is a state historic marker on the sidewalk.

• Old Daisy Theater
329 Beale St.

Another grand old theater where movies and touring acts played, this one is pretty much closed but still standing. You can look at the mosaic entranceway and old ticket booth under the painted ceiling of the outdoor foyer. It houses some offices, and shows are held there occasionally, but the building is generally closed to the public.

The 1929 short film *St. Louis Blues*, starring Bessie Smith, had its world premiere at the Daisy, and Bessie attended.

• Monarch Club
340 Beale St.

Currently occupied by a bar called Dick's Last Resort (901-543-0900), this is perhaps the street's loveliest building. In its heyday, from 1902 to about 1920, the Monarch Club was the fanciest joint on Beale—and the most notorious. It was dubbed the "castle of missing men" because so many murders were committed there. Owned by politician and alleged gangster Jim Kinnane, it is probably the club where Robert Wilkins wishes he were in his 1935 "Old Jim Canans":

> *I wisht I was back at Old Jim Canans*
> *I'd stand on the corner and wave my hand*
> *And if you don't b'lieve that I'm a drinkin' man*
> *Said, baby, stop by here with your beer can.*

Born in Hernando, Mississippi, and resident of Memphis for many years, Wilkins later became the *Reverend* Robert Wilkins and changed the words of his old blues numbers to make them religious (such as "That's No Way to Get Along," about women mistreating him, which became the biblical "Prodigal Son"). But he certainly bragged about partying down at Jim Kinnane's. The song refers not only to beer drinking but also to whiskey, playing the dozens, and sniffing cocaine. Perhaps that was just to please the audience, though—Ishmon Bracey, another bluesman-turned-minister, said of Wilkins, "Didn't drink nothing but a little wine. I never saw a man drink so little."

Delta blues-singing pianist Louise Johnson also liked the Monarch, or knew that her audiences did. She opens her 1930 "On the Wall" (with Charley Patton in the studio making spoken comments) by announcing:

> *Well, I'm going to Memphis, gon' stop at Jim Kinnane's,*
> *I'm going to show these womens how to treat a man*

Another verse has her stopping at "Church's hall" to show the women "how to cock it on the wall." "Church's hall" was the auditorium in **Church's Park**, east of Fourth Street on Beale. Established in 1899 by Robert Church, a real-estate magnate said to be the South's first black millionaire, the park was an early center of black social life. The auditorium is no longer standing.

- **W. C. Handy Home**
  352 Beale St.
  (901) 522-1556

The building is open from 10 A.M. to 4 P.M. Tuesdays through Saturdays. An admission charge includes a tour.

The delightful, thorough tour of W. C. Handy's home given by Mattie Sengstacke is probably the best deal in town. Mrs. Sengstacke is familiar not only with Handy's life but also with Memphis history, the Civil Rights Movement, and the African American press, among other subjects.

The house is tucked into the corner of the Beale Street Historic District, back a way from the street. It was moved to Beale from its original location at 659 Jennette Street, ten blocks to the south, which is where Handy actually lived while he was in Memphis—from about 1905, when he came here from Clarksdale, Mississippi, until 1918, when he moved to New York.

A simple brick shotgun house, it is painted plain gray on the outside and white on the inside. Visitors can see musical instruments and clothing of the type associated with Handy, but not his actual belongings (some of those are in another Handy museum, at his birthplace in Florence, Alabama).

A trained, professional musician, Handy championed and commercialized the blues, which had been a folk music passed on strictly through the oral tradition. He wrote and published compositions with elements of the blues in their melodies and lyrics and with the word "blues" in their titles, thus bringing that form into the mainstream of popular music and creating the first blues craze. Although he accepted the title "Father of the Blues," even using that as the name of his autobiography, Handy did not create the blues and never claimed to.

The Handy house in Memphis contains the published sheet music of many of his songs, photographs of him and his family throughout their lives, and some of his letters. Handy tapes, books, and T-shirts are available for purchase.

- ## The Midway
  357 Beale St.

Many musicians claimed to have played at the Midway. Memphis Slim insisted, however, that he and Roosevelt Sykes were the only two blues singers who played there, "because guitar players couldn't play nowhere in those days but in the park or in the street somewhere." The Midway remained open as a pool hall into the late 1960s, when most of the other joints had become pawnshops, barber shops, laundries or were closed.

The building has been demolished. The site lies outside the Beale Street Historic District, which ends at Fourth Street.

- ## Solvent Savings Bank
  386 Beale St.

Walk across Fourth Street—the limit of the usual tourist section of Beale Street—to find this handsome red-brick two-story building that once housed Pace and Handy Music Publishing. Solvent Savings itself was the city's first black-owned bank, established in 1906. Pace and Handy Music opened shop as a tenant upstairs, 392 Beale, the following year.

- ## Center for Southern Folklore
  Pembroke Square at Peabody Place, 119 S. Main St.
  (901) 525-3655

The Center for Southern Folklore (not to be confused with the Center for the Study of Southern Culture at the University of Mississippi) is a nightclub, coffee bar, art gallery, and bookstore with live music and other cultural events at noon and in the evening. It also is a nonprofit corporation that aims "to preserve, defend and protect the music, culture, arts and rhythms of the South." It produces the annual Memphis Music and Heritage Festival, held on Labor Day weekend.

The center often features live blues at lunchtime. The late Mose Vinson was a regular until his death in 2002. Vinson, a native of Holly Springs, Mississippi, was a longtime participant in the Memphis music scene—he played on such 1950s Sun recordings as James Cotton's "Cotton Crop Blues" and Jimmy DeBerry's

"Take a Little Chance." The Fieldstones, longtime house band at the beloved Memphis jook Greens Lounge (destroyed by fire in 1998) also play at the center.

- ## The Peabody
  149 Union Ave.
  (901) 529-4000

The Peabody's giant neon sign glows above Beale Street. An elegant and expensive old hotel, the Peabody might seem a world apart from the raucous street life of Beale. But it has an important place in blues history as a site of field-recording trips by northern record companies in the 1920s and 1930s. The companies would rent a room at a hotel in a southern city, then call for blues singers for auditions and on-the-spot recording sessions.

Among the artists who recorded at the Peabody in 1929 were Furry Lewis, Charlie McCoy, Walter Vincent (aka Vincson), Speckled Red, Robert Wilkins, Jenny Pope, Big Joe Williams, Jed Davenport, Garfield Akers, Jim Jackson, Joe Callicott, and Kid Bailey.

Mississippi bluesman Eugene Powell, who recorded as Sonny Boy Nelson at the St. Charles Hotel in New Orleans in 1936, provides some insight into a process that was probably about the same at the Peabody, the King Edward in Jackson, or any of the other hotels that served as temporary recording studios:

> I remember we worked all night. The machine was sitting in the middle of the room, but we was way upstairs in the air, in another part of the house. The place was about seven or eight stories high, and we was way up there, playing music, to be out of the noise and other stuff, cars, or they would get caught on tape—they put those big sheets up over the windows to muffle all that music and stuff. The guys that recorded us they were nice fellas, they just recorded whatever we wanted to play. They didn't tell us how to do nothing. So we was making some good records.

The Peabody also sometimes provided work for Memphis jug bands at stag parties for white businessmen. Those were good gigs, because the businessmen would get drunk and tip well, especially when the bands played requested pop hits.

Now inside the Peabody lobby, **Lansky's** still features the flashy men's clothing it has specialized in since the 1950s, when it was the place where Beale Street's hippest bought their threads. At least one dreamy-eyed young white boy—Elvis Presley—would gaze into the store's windows and say hello to its proprietors. As soon as he got a few bucks, Presley began buying clothes at Lansky's. Even before he started performing, Presley stood out from the white working-class crowd for his unconventional dress, which, like his music, derived almost directly from blacks. Bernard Lansky, who still owns and operates the store, proudly proclaims himself "Clothier to the King" on his signs and business cards. B. B. King, Bobby "Blue" Bland, and Rufus Thomas have also shopped at Lansky's.

When Elvis was hanging out there, Lansky's was at 126 Beale St., where, appropriately, the nightclub **Elvis Presley's Memphis** (901-527-6900) is today. The club maintains a Lansky's display in its side window. Nearby and across the street stands a giant Elvis statue that was unveiled during Elvis week 1997.

- **Beale Street Walk of Fame**

Brass notes on the sidewalk honor people who have been important in Memphis music history. Many blues musicians as well as those from other genres are so recognized, as are business people, public officials, and other nonmusicians who have had significant roles on Beale.

- **Gayoso Street**

North of Beale and parallel to it, this street was full of high-class whorehouses around the turn of the twentieth century. It was the Memphis equivalent of New Orleans's famed Storyville district. Like Storyville, it featured light-skinned black prostitutes who catered to wealthy white customers. And, as in Storyville, each club had a pianist playing standards, ragtime, and early forms of blues and jazz.

- **Memphis Rock 'n' Soul Museum**
  145 Lt. George W. Lee Ave., in the Gibson Guitar Building
  (901) 543-0800

The Smithsonian Institution designed this as a traveling exhibition, but Gibson provided a permanent home at its plant in Memphis, which opened in 2000.

The admission price includes an audio tour, featuring speech and music, through the museum's photos, artifacts, and re-creations. The portable CD players also allow visitors to listen to a choice of dozens of classic Memphis tunes, including such obscure gems as Elder Curry's "Memphis Flu" and Phineas Newborn, Jr., and Trio's "No Moon at All," as well as the standard classics. The opening video is a good introduction to Memphis music—make sure to stay for Carl Perkins's "Matchbox" at the end. Among the museum's treasures are a piece of the Grand Ole Opry transmitter, a 1934 Seeburg jukebox, the drums Al Jackson played on "Dock of the Bay" and "Green Onions," and the sax on which Ben Branch played "Precious Lord, Take My Hand" for Martin Luther King, Jr., just before King was killed. Hours are 10 A.M. to 6 P.M. Sundays through Thursdays and to 8 P.M. Fridays and Saturdays. Tours of the plant also are available.

FESTIVALS

The Memphis Music and Heritage Festival (Labor Day weekend), BluesFirst/International Blues Challenge (in late January), the Handy Awards (in April), and Memphis in May's Beale Street Music Festival (early in May) are blues-filled festivals held on and around Beale.

The **Music and Heritage Festival**, presented by the Center for Southern Folklore, is Memphis's answer to the New Orleans Jazz and Heritage Festival. Both are celebrations of the music and folk traditions of their area. But while the event in New Orleans draws hundreds of thousands, the Memphis fest attracts small, mostly local audiences. It is delightful and free, held on outdoor stages and inside the center.

BluesFirst/International Blues Challenge, presented by the Blues Foundation, combines a conference for blues societies and fans with a competition for unsigned blues acts. It all happens along Beale Street. The Blues Foundation also presents the Handy Awards, the blues world's equivalent of the Grammys. The awards event features plenty of live music. Tickets and information on both events are available through the Blues Foundation's web site, www.blues.org.

Memphis in May is the city's biggest celebration, and includes many other events besides the two-day music festival, which is held in the riverside Tom Lee Park and on Beale. There are several pop headliners, but also a blues stage with national and regional acts.

Away from Beale Street

• Crump Boulevard

This street is named after Edward Hull Crump, who was born in Holly Springs, Mississippi, in 1874, moved to Memphis as a young man and became mayor in 1909. He was reelected twice, then resigned in 1916 amid legal pressure over his refusal to enforce state prohibition law. However, like other local political bosses in U.S. cities, Crump firmly controlled Memphis politics until his death in 1954.

W. C. Handy composed "Mr. Crump Don't Like It" as an *instrumental* campaign ditty for Crump in his first campaign. Listeners, however, would sing along, expressing their feelings about Crump's reform plans. Those comments became the lyrics to the song:

> *Mr. Crump won't 'low no easy riders here*
> *We don't care what Mr. Crump don't 'low*
> *We gon' to bar'lhouse anyhow—*
> *Mr. Crump can go and catch hisself some air!*

Handy transformed the song into his "Memphis Blues." But "Mr. Crump" lived on as a Memphis staple, notably in a 1927 recording titled "Mr. Crump Don't Like It" by the Beale Street Sheiks (Frank Stokes and Dan Sain).

• Bridges

Bluesman-turned-rock pioneer Chuck Berry wrote the classic "Memphis, Tennessee" about trying to reach by phone a little girl who lived "on the south side, high upon a ridge, just a half a mile from the Mississippi bridge." The location of the fictional girl's home is probably not specific. The bridge, however, would be the Memphis-Arkansas Bridge that crosses the Mississippi River at Crump Boulevard—*not* the flashy new M-shaped Hernando de Soto Bridge farther north. The Memphis-Arkansas Bridge, originally named the E. H. Crump Bridge, was completed in 1949. To cross Berry's bridge, take Interstate 55 north.

Half a mile south of there would put you at about McLemore Avenue.

The Hernando de Soto Bridge was completed in 1972, too late for Chuck Berry's song. But it does have a music-oriented **welcome sign.** Driving over the bridge into Memphis from West Memphis, notice the sign that greets you from atop a storage silo to the right: "Memphis, Home of the Blues, Birthplace of Rock 'n' Roll." The "I" in Memphis is in the form of a guitar. The sign, installed in September 1999 by Shelby County government with private donations, lights up at night.

- **WDIA**
  112 Union St.

WDIA is no longer at its original location (2267 Central Ave.). A state historic marker in front of station's *current* location identifies WDIA as "the Goodwill Station" and notes that its all-black format made it the top-rated Memphis station in the early 1950s. The sign names Nat D. Williams as the station's first black deejay and identifies some of its other well-known deejays from over the years, including blues singers B. B. King, Rufus Thomas, and Dwight "Gatemouth" Moore (although his name is spelled incorrectly and his nickname is left off).

The station is on the third floor of the building. Its waiting room contains paintings of its deejays by Memphis artist George Hunt. The best way to appreciate WDIA is to turn on your radio to 1060 AM and listen to it—especially on Saturdays, when it plays all blues.

In 1949, WDIA became the first black-format (although white-owned) radio station. It billed itself "The Mother Station of the Negroes." Joe Hill Louis, "the Be-bop Boy," a one-man band who played the blues in parks and at ball games (and recorded at Sun Records) was the station's first Pep-ti-kon Boy, singing live commercial jingles for the patent medicine. The next Pep-ti-kon Boy was B. B. King.

King, a new arrival from Mississippi, had played one night at the Sixteenth Street Grill in West Memphis, filling in for regular performer Sonny Boy Williamson. The club's owner, a Miss Annie, told King he could work there six nights a week if he, like Williamson, had a radio show on which to publicize the Cafe gigs.

Sun Studio, 706 Union Avenue, Memphis

King scrambled to WDIA, where he won the radio spot by instantly writing a Pep-ti-kon jingle. King biographer Sebastian Danchin cites that moment as "the point where his career really took off." King worked at the station until 1953, when he turned his show over to Rufus Thomas.

- **Sun Studio**
  706 Union Ave.
  (800) 441-6249 or (901) 521-0664

Bob Dylan reportedly kissed the studio floor when he visited. Best known as the place where Elvis Presley made his first recordings, Sun Studio would be a major musical shrine even if Elvis had never stopped by.

At Memphis Recording Service (as it was called in its first few years, before the Sun label was founded), Sam Phillips oversaw raw, wild blues sessions, including the wonderful early recordings of Howlin' Wolf, "Dr." Isaiah Ross, B. B. King, Big Walter Horton, James Cotton, Rufus Thomas, Little Junior Parker, and Little Milton. Jackie Brenston's 1951 "Rocket 88" (featuring Ike Turner as pianist and bandleader), often considered the first rock 'n' roll record, was another in the series of important, influential, and just plain great tracks recorded here.

On the eighteen-year-old Presley's first session at the studio in 1953, he chose to record the decidedly non-blues, non-rock 'n' roll "My Happiness" and "That's When Your Heartaches Begin." Presley returned to Sun on July 5, 1954, however, with Scotty Moore and Bill Black, and cut a cover of Mississippi bluesman Arthur Crudup's "That's All Right" that would launch Presley's career and the national rock 'n' roll craze.

Phillips soon sold Elvis's contract to RCA. But Phillips's attention had shifted from blues to white rock 'n' roll. He recorded hits for Carl Perkins, Johnny Cash, Jerry Lee Lewis, Roy Orbison, and Charlie Rich. Despite all his success with rockabilly, however, Phillips has always called Howlin' Wolf his greatest discovery.

"My feeling was that there was more talent, innately natural, in the people that I wanted to work with—Southern black, Southern country white—than there was in the people who wrote down arrangements," Sam Phillips told an interviewer in 1994, concisely stating the philosophy that guided him and his studio.

Phillips moved his operations to 639 Madison Avenue in 1960 and kept Sun going there until 1968, but the company was no longer a vital force in popular music. Phillips retired in 1969 and died in 2003. His son Knox still operates the Madison Avenue studio as Phillips Recording Service.

Except for occupation by a few short-lived businesses, the original Sun Studio was empty and unused from 1960 to 1985. Looking much the way it always did, it has reopened as an active recording studio as well as a tourist attraction. B. B. King returned to Sun in 1987 to record "When Love Comes to Town" with Irish rock superstars U2, who also recorded three other songs here for their album *Rattle and Hum*. Bonnie Raitt, Ringo Starr, and the Stray Cats also have recorded here in recent years.

If you get inspired, studio time is available at competitive prices. You can also book a special souvenir session, in which you sing to a prerecorded background and take home a CD or tape of yourself.

In the half-hour studio tour, for which there is a fee, you can pose for pictures at the microphone Elvis used. The guide tells the amazing history of Sun, and plays samples of many of the songs recorded here, including some blues numbers. Tours are given from 10 A.M. to 6 P.M. daily.

Entrance to the gift shop, upstairs, is free, and it has exhibits of photographs and equipment. Tapes and CDs of all the Sun artists are available. In the 1950s, the gift shop space was Taylor Boarding Home, where many of the white artists stayed while they were recording. Blues pianist Mose Vinson worked there as a custodian. Vinson did get to play on some of the sessions.

The Sun Studio Cafe, downstairs, is a working restaurant that also has a small gift shop. It looks about the way it did in the old days, when it was the Taylor Cafe, where the studio staff and artists would hang out and work out deals.

- **Graceland, Elvis Presley's home and grave**
  3734 Elvis Presley Blvd.
  (800) 238-2000 or (901) 332-3322

The most visited place in Memphis and probably the most popular music-related site in the world, Graceland is the house Elvis bought in 1957, when he was a twenty-two-year-old star. He lived here until he died twenty years later.

You can get a free peek at the outside of the house by walking across the street from the parking area and looking over the stone wall. The wall and sidewalk in front of the house are covered with graffiti from fans. A state historic marker there sums up Presley's career:

Elvis Aaron Presley

Elvis Presley was born in Tupelo, Mississippi on January 8, 1935, the son of Vernon and Gladys Presley. He moved to Memphis in 1948. Soon after signing a contract with Sun Records in 1954 he achieved tremendous popularity. His musical and acting career in records, movies, television, and concerts made him one of the most successful and outstanding entertainers in the world. He died on August 16, 1977 and is buried here at his Memphis home, Graceland.

The Meditation Garden, which contains the graves of Presley and his mother, father, paternal grandmother, and a monument to his stillborn twin brother, is open free of charge from 7 to 8:30 A.M. daily.

To see any other part of the property, you must take a tour. The tours are offered from 9 A.M. to 5 P.M. Mondays through Saturdays and 10 A.M. to 4 P.M. Sundays. Graceland is closed on Thanksgiving, Christmas, and New Year's Day. The mansion tour is not given on Tuesdays from November through February. The platinum tour, which includes everything, costs $22 for adults, $11 for children seven to twelve years old, and $19.80 for students and senior citizens. For lesser fees one may select parts of the platinum tour—the mansion tour (the house, grounds, and grave), the Elvis Presley Auto Museum, the Lisa Marie and Hound Dog II airplanes, or the Sincerely Elvis exhibit of artifacts. Photography is permitted at Graceland, but only without flash. Video and audio recording are prohibited.

Built in 1939, Graceland already had its name when Elvis purchased it for a hundred thousand dollars and moved his family into it. It became the hangout for his large entourage of male friends, along with a changing cast of women. Fans would wait outside, hoping to catch glimpses of Elvis, and he often obliged them by coming out to chat and sign autographs.

The house is a palace of period kitsch. It has stained-glass peacocks, a Hawaiian-themed Jungle Room with an indoor waterfall and green shag carpeting on the floor and ceiling, a basement poolroom with fabric-covered walls, a firing range, and televisions everywhere (including three side by side in one room, so Elvis could watch all three channels simultaneously, an idea he got from President Lyndon Johnson). Much of it is left as it was when it was a family home. Other areas display gold records, portraits made by fans, clothing from Elvis's movies and concerts, guns given him by police officers, and other goods.

The mansion tour includes an audio guide with comments from Elvis's ex-wife, Priscilla, about life at Graceland: "One time it was meatloaf. Meatloaf every night for six months."

Many visitors become teary-eyed at the end of the tour when they arrive at the Meditation Garden, the final resting place for Presley and his family members. (Minnie Mae Presley, who died May 8, 1980, about a month before her ninetieth birthday, outlived her son, daughter-in-law, and famous grandson to become the most recent occupant of the garden.)

August 10–16 of each year is Elvis Week; it draws thousands of hardcore fans for special events, including an overnight candlelight vigil at the grave beginning on August 15.

• Stax Museum of American Soul Music

926 E. McLemore Ave.
(888) 942-SOUL or (901) 942-SOUL

Open 9 A.M. to 4 P.M. Mondays through Saturdays, 1 to 4 P.M. Sundays. There is an admission charge.

Memphis is known for the blues and for rock 'n' roll. But in the 1960s and 1970s, it also was home of the great soul record company Stax. Jim Stewart (the "St") and Estelle Axton ("ax"), brother and sister, turned an old movie theater into "Soulsville USA," as its marquee proclaimed. With house band Booker T and the MGs, Stax created a Memphis soul style that challenged Detroit's Motown artistically and financially.

Besides the artists mentioned on the historic marker, Stax also made a 1963 album by jug-band bluesman Gus Cannon. And the company's biggest hit ever was the 1968 "Who's Making Love" by urbane bluesman Johnnie Taylor, who went on to make many successful records for Jackson-based Malaco before his death on May 31, 2000.

The museum is on the lot where Stax stood at the northwest corner of McLemore Avenue and College Street, across College from Shirley's Beauty Salon. In July 1980 Union Planters Bank sold the building, for ten dollars, to Southside Church of God. The church never followed through on a plan to turn it into a community center but refused to sell it to anyone who wanted to make it a monument to Stax, allegedly because the company's product was the devil's music. The building was torn down in 1988. A bit of the lobby's checkerboard slate-tile floor was all that remained, with parts of a concrete foundation. A state historic marker reads: "On this site stood Stax Records, Inc. which boasted such stars as Otis Redding, Rufus and Carla Thomas, Isaac Hayes, the Staple [sic] Singers, Albert King, the Bar-Kays and many others. It relied upon its deep soul roots to carry it through struggling from a back-street garage in 1957 to become a multi-million-dollar organization."

The site has been redeveloped as a museum with future plans for a music academy. The city and private donors are sponsoring the project, which is intended to rejuvenate the neighborhood.

Part of the original neon Stax sign is inside the **Rum Boogie Cafe** on Beale Street. And **Shangri-la Records**, 1916 Madison St. (901-274-1916), sells bricks from the Stax building for ten dollars.

- ## Memphis Minnie's Final Residence
  1355 Adelaide St.

This is where Memphis Minnie and Ernest "Little Son Joe" Lawlers, her third and final husband and her musical partner, lived from about 1960 to the end of their lives, staying with Minnie's sister Daisy. Having had a stroke and suffering from asthma, Minnie was in a wheelchair by then. Photos of her from that period, sitting on the house's porch, have been published in books and magazines. Lawlers died in 1961. Minnie lived until August 6, 1973. The old, white, wood house is near the corner of Olive Street. It has red-and-white awnings and well-maintained shrubs and lawn; the porch still looks inviting. Resist the temptation, though, because this is a private residence.

- ## Wild Bill's Lounge
  1580 Vollintine Ave. (at Avalon St.)
  (901) 726-5473

This north-of-Midtown jook joint is in a long, old commercial building that also houses a dry cleaner, a deli, and three beauty shops.

Inside, it's a box about thirty feet wide by seventy feet long, with a kitchen in the back that cooks up chitterlings, beef stew, fried chicken, and all the trimmings. The room is bright orange, with Christmas lights strung all about and dozens of photos on the walls. It's full of long rows of tables—if you come alone, you'll be seated with other people.

The live music happens most Friday, Saturday, and Sunday nights, when house band the Hollywood All Stars holds court. Wild Bill, the club's owner, sits at the front door and opens it to let you in and collect your five-dollar cover. Bill also has his own way of letting the band know when break time is over—he picks up a drum stick and bashes a few drums and cymbals.

You walk in right onto the dance floor. Either start dancing immediately or take your seat and order a drink. The beer prices can't be beat: $3.50 for a forty-ounce bottle, served with a glass.

Furry Lewis's grave, Hollywood Cemetery, Memphis

- ## Live Blues Elsewhere in Memphis, Off Beale Street

In Midtown, look for acoustic bluesman Robert "Wolfman" Belfour at Murphy's and occasional visiting blues acts at Otherlands, the Hi-Tone, or the Young Avenue Deli. The Hard Luck Cafe, a downhome-looking jook at McLemore Avenue and Third Street, recently has been advertising live blues. Check the weekly *Memphis Flyer* or the Friday edition of the *Commercial Appeal* for listings of who is playing where.

- ## Furry Lewis's Grave
  Hollywood Cemetery, 2012 Hernando Road

Park at the entrance and walk around the office and straight up the path that leads into the cemetery. Turn left at the third intersection and then look to the left. Furry's gravestones (one upright and one flat) are there, facing away from the entrance.

The flat one reads:

> *Walter "Furry" Lewis*
> Blues Man
> Mar. 8, 1893
> Sept. 14, 1981

The upright stone disagrees on the birthdate, listing it as March 6 (the more commonly accepted date). It also says, "When I Lay My Burden Down," with an etching of a guitar.

Walter "Furry" Lewis, the street sweeper on Beale Street for forty years, also was a bluesman who recorded in the 1920s, playing delicate guitar arrangements on such pieces as "Kassie Jones" and "Turn Your Money Green."

Furry emerged from a long musical retirement to become the star of the blues revival of the 1960s and 1970s. He not only made new recordings and played concerts and festivals but also appeared on *The Tonight Show* with Johnny Carson (where he quipped, "Why should I marry when the man next door has a wife?") and in *W. W. and the Dixie Dance Kings* with Burt Reynolds. He was also an opening act for the Rolling Stones.

• West Memphis, Arkansas

West Memphis, Arkansas, sits right across the Mississippi River from Memphis, Tennessee. In the 1940s through the 1950s, West Memphis was a hotbed of blues. Sonny Boy Williamson II, Howlin' Wolf, and B. B. King all played in its clubs. Most of the action was on Eighth and 16th streets south of Broadway. KWEM, the radio station where B. B. King was a guest on Sonny Boy's show in 1948, was at Broadway and 12th Street. It is gone, replaced by a large bank building.

• Albert King's Grave

To get there: From Memphis, take Interstate 55 north across the river into West Memphis, switch to Interstate 40 west and continue to exit 271, which is Arkansas Highway 147. Drive south on 147, through the Arkansas Delta, which is even more desolate and less populated than its Mississippi equivalent across the river. After 3 miles you will come to Paradise Gardens Cemetery, a huge burial ground in the midst of this isolated area. Turn into the cemetery.

Albert King is buried in the right front corner, near the Dr. Martin Luther King Jr. Park and a large, white, raised monument, surrounded by benches, honoring Martin Luther King. There are wooden street signs inside the cemetery marking the paths Martin Luther Kingsway and Albert Kingsway. (Martin Luther King is not buried here.) Although he is in a huge cemetery, Albert King lies alone; no other graves are in his part of the grounds, which he shares only with the Martin Luther King monument.

Albert King's gravestone is flat, and the whole grave is covered with gravel and bordered by two rows of raised bricks. A bronze

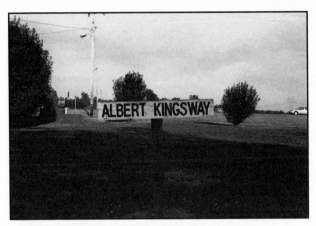

Sign near Albert King's grave, Paradise Grove Cemetery, Edmondson, Arkansas

plaque on the marble stone depicts King's trademark Flying V guitar, properly oriented for a left-handed player. It reads:

'I'LL PLAY THE BLUES FOR YOU'

Albert Nelson King

April 25, 1923–December 21, 1992

Born under a bad sign in the Mississippi Delta, Albert King rose to greatness as a true giant of blues music. With his commanding presence, powerful voice, and stinging single-note guitar style, Albert King played the blues for the world, and forever changed the way the world would play the blues.

Dedicated to the memory of Albert King from his many fans and friends.

Early in his career, Albert King tried to pass himself off as fellow Indianola native B. B. King's brother, even changing his last name from Nelson to King. There was no need for the charade. Albert was a fine singer and a killer guitarist with a style all his own, based on bending the strings *way* across the fingerboard. He found his greatest success in the late 1960s, on Memphis's Stax label, where he recorded such songs as "Born Under a Bad Sign" and "I'll Play the Blues for You" backed by Booker T and the MGs. King has greatly influenced many blues and rock guitarists, including Eric Clapton, Robert Cray, and Stevie Ray Vaughan.

The Delta

chapter 3

DOWN HIGHWAY 61

Highway 61

To get there: Memphis's Third Street becomes Highway 61. From downtown
Memphis, head south on Third Street. From Memphis International Airport,
take I-240 west toward downtown; after 2 miles switch to I-55 north, and
then, after another 1½ miles, take the Highway 61 south exit.

> 61 Highway is the longest road I know
> She run from New York City down to the Gulf of Mexico

Thus sang Mississippi Fred McDowell. Other versions put the
starting point in Detroit and have it end at the border of New
Mexico. Actually, it extends past Duluth, Minnesota, up to Thun-
der Bay, Ontario, Canada, and down to New Orleans. Highway 61
runs the full length of the Mississippi Delta, Memphis to Vicksburg, passing through or near most major towns.

Big Joe Williams and Howlin' Wolf sang of the other main
Delta highway: "I'm going to get up in the morning, hit Highway
49." Since most bluesmen were rambling types, their songs often
mention 49, 61, or 51, which skirts the Delta's east border and
connects Jackson to Memphis.

When walking or driving these roads today, you probably will not be literally in the footsteps of the old blues singers, because the road alignments have changed. In many places the Old Highway still exists, parallel to the new road. It usually passes through the centers of towns.

Walls

• Memphis Minnie's Grave

To get there: From the intersection of Highway 61 and Highway 302, go west on 302, past the Walls turnoff and across the tracks. Follow the road as it makes a sharp left, then take the first right onto Old Highway 61. Proceed 2 miles to an intersection with a sign reading "Church." The sign refers to a church different from the one you are seeking, but turn right at that intersection anyway, onto Norfolk Road. Follow Norfolk for less than a mile, until you see New Hope M. B. Church on the right, with a cemetery before it.

Minnie's grave has the tallest stone in the small cemetery. After parking in the church lot, walk parallel to the road you came up, in the direction you came from, until you get to that tall stone.

Two pink roses, with green leaves, are painted into the angled top of the stone, which stands about four feet tall. Commissioned by the Mount Zion Foundation, it also features a photo of Minnie and reads:

Lizzie "Kid" Douglas Lawlers
AKA
Memphis Minnie
June 3, 1897
Aug. 6, 1973

The back of the stone features this lengthy, philosophical inscription:

The hundreds of sides Minnie recorded are the perfect material to teach us about the blues. For the blues are at once general and particular, speaking for millions but in a highly singular, individual voice. Listening to Minnie's songs, we hear her fantasies, her dreams, her desires, but we hear them as if they were our own.

One of the few female singer-guitarists in blues, and one of the very best blues guitarists of either gender, Lizzie "Memphis Minnie" Douglas was born in Algiers, Louisiana, in 1897, and moved

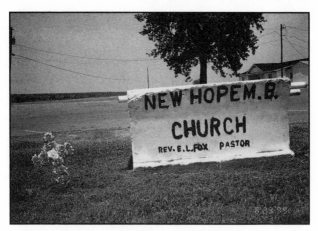

Church cemetery where Memphis Minnie is buried, Walls

to a farm near Walls with her family around 1904. By the time she was in her teens, she was slipping off to Memphis to play on the street around Handy Park.

When she started recording in 1929, at age thirty-two, Kid Douglas became Memphis Minnie, a Chicago-based blues star who would record about two hundred sides. "Memphis Minnie can make a guitar speak words, she can make a guitar cry, moan, talk and whistle the blues," wrote Big Bill Broonzy, himself no slouch. Minnie bested Broonzy in a blues contest in 1933 in Chicago, although he stole her prize, ran off, and drank it.

Lovely, petite, hard-drinking, hard-cursing, tobacco-chewing, and ready to fight if necessary, Minnie was a musical genius, a celebrity and a real character. Although she had a long career with many hits, Minnie fell into poverty in her old age. She moved back to Memphis in the 1950s and died there in 1973. Her family brought her body back to Walls for burial.

The **town of Walls** itself is small and unremarkable, with an auto-body shop, a dense trailer park, a bank, a church, a gas station, and a tavern making up its business area. Across the tracks, on West Railroad Avenue in the town's old black section, is a closed-up cafe that might be the sort where Minnie played on her visits. She toured the South regularly after becoming a successful, Chicago-based musician. Minnie would also come home to Walls to visit, sometimes for weeks or months, when she wasn't touring.

Robinsonville

To get there: If you ask at one of the casinos how to get to Robinsonville, you will probably get a puzzled look and be told, "You're in Robinsonville." But the casinos actually are a few miles from the town itself. From the intersection of highways 61 and 304, go west 1 mile on 304 to the first light, which is Old Highway 61. Turn left and you are in Robinsonville.

This tiny town, now ringed with casinos, is where young Robert Johnson bombed out when he took the stage at a jook joint where Son House and Willie Brown were playing. Howlin' Wolf also farmed and played in the area. "A lot of corn whiskey was cooked around Robinsonville" is how one longtime resident explained the town's great number of musicians.

The Hollywood Cafe, on the left, is a real restaurant, not a jook joint. Turn left at the Hollywood Cafe and then immediately right onto Front Street to see Foster's Cafe, an abandoned and very dilapidated old jook joint with a still-readable sign. That is the only reminder of the days when some of the Delta's greatest bluesmen lived near this town and played in the jooks and on the streets.

- ## Kirby-Wills Plantation

  To get there: A modern Kirby-Wills Plantation sign, lettered vertically on a pole on the east side of Highway 61, can be seen across from the Tunica Visitors Center, 2.4 miles north of the intersection of highways 61 and 304. There is a smaller, older sign in front of a group of buildings 1.1 mile farther north.

Charley Patton's 1929 "Joe Kirby Blues" refers to the owner of this plantation, who apparently gave Patton the blues, although the song doesn't provide specifics. It does mention a girlfriend in the area:

> *I'm goin' where the Green River never do run down*
> *'Cause the woman I love, Lordy, she's living in Robinsonville town.*

(Green River, which also gets a Patton song of its own, "Green River Blues," was a stream near Lake Cormorant, with a mill owned by the Memphis-based Green River Lumber Company.)

The woman Patton sings about is likely singer-pianist Louise Johnson, who lived at Kirby-Wills and entertained at a jook there. Besides being a fine musician, Johnson is significant as one of the few women who played self-accompanied Delta blues. This concept was so unfamiliar to scholars and fans that for years they tried to determine which male pianist had backed Johnson on her records. Son House cleared up the mystery by explaining that she backed herself.

Foster's Cafe, an abandoned jook joint on Front Street, Robinsonville

Johnson was also part of the most famous love triangle in the blues world. In 1930, Charley Patton recruited her and Willie Brown, who were both living at Kirby-Wills, to join him and Son House on a trip to record at the Paramount studio in Grafton, Wisconsin.

Johnson, who was about twenty-five, had been romantically involved with blues-star Patton, about fifteen years her senior. The two of them began the trip sitting together in the front seat of the chauffeur-driven, moonshine-stocked car. But they began arguing after a while, and Johnson switched seats with Brown. House, who was closer to Johnson's age, began sweet-talking her in the back seat. Even House was surprised, however, when they got to their hotel in Grafton and Johnson told him the two of them would share a room.

The romantic intrigue didn't stop anyone from recording top-quality music the next day. You can plainly hear the men shouting in the background on Johnson's songs. It's hard to tell if they are being encouraging or rude.

Plantation where blues singer-pianist Louise Johnson lived, Robinsonville

- **Abbay and Leatherman Plantation**

    To get there: From highways 61 and 304, head west on 304 (Casino Strip Boulevard) for 4.0 miles. The two buildings are on your right, on the north side of the road.

This is where Robert Johnson spent most of his childhood. His mother, Julia Dodds, and stepfather, Dusty Willis, brought Robert here from Memphis (where he had been living with his mother's previous husband) in about 1918, when he was seven. Robert grew up here, picking up the jew's harp, then the harmonica, and then the guitar, and pestering Brown and House to teach him more about music.

Johnson left the area to return to Hazlehurst, his hometown, sometime after 1930. He came back to Robinsonville a few years later and astounded everyone with his guitar virtuosity, provoking the idea that he might have struck a bargain with the devil.

Abbay and Leatherman once employed 450 families, but the number is down to 11. The original plantation office building, a white-painted brick building with a sign reading "Abbay and Leatherman," is standing and still in use as the office. The plantation is still owned and operated by the Leatherman family, which bought the land from the Indians around the 1830s. The office, which dates from that era, also used to serve as the commissary

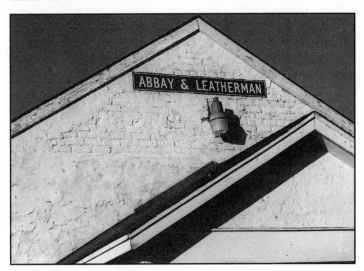

Plantation where Robert Johnson grew up, Robinsonville

where the workers shopped with scrip. Next to it is a small county jail of the same vintage.

• Commerce

To get there: The land that once was Commerce is on the north side of Casino Strip Boulevard (Highway 304) just east of the levee, or kitty-corner from the Exxon/Full House store two lights west of the Abbay and Leatherman plantation building. The only reminders of the town are the Commerce Landing Center, a Commerce Development sign, and Commerce Baptist Church, all along Casino Strip Boulevard.

This settlement was where many of the workers at Abbay and Leatherman Plantation lived. Robert Johnson lived here as a boy and attended school here. Writer Samuel Charters visited Commerce in the early 1970s and wrote that it "isn't much more than two rows of shacks," with a dirt road that led from Commerce past the plantation buildings to Robinsonville. The settlement has since been demolished.

• Bluesville

To get there: From Casino Strip Boulevard (Highway 304), follow the signs to the Horseshoe Casino.

The *name* of this thousand-seat nightclub inside the Horseshoe Casino may be a tribute to the area's blues traditions. And its décor follows a blues theme, with faux peeling-plaster walls and tin roofs over guitar-, harmonica- and piano-shaped bars. But its entertainment lineup generally is anything but the blues. LeAnn Rimes, Martina McBride, the Doobie Brothers, and Ronnie Milsap were the coming attractions advertised recently.

- ### The Blues and Legends Hall of Fame Museum

Inside the Horseshoe Casino, this museum, which is open 9 A.M. to midnight seven days a week, aims to cover the blues heritage not only of Robinsonville or even of the Mississippi Delta but of the whole world. It falls short of that lofty goal, but it is well worth visiting anyway.

Among its treasures are W. C. Handy's 1929 bill of sale for "St. Louis Blues" to RCA for two hundred dollars; a Lightnin' Hopkins song list that includes "Please Release Me" and "Jolie Blonde"; Memphis Minnie's hand-lettered wood grave marker (which has been replaced by a stone at her grave); Big Mama Thornton's bitten-up harps; and two of Furry Lewis's guitar cases.

There also are exhibit cases for several dozen blues artists. Each case contains a wildly colored portrait by Memphis artist George Hunt, records, an instrument of the type the artist used, and other relevant artifacts (guns are included in Bukka White and Big Mama Thornton's cases).

The museum has guitars actually used by a few of the artists, such as Bo Diddley, Stevie Ray Vaughan, Bukka White, and Albert King. There are plenty of photographs by Oxford-based music photographer Dick Waterman. And a few exhibits that don't have much to do with the blues—an array of Dylan-signed harmonicas and a display of San Francisco rock posters—are interesting nonetheless.

Tunica

Now known mainly as the center of the casino region, Tunica once was a lively blues town, with a number of clubs and gambling dens run by a man named Hardface. The north end of Main Street has some old storefronts reminiscent of these days.

- **Tunica Museum**
  1 Museum Blvd. (next to Paul Battle Arena on Highway 61 about 4 miles north of Tunica's commercial strip)
  (662) 363-6631

This well-funded museum covers the natural and cultural history of the area. It includes a reproduction of a jook joint, with recorded commentary by blues drummer Sam Carr, a native and resident of the area. It also presents occasional blues exhibits and programs.

- **Nickson's Disco Club**

On Magnolia Street, off Main Street at the south end of downtown, this big, friendly jook joint lacks live music but has a deejay on weekends. The jukebox is blues-rich. An unnamed white building next to it offers live music on Saturdays from the Soul Constructors, a local band.

Lula

To get there: From Highway 61, take Highway 49 west and follow the sign into town.

Son House and Charley Patton were both living in Lula in about 1930, and both composed songs about the town's severe dry spell and recorded them that year. House's "Dry Spell Blues" declared that it was

> So dry old boll weevil turn up his toes and die
> No, ain't nothing to do—bootleg moonshine and rye.

While Patton's "Dry Well Blues" observed:

> Way down in Lula, hard living has hit.
> Lord, your drought came and caught us and parched up all
>   the trees.

The Lula well that "was gone dry" in Patton's song was probably the main one for the town, which feeds the water tower that stands today. You can wash your clothes in that well's water and then give them a "dry spell" at the town's laundromat.

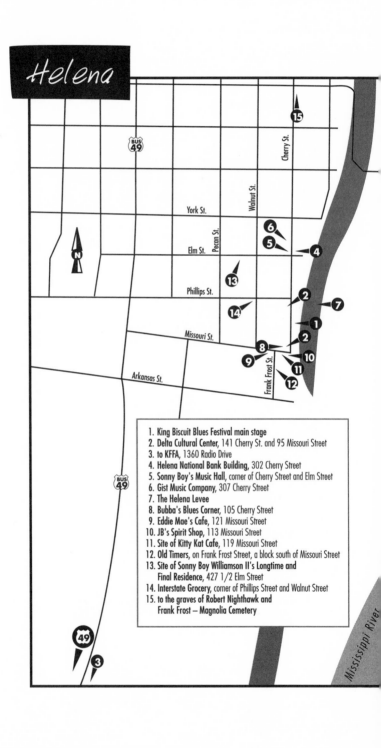

Helena

1. King Biscuit Blues Festival main stage
2. Delta Cultural Center, 141 Cherry St. and 95 Missouri Street
3. to KFFA, 1360 Radio Drive
4. Helena National Bank Building, 302 Cherry Street
5. Sonny Boy's Music Hall, corner of Cherry Street and Elm Street
6. Gist Music Company, 307 Cherry Street
7. The Helena Levee
8. Bubba's Blues Corner, 105 Cherry Street
9. Eddie Mae's Cafe, 121 Missouri Street
10. JB's Spirit Shop, 113 Missouri Street
11. Site of Kitty Kat Cafe, 119 Missouri Street
12. Old Timers, on Frank Frost Street, a block south of Missouri Street
13. Site of Sonny Boy Williamson II's Longtime and
    Final Residence, 427 1/2 Elm Street
14. Interstate Grocery, corner of Phillips Street and Walnut Street
15. to the graves of Robert Nighthawk and
    Frank Frost — Magnolia Cemetery

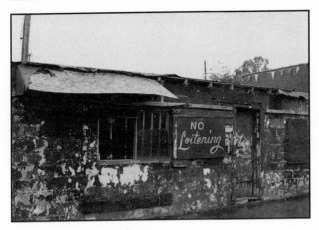

Club on Walnut Street, Helena

Helena, Arkansas

To get there: From Highway 61, take Highway 49 west, crossing the bridge into Arkansas. At the T in the road, turn right and drive about two miles, into Helena.

In the 1930s through the 1950s, this Mississippi River port town was notoriously "wide open"—an easy place to get your fill of liquor, gambling, prostitution, and music.

Bluesman Cedell Davis, who was born in Helena in 1926, remembered the old days in a 1976 interview: "They could go to town and stay there 'til maybe 9 or 12 o'clock [in Mississippi towns], they'd get out, you see. But now, Helena, you didn't have to worry about no time, see, wasn't no time—all night, see, because the joints stayed open all night, all day, you know what I mean like that. Well, anything that you wanted to spend money on or buy, it was there. All you had to do was look around, it was there."

Robert Johnson lived here for much of the last five years of his life, which ended in 1938. He stayed with girlfriend Estella Coleman, who was fifteen years his senior, and gave music lessons to her son, Robert Lockwood, Jr., who was only four years younger than Johnson. Howlin' Wolf is another blues star who was a resident of Helena for a while. Slide guitar master Robert Nighthawk was a native. Pianist Roosevelt Sykes was born here and started his career by playing in Helena joints for "a dollar and a red pop." Countless others stopped by to play in its many clubs.

But the town's proudest blues son, the king of Helena's blues scene and the man who broadcast it over the air, was Sonny Boy Williamson II, aka Rice Miller. Star of *King Biscuit Time*, the first blues radio show, Williamson was the center of a group of musicians that included Lockwood, Pinetop Perkins, Houston Stackhouse, Johnny Shines, Dudlow Taylor, and Peck Curtis. Although he was born in Glendora, Mississippi, it was in Helena that the great blues harpist became widely known. Through his radio fame, he attracted the attention of Jackson record producer Lillian McMurry, who would record him.

• King Biscuit Blues Festival

Held on the second weekend of October, this huge, free, three-day festival takes place on three stages in historic downtown Helena. The setting contributes as much as the music does to the good feeling here. At the main stage, the audience sits on the levee. Vendors set up in the streets, including local folks selling home-cooked foods. Musicians, too, are allowed to set up and play in the street, and some top-notch ones do. Local stores, bars, and restaurants stay open, many of them enjoying their busiest days of the year.

There is an acoustic/heritage stage with intimate performances from acoustic or smaller-group acts and a gospel stage (indoors, a good place to go if it starts to rain). The spirit of Sonny Boy Williamson seems to hover over the proceedings, inspiring the performers and relaxing the audience.

One problem you might have at King Biscuit is finding a place to stay. Try to make your reservations early, and look for rooms in communities within an hour's drive (in Arkansas or Mississippi), since there aren't many right in Helena. Another option is low-cost camping at the volunteer fire department's campground right at the festival.

• Delta Cultural Center
141 Cherry St. and 95 Missouri St.
(870) 338-4350

The center's two facilities, a block apart, are open from 10 A.M. to 5 P.M. Mondays through Saturdays and 1 to 5 P.M. Sundays. Admission is free.

The Cherry Street location features a permanent "Sounds of the Delta" exhibit and changing art exhibits. Blues is not the only thing on the menu. There are photos of east Arkansas-connected musicians in various genres, including Louis Jordan, Levon Helm, Al Green, and Rosetta Tharpe, along with bluesmen Johnnie Taylor, Howlin' Wolf, Albert King, Robert Lockwood, Jr., Robert Nighthawk, Cedell Davis, Harmonica Frank Floyd, Roosevelt Sykes, and Junior Wells.

And it covers the story of *King Biscuit Time*. The radio program started in November 1941 and became such a hit that Interstate Grocery was soon selling Sonny Boy Meal along with its King Biscuit Flour (both are still available in local groceries).

The announcer would start the program by saying, "Pass the biscuits, 'cause it's King Biscuit Time," and then Sonny Boy Williamson and Robert Lockwood, Jr., would sing:

> *Good evenin', everybody, tell me how you do*
> *We're the King Biscuit boys and we've come out to play for*
>   *you.*
> *Every mornin' for my breakfast, put King Biscuit on my table*
> *I'm invitin' all my friends and all my next-door neighbors.*

The museum has some drums that Peck Curtis played on the show. And, best of all, it still has the show itself. Yes, *King Biscuit Time* came back on the air in 1986, after six years off. And "Sunshine" Sonny Payne, who took over from original announcer Herb Langston in 1953, is still the host. He broadcasts live from the Delta Cultural Center on Cherry Street from 12:15 to 12:45 P.M. weekdays—unless there is a St. Louis ballgame—on KFFA, 1360 AM. Visitors are welcome, and Sonny will likely ask you to say a few words on the air.

The Missouri Street facility, in a restored 1912 train depot, is a small but well-designed museum covering all aspects of Arkansas Delta life and history, starting with prehistoric Indians and continuing with farming, the river, the Civil War, home life, and other subjects.

- **KFFA**
  1360 Radio Dr.
  (870) 338-8361

  To get there: From downtown Helena, head south on Highway 49B, past the turnoff for the Mississippi Bridge and on toward West Helena on Highway 49. Turn right at a light 3.0 miles past the bridge turnoff, and then bear to the right at the fork, onto Highway 185. Go 0.7 miles and look for the Sonny

Boy trailer in a field on the right. The station's offices and transmitter are just past that, on Radio Drive.

"Oh, yes! I used to listen to Sonny Boy and them all the time ... When *King Biscuit Time* was on, everybody stopped working in the fields to listen to them," said B. B. King.

The original KFFA building, on Walnut Street, has been torn down. Its next home, starting in the 1960s, was on the fifth floor of the tallest building in town, the **Helena National Bank Building** (then called the Solomon Building), 302 Cherry St. KFFA's studio and offices are now based in a trailer outside of town, next to its transmitter.

When he's not downtown doing *King Biscuit Time*, Sonny Payne works at the office, selling ads for the station. The original Sonny Boy logo-painted King Biscuit trailer, from which Sonny Boy and his comrades would play at gas stations and grocery stores throughout the countryside, is parked in a field near KFFA. It comes into town for the King Biscuit Festival.

- **Sonny Boy's Music Hall**
  Corner of Cherry St. and Elm St.
  (no phone)

An old mosaic in the walkway gives away this building's former existence as a J. C. Penney's. Now it is run by the Sonny Boy Blues Society, which hosts occasional shows in it, especially during the blues festival.

- **Gist Music Company**
  307 Cherry St.
  (870) 338-8441

Sonny Boy Williamson II, Robert Lockwood, Jr., and the other *King Biscuit Time* entertainers used to stop by this store after doing their show at the building across the street.

"They didn't buy much," says owner Morris Gist. "They didn't have much money." They would even repair a broken guitar string if possible, by tying a knot in it.

Gist started in the music business by selling records on Helena streets, with a windup Victrola to play them on, as a child during the Depression. From there he got a jukebox route, and eventually opened this store in 1953. "We didn't change a thing," Jean Gist says of the furnishings. "We like it like this." It still has the original high ceilings, old wood cabinets, and friendly owners.

• The Helena Levee

A brick walkway along the levee affords fine views of the harbor, the river, and some of Mississippi on the other side. Also notice the mural of blues artists on the levee wall near the Delta Cultural Center.

• Bubba's Blues Corner
105 Cherry St.
(870) 338-3501

Bubba Sullivan operates not just a record store but Helena's blues information center from the corner of a large antique store run by his wife. An Arkansas native who has been a blues fan for a long time, Sullivan is happy to discuss local history, the King Biscuit Festival, 1930s blues legends, or the latest hits. He plans to install a blues walk of fame in the sidewalk outside the store, commemorating deceased musicians who have played at King Biscuit (Luther Allison and Johnny Copeland are the first two scheduled for the honor). And, of course, Sullivan sells CDs, tapes, and vinyl records, including hard-to-find items, along with T-shirts, books, and videos.

• Eddie Mae's Cafe
121 Missouri St. (corner of Frank Frost St.)
(no phone)

"Home of Bluesman Frank Frost," the window proclaims, and it has an airbrushed portrait of the late singer-harpist-keyboardist. Frost lived and died in the apartment next to this restaurant/jook, which was owned by his longtime girlfriend Eddie Mae Walton. Walton died in 2002, and the club reopened under new management. There is live music here during King Biscuit Festival. Otherwise, it's open for food, drink, and jukebox blues.

• JB's Spirit Shop
113 Missouri St.

In Chris Hunt's 1992 documentary film *The Search for Robert Johnson*, John Hammond, Jr., interviews Johnny Shines inside this liquor store. In the film, Hammond and Shines also go outside onto two corners of Missouri and Frank Frost streets to play the blues, separately, simulating an old-fashioned "cutting contest." They wind up playing together in front of Eddie Mae's Cafe.

• Site of Kitty Kat Cafe
119 Missouri St.

This abandoned storefront, with no sign, was a jook joint where Robert Johnson used to play, according to Bubba Sullivan.

• Old Timers
On Frank Frost St. a block south of Missouri St.
(no phone)

A very downhome, friendly jook joint, this plain room has a refrigerator, but the beer is served from coolers, which also function as seats (there are some couches and chairs). Many customers bring their own bottles of liquor. Although young adults are welcome, the joint's name reinforces its role as a place where people in their late thirties and up can feel comfortable. A pool table is available and there is dancing, usually to a jukebox. Jam sessions take place from 4 to 7 P.M. Sundays, but don't expect any big names. "If you can halfway play your instrument, you can come and jam," one regular explains. Food is served—chili, sausages, barbecue, and hog maws.

• Site of Sonny Boy Williamson II's Longtime and Final Residence
427½ Elm St.

Helena was where Sonny Boy first made his fame, on the *King Biscuit Time* broadcasts. And the town was his home, on and off, throughout his life. From 1941 on, whenever he was staying in town, he rented a room in the boardinghouse on this site. In 1964 he came back for what he somehow knew was the final time. He told people he had come home to die. On May 25, 1965, he died in his sleep in his room in the boardinghouse.

The Sonny Boy Blues Society tried to raise funds to buy the building and restore it as a museum and concert hall. The effort failed, and the owner demolished it. The tile floor is about all that remains.

Former site of Interstate Grocer, the company that sponsored the
radio show *King Biscuit Time,* featuring Sonny Boy Williamson II,
Helena

- **Interstate Grocery**
  Corner of Phillips St. and Walnut St.

You can still see the painted-on name on this huge, two-story
brick building, the plant that once made King Biscuit Flour and
Sonny Boy Meal. Sonny Boy and the other musicians often
worked menial jobs at the plant besides playing on the radio show.
A tire business now occupies part of the building.

- **Graves of Robert Nighthawk and Frank Frost**
  Magnolia Cemetery

  To get there: From the north end of Cherry Street, circle around onto Perry
  Street. Three blocks past the traffic light, turn right onto College Street. Con-
  tinue 0.8 mile, through residential neighborhoods, until you see the sign for
  Magnolia Cemetery. Turn at the sign and go another 0.2 mile to the cemetery.

Helena's Sonny Boy Blues Society plans to erect markers for
both of these bluesmen. In Nighthawk's case, the marker will be
near the entrance to the cemetery, since no one knows the exact
spot where he is buried.

Robert Nighthawk, a Helena native who lived from November
30, 1909, to November 5, 1967, was a distinctive and influential
musician on both the harmonica (on which he recorded under
the name Robert Lee McCoy) and the guitar. He first recorded on

May 5, 1937, with Sonny Boy Williamson I and Big Joe Williams, and continued to record into the 1960s. He is most famous for his slide-guitar work, which influenced Muddy Waters, Elmore James, and Earl Hooker. He took the name "Nighthawk" while he was playing regularly on KFFA, after his signature tune, "Prowling Nighthawk." He is the father of the great Delta blues drummer Sam Carr, who worked with Frank Frost until Frost's death in 1999.

Frost, who was sixty-three when he died, was an Arkansas native who learned harmonica from Sonny Boy Williamson II. He also sang and played keyboards. Frost, Carr, and guitarist Big Jack Johnson made up the Jelly Roll Kings, who recorded several albums together and were a longtime favorite in Delta jook joints. Frost also recorded several albums under his own name, and played a musician in the 1986 film *Crossroads*.

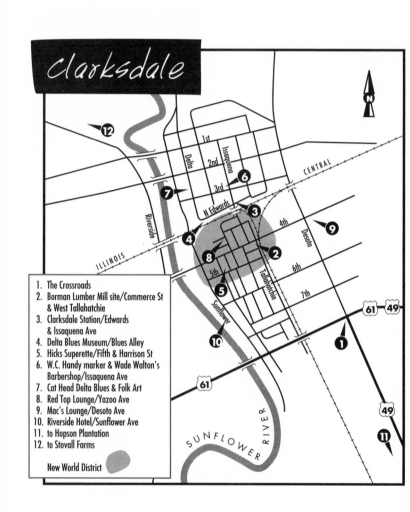

Clarksdale

1. The Crossroads
2. Borman Lumber Mill site/Commerce St & West Tallahatchie
3. Clarksdale Station/Edwards & Issaquena Ave
4. Delta Blues Museum/Blues Alley
5. Hicks Superette/Fifth & Harrison St
6. W.C. Handy marker & Wade Walton's Barbershop/Issaquena Ave
7. Cat Head Delta Blues & Folk Art
8. Red Top Lounge/Yazoo Ave
9. Mac's Lounge/Desoto Ave
10. Riverside Hotel/Sunflower Ave
11. to Hopson Plantation
12. to Stovall Farms

New World District

chapter 4

THE CLARKSDALE AREA

Clarksdale

When the railroads supplanted the river as the area's main artery, inland Clarksdale's importance surpassed that of older riverside towns like Vicksburg and Natchez. Clarksdale's location became even more strategic when the highways came in. The Illinois Central Railroad and highways 61 and 49 all intersected here, helping make it the richest town in the Delta, the cotton capital.

Naturally, the music followed. "I made more money in Clarksdale than I had ever earned," W. C. Handy boasted. "This was not strange. Everybody prospered in that Green Eden." A cultural hot spot even in Handy's day, Clarksdale was already an important blues town in the mid-1920s, when Son House learned to play guitar there from a man named Lemon (who had earned that nickname by mastering Blind Lemon Jefferson's recordings). The torch would pass when Muddy Waters learned from House in a nearby plantation jook a decade later.

The town's blues heritage continued through the postwar electric period, when Clarksdalians Junior Parker and Ike

Old Greyhound bus station, Third Street and Issaquena Avenue, Clarksdale (Since this photograph was taken, the station has been restored and now houses the Clarksdale Welcome Center.)

Turner, among others, would make their names. In recent years such artists as Big Jack Johnson and James "Super Chikan" Johnson have come from Clarksdale. One native Clarksdalian who left town in 1931, at age fourteen—John Lee Hooker—became a superstar in his old age.

With twenty thousand residents, Clarksdale is one of the Delta's larger cities but still a small town. (The motto that appears on signs— "Welcome to Clarksdale, Home of the Big Frog"— does *not* refer to a blues artist named the Big Frog. It's an invitation to companies to move to a town where they can be big frogs in a small pond.)

Besides the places listed below, there is sometimes live music at the Junction (11 miles north of Clarksdale on Highway 61 at Jonestown Rd., 662-358-4750), Red's (Sunflower and Martin Luther King avenues), and occasionally at other places, especially around festival time.

• The Crossroads

When local residents speak of the Crossroads, they mean the intersection of the Delta's two main highways, 49 and 61. That intersection is clearly *not* the place Robert Johnson sang about in his "Cross Road Blues":

> *I went to the cross road, fell down on my knees*
> *Asked the Lord above, "Have mercy, save poor Bob if*
> *you please."*

Johnson was almost certainly referring to a lonely country crossroads, not a busy intersection next to a big town. If Johnson or any other bluesmen sold their souls to the devil at a crossroads, they would probably have picked a more remote location. And even though the devil appears in some other Johnson songs (especially "Me and the Devil Blues"), "Cross Road Blues" makes no such reference. "The Lord above" is the only supernatural being Johnson deals with in this song.

Still, this Crossroads is important for what it is: the intersection of the two main blues highways, the roads on which countless blues singers and other Delta folks walked or rode as they sought work, migrated north, or just rambled. The highway alignments have changed over the years, however, so the Crossroads hasn't always been in this spot. With the new bypass outside town, the Crossroads may be relocating again.

The intersection itself isn't so romantic to look at these days. Delta Donuts and Abe's Bar-B-Q ("get your souvenir T-shirts here") are somewhat more interesting than the chain gas stations and convenience stores. The highway sign itself, with both numbers on it, might be worth stopping at for a moment of silence or a photo. Just be careful if you stop—it's a very busy intersection. Recently, a garish "crossroads" sign, twenty feet high with lights and blue guitars, has appeared at the intersection.

And before you get down on your knees, one more point: this juncture is not technically a crossroads of 49 and 61. It's actually only a T-intersection of the highways, because what looks like the extension of 49 is Desoto Avenue west of 61. The two highways join into one as you head north from this spot. They break apart again twenty-two miles north, near Moon Lake, where 61 continues north and 49 heads west to the Helena bridge. So if a three-way intersection is enough for you, that spot is another Crossroads.

The 1986 movie *Crossroads*, starring Karate Kid Ralph Macchio as a Juilliard student who hooks up with Willie Brown to seek a lost Robert Johnson song, revived the pop-mythology concept of a bluesman going to a crossroads to make a deal with the devil. (The crossroads in the movie was in Beulah, Mississippi.)

Throughout rural Mississippi, people refer to the intersection of the two most important roads in their area as "the cross-

roads." Since Robert Johnson was a rambling guy, it is impossible to tell which crossroads he is talking about, if any in particular, in his song.

Arkansas bluesman Robert Lowery, who sings a version of Johnson's "Cross Road Blues," introduces the song by explaining that
one is sometimes torn between two women who live down different
roads, so you stand at the crossroads wondering which to visit.

Years before Johnson's recording, Charley Patton had referred
to the crossroads in his 1929 "Joe Kirby Blues":

> *I was standing at the crossroad bidding my rider goodbye*
> *Train blowed for the crossroad, Lord, she started to fly.*

Patton's verse contains no suggestion of anything supernatural. Yet he does cast the crossroads as a significant and dramatic
place, a place where you might bid a lover goodbye and start a new
phase of life.

In the West African Yoruba religion—elements of which per-
sist in African American folk belief—crossroads belong to the god
Eshu, also called Elegba, Elegbara, or Legba. The crossroads is
where one recognizes truth and makes life-changing decisions.
Eshu is the messenger god, a childless wanderer, a mischievous
and creative spirit. Missionaries and others familiar with both
Yoruba and Christian beliefs sometimes equated Eshu with the
devil. So, by the 1930s in Mississippi, the Yoruba concept of going
to the crossroads to pray to Eshu for inspiration had changed into
meeting the devil there to exchange one's soul for musical gifts.

There is no evidence that Robert Johnson ever claimed he had
made a crossroads deal with the devil or anyone else. Some other
people attributed such a deal to him, however, to account for his
seemingly overnight transformation from inept to masterful musician. Son House and Willie Brown had known Johnson as a
pesky kid who would pick up their guitars and make unmusical
noise while they were on break. But one day, after they hadn't seen
him for a year or so, he picked up a guitar. "And man! He was so
good!" House related many years later. "When he finished, all our
mouths were standing open. I said, 'Well, ain't that fast! He's gone
now!'" But what had actually made the difference, of course, was
another age-old tradition: sitting down and practicing for hours
on end, or "woodshedding," as jazz musicians call it.

Another Delta bluesman *did* claim to have made a supernatural deal. That was Tommy Johnson (no relation to Robert). Tommy Johnson's brother, LeDell, told researcher David Evans the exact procedure:

> He said the reason he knowed so much, said he sold hisself to the devil. I asked him how. He said, "If you want to learn how to play anything you want to play and learn how to make songs yourself, you take your guitar and you go to where a road crosses that way, where a crossroad is. Get there, be sure to get there just a little 'fore 12 o'clock that night so you'll know you'll be there. You have your guitar and be playing a piece there by yourself. You have to go by yourself and be sitting there playing a piece. A big black man will walk up there and take your guitar, and he'll tune it. And then he'll play a piece and hand it back to you. That's the way I learned to play anything I want."

Note that LeDell did not specify a particular crossroads. So if you're interested in trying it, any lonely Delta crossroads ought to work. And by the way—it wouldn't hurt if you also spent several years practicing every day.

• The Clarksdale Mill

In "Moon Going Down," Charley Patton sings:

> *Oh where, where were you now, baby, Clarksdale mill burned down?*
> *Oh where, where were you now, baby, Clarksdale mill burned down?*
> *(Spoken: Boy, you know where I was) I was way down Sunflower with my face all full of frown.*

He apparently was referring to a fire at the Borman Lumber mill, which once occupied the now-vacant lot at Commerce Street and West Tallahatchie. The mill burned down shortly before Patton recorded the song, in 1930. It is unclear what business Patton had on nearby Sunflower Avenue. But a clue might come later in the song, when he sings about the green house over yonder full of the "finest young women, Lord, a man 'most ever seen." The Bottoms, the area along the Sunflower River now occupied by the Martin Luther King Community Park, was once a red-light district.

• Clarksdale Station

At Edwards and Issaquena avenues sits Clarksdale Station, built in 1926. This is the passenger depot where Muddy Waters bought his ticket, sat in the colored waiting room, and boarded the train to Chicago in 1943. Thousands of other black Clarksdalians, probably including other blues singers, made that trip from the same spot. And tens of thousands of others began the same kind of trip from similar train stations in other towns. But somehow Muddy is the classic example of that whole mass migration—the rural southerner saving up to buy the ticket, quitting his job at the plantation, packing up his guitar and a few other belongings, telling his woman he'll send for her. Of course, Muddy *did* find fame and fortune in Chicago. Many did not, and some soon made the return trip back south.

Coahoma County and the county chamber of commerce have purchased and renovated the depot as part of the Blues Alley project that also includes the Delta Blues Museum. Clarksdale Station has spaces for a nightclub, restaurants, and shops, which are for lease to private tenants.

There hasn't been passenger service to Clarksdale for several decades. But if the county's plan is carried out, the trains may roll again—to take tourists from Clarksdale to Lula, where they will be shuttled to the casinos along the Mississippi River.

• Delta Blues Museum

Old Freight Depot, 1 Blues Alley. The museum also has public archives on the second floor of the Carnegie Public Library, 114 Delta Ave. (662-627-6820; the Web site is www.deltablues museum.org).

Hours are 10 A.M. to 5 P.M. weekdays, to 2 P.M. Saturdays, with extended hours during festivals.

In October 1999, the Delta Blues Museum finally made its long-planned move to the Freight Depot, from its original home in the library. A 1918 brick building, the new digs are grander and more suitable to the museum's subject matter. However, the twelve-thousand-square-foot space is *too* big for the museum's modest collection. The staff is filling the extra space with changing photo exhibits while it tries to raise the $1.2 million needed for new permanent exhibits.

The small but interesting collection includes an oil drum from the company Big Jack Johnson, "the Oil Man," used to drive a

Illinois Central Railroad Freight Depot, built in 1918, home of the Delta Blues Museum since 1999, Clarksdale

truck for. The old gravestone for Mississippi Fred McDowell (misspelled "McDewell") is here. There are a metal guitar slide Lonnie Pitchford made from a leg of his kitchen table and a beat-up barber chair once used by singing barber Wade Walton. A rather creepy wax likeness of Muddy Waters sits in a chair. And there are signs from buildings that no longer exist, such as Clack's Grocery, where Alan Lomax recorded Son House.

A series of panels uses words and photos to showcase the astounding number of Mississippi musicians—in blues and other genres—who have achieved national renown. Another exhibit shows the development of stringed instruments, beginning with the African gourd banjo. And a display case is devoted to the underappreciated singer-drummer-harpist Big Mama Thornton. The changing blues-related photo exhibits generally are by nationally prominent photographers.

The museum gift shop is a great place to buy books, magazines, calendars, CDs, tapes, postcards, T-shirts, or hat pins. Many of the books and recordings are local or otherwise hard to find.

The museum also functions as a crossroads for blues travelers from all over. Blues-influenced rock stars Jimmy Page and Robert Plant shopped enthusiastically when they stopped by in 1998, fulfilling the title of their album of that year, *Walking into Clarksdale*. Many blues musicians drop in occasionally. And foreign visitors come in a steady stream to this little museum in a small Mississippi town.

From 3 to 5 P.M. Mondays through Thursdays, Clarksdale bluesman "Dr." Mike James uses the museum as a classroom where he teaches schoolchildren to play the blues on various instruments. Those who learn their lessons well may be asked to join James's band, the Interns. Some of the students also have formed their own bands, including Pure Blues Express, an all-girl group. Others have joined established groups in the area. The class sessions are open to the public.

- **Sunflower River Blues and Gospel Festival**
  (800) 626-3764

Probably because it happens in the dead of the Delta summer, early August, Clarksdale's annual blues festival has always drawn far fewer people than the festivals in Greenville (September) and Helena (October).

Don't let the heat scare you off, though. The smaller attendance at Sunflower gives it an intimate charm that the other two major Delta blues festivals lack. At Sunflower, it is easy to get close to the stage, to run into a performer in the crowd, or to get to a portable toilet.

The music also sets Sunflower apart. Its performers all are Mississippi natives or have strong connections to the state. The emphasis is on deep, traditional blues, not the blues-rock or soul-blues that dominate other festivals throughout the country. And admission is free!

- **New World District**

The railroad tracks separate Clarksdale's downtown (which was traditionally for whites only, except for blacks who had jobs there) from the longtime center of black life, commerce, and music, the New World. Issaquena Avenue and Fourth Street (now called Martin Luther King Avenue) are its main drags.

Although bandleader W. C. Handy mainly made his living at plantation dances, store openings, and political rallies when he lived in Clarksdale in the first decade of the century, he also jammed in New World joints—apparently playing something other than blues, however. In his autobiography, Handy praised the neighborhood's brothels full of "lush octoroons and quadroons from Louisiana, soft cream-colored fancy gals from Mississippi towns," and noted that "just beyond this section lived some of the oldest and most respectable Negro families."

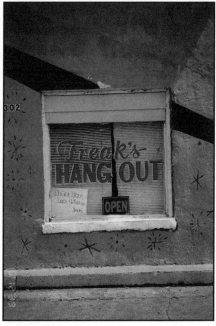

Window of business in the New World district, Clarksdale

The New World was still hopping in 1942, when folklorist Alan Lomax visited on a song-collecting trip and caught a young Honeyboy Edwards singing an Uncle Sam blues on a street corner. Lomax observed, "Peanut vendors and Mexican hot-tamale salesmen peddled their wares. Fried catfish was proclaimed available in every restaurant window. Wagons bulging with huge green watermelons stood at every corner. Inside the bars—the Dipsie Doodle, the Red Wagon, the Chicken Roost, and Catfish Bill's—jukeboxes moaned and blasted."

These days, the cathouses are gone and the food and drink choices are more limited, although a tamale man still sets up his cart at MLK and Issaquena. The New World is still the liveliest part of town. People walk in and out of bars or nearby churches, chat on the sidewalks, or drive slowly through. In the bars, gamblers will offer to play you a game of checkers, dominos, or Ping-Pong, as well as dice or cards. The blues is still heard, but usually only on jukeboxes or deejay turntables. Another part of Lomax's description could almost apply today: "Slick young sheiks in Harlem drape-shape coats, watch chains hanging below the knees of their peg-top trousers, watched the chicks go by, some in poor cotton dresses, some in the latest fashions."

On July 6, 1999, President Bill Clinton strolled down Issaquena Avenue in one stop on his tour of the nation's poorest places. Clinton posed for photographers in front of the New Roxy theater. Later he and his party ate ribs and tamales in a back room of **Hicks Superette**, Fifth and Harrison streets. A board near the counter commemorates that occasion with photos and a copy of a handwritten letter of thanks from Clinton. After Clinton's meal, at owner Eugene Hicks's suggestion, the president went outside and shook hands with townspeople who had been waiting in the heat to see him. (Clinton apparently had left his saxophone at home—there is no record of him playing the blues in Clarksdale.) Something about this downhome eatery attracts big names—John F. Kennedy, Jr., and his date dined there, sitting at a counter in the main room, during their 1991 visit to the town. There are no photos of Kennedy because, Hicks says, "I didn't know who he was, until later."

- ## W. C. Handy Home Marker
  Issaquena Ave. near Third St.

Handy, the "Father of the Blues," was a native of Florence, Alabama, and is most associated with Memphis. But he also lived in Clarksdale for a few years, beginning in 1903, when he was thirty, and took a job leading a black Knights of Pythias band—a nonblues, society band that he built up into a nine-piece orchestra. It was while Handy was living in Clarksdale—but waiting for a train at the Tutwiler depot—that he had the dramatic, career-changing introduction to the blues he describes in his autobiography.

A historical marker stands in front of the empty lot where Handy's house was.

- ## Wade Walton's Barber Shop
  317 Issaquena Ave.

The late Clarksdale barber Wade Walton was "discovered" as a musician by British blues scholar Paul Oliver in 1960. He made a fine album on Bluesville, *Shake 'Em on Down*, shortly after that, and sang and played guitar and harmonica at local nightspots and festivals. But, as he humbly admitted, barbering was his occupation and music just a pastime.

Even if he hadn't been a musician, Walton would merit a place in blues history as the barber to such luminaries as Sonny Boy Williamson II, Ike Turner, and Howlin' Wolf. When Allen Ginsberg visited Mississippi in 1983 or 1984, Wade Walton's Barber Shop was the first place he wanted to go. The blues-singing barber cut the beatnik poet's hair.

Walton appears in the documentary film *Deep Blues*, wearing an impossibly loud suit—plaid, with huge lapels—as he works and plays in his shop. He managed to combine both his interests when he played percussion by sharpening his razor against a leather strop, scraping, clanging, and swishing out a beat, as he did with guitarist Big Jack Johnson on "Close Shave Boogie" on the 1990 compilation album *Clarksdale, Mississippi: Coahoma the Blues* (available at the Delta Blues Museum gift shop) and with guitarist R. C. Smith on "Barbershop Rhythm" on the 1960 compilation *I Have to Paint My Face*. The 1990 album also includes Walton accompanying himself on guitar as he sings "Leaving Fourth Street," his lament about being forced to relocate from his longtime location at 304 Fourth St. in 1989. It concludes with the lines:

> *I knew all the time that I wasn't treated fair*
> *But if you come to 317 Issaquena, I can still cut your hair.*

All of Walton's musical instruments are depicted in the mural on the building: a harmonica, a guitar, and a razor strop, with razor. "Attention: No cameras or any recording devices beyond this point," warns a sign at the front door.

Walton died January 10, 2000, at age seventy-six, at a hospital in St. Louis, after a brief illness. He is buried at McLaurin Gardens in Lyon, just north of Clarksdale on Highway 61. The barbershop has closed, but the city has purchased the building. There are plans to turn it into a museum.

- **WROX**
  330 Sunflower Ave.
  (662) 627-1450

One of the nation's first blues radio stations, WROX was originally based at 317 Delta Ave., in the building now occupied by

Bluestown Music and Studio 61 recording. It then moved down the street to 257 Delta for a time in the 1950s, a time when Ike Turner worked there first as a janitor, then as a deejay. Elvis Presley gave a live performance on the station during that time. Then it relocated to the second floor of the McWilliams Building (Third Street and Delta Avenue, site of the closed Alcazar Hotel), and stayed there for most of the reign of Early "The Soul Man" Wright. In the early nineties it moved back to 317 Delta. In 1998, an out-of-town chain purchased WROX and converted it to talk format, with off-site programs. Happily, in 2003 WROX came back as a local, all-blues-format station. It can be heard at both 1450 AM and 92.1 FM.

The new ownership restores the tradition established during the long run of a unique radio personality. Eighty-three when he retired, Wright had been on the air for fifty-one years. When he started, he was one of the few black deejays in the country, on one of the first stations to play blues records (KFFA in nearby Helena already had a blues program, but its announcers were white). And his charming style and format remained virtually the same throughout his five-decade career.

Wright's daily blues and gospel shows were a favorite of residents and visitors alike. Teenagers in the fifties and sixties would honk their horns from the street outside the studio (which was not soundproof) in the McWilliams Building, hearing the horns on the air and shouting their requests to Wright when he came to the window. Howlin' Wolf, B. B. King, Little Milton, Bobby Rush, and Clarksdale native Ike Turner were among the blues artists who would stop and visit with Wright, live on the air, whenever they were in town. The not-so-famous—friends, strangers, locals, and tourists—also were welcome as guests on Wright's show.

Wright's on-air manner defied radio convention and delighted his listeners, many of whom made tapes of his shows. In a deep, slow voice, he spoke in a downhome vernacular. And he left long breaks of silence when he stopped to look for a record or take a drink of water. Wright and his studio—at the McWilliams location—are in a scene in the film *Deep Blues*, in which Wright interviews Big Jack Johnson on the air. "Ladies and gentlemen, I got a very extinglished guest here in the studio with me tonight," Wright begins.

Wright died December 12, 1999. He is buried at Heavenly Rest Cemetery, on Highway 61 just north of Clarksdale.

The building now houses Bluestown Music, which sells musical instruments, and Studio 61, a recording and production studio. Bubba O'Keefe, owner of Sunflower River Trading Company, plans to turn the second floor of 257 Delta into a WROX museum.

- **Cat Head Delta Blues & Folk Art**
  252 Delta Ave.
  (662) 624-5992

In an appropriately weathered building, this store is a treasure house for blues lovers. It stocks blues recordings, folk art, photographs, and related books and magazines. Fill in your Blind Lemon Jefferson collection, pick up a hand-labeled CD by an obscure local act, or maybe even find an out-of-print blues book here. There is a good selection of blues videos, too. Owners Roger and Jennifer Stolle are founts of knowledge on live blues and other events throughout the Delta. They post such information on their web site, www.cathead.biz, and also e-mail regular updates on blues happenings. The store also hosts frequent in-store performances and book signings, especially around festivals and holidays.

- **Ground Zero Blues Club**
  0 Blues Alley
  (662) 621-9009

This large club and restaurant, decorated jook-joint style, opened in 2001. One of its owners is actor Morgan Freeman, who grew up in Greenwood and lives in Charleston, Mississippi. The club was featured in the 2003 Starz! TV documentary *Last of the Mississippi Jukes*, including a scene of Alvin "Youngblood" Hart, Sam Carr, and Clarksdale bassist Anthony Sherrod playing on the Ground Zero stage.

Ground Zero presents live music regularly, although not always blues.

- **Red Top Lounge (aka Smitty's)**
  377 Yazoo Ave.
  (no phone)

This nightclub's facade was the backdrop for the wild cover photo on the Jelly Roll Kings' 1979 album *Rockin' the Juke Joint*

Down. The three Kings—Big Jack Johnson, Frank Frost, and Sam Carr—stand in front of the Red Top Lounge with their instruments, Jack looking especially dapper in a pink suit, wicked process, and oversized sunglasses, and playing a Beatle-style bass.

The Jelly Roll Kings were the house band for years at this large club, which also hosted shows by many other local and traveling blues acts. The club closed permanently in 2003.

- **Mac's Lounge**
  426 Desoto Ave.
  (no phone)

In the film *Deep Blues*, Big Jack Johnson and his band perform "Catfish Blues" and "Daddy, When Is Mama Coming Home?" at a 1990 Halloween party at the Pastime Lounge. That sequence includes a brief scene of a white-suited man dancing and prancing outside the club, in front of a smoking Boss Hog's Barbecue trailer. A photo of that dancer also appears on the cover of the *Deep Blues* soundtrack album. (Boss Hog's is at 1410 N. State St., 662-627-5264.)

The Pastime has since become Mac's Lounge. It has not had live music lately, but a deejay spins tunes on Thursday and Saturday nights.

- **Riverside Hotel**
  615 Sunflower Ave.
  (662) 624-9163

In the predawn hours of September 26, 1937, Bessie Smith, the Empress of the Blues, and her friend and driver, Richard Morgan, were driving from Memphis to Clarksdale on Highway 61, riding in Bessie's old Packard. They planned to stop in Clarksdale before heading to Darling, Mississippi, for a show there.

But somewhere about sixteen miles north of Clarksdale (the exact spot is unknown and the question is probably meaningless now, because the road has been widened and realigned several times since), the Packard struck a stopped truck that was partly blocking the narrow highway. The car rolled over and its wood roof was sheared off. Morgan was unhurt, but Smith's arm was badly injured, and she was bleeding profusely.

The truck driver drove off toward Clarksdale. Morgan flagged down a car that came by immediately; amazingly, it contained a physician, Dr. Hugh Smith, who was going fishing with his friend Henry Broughton. Smith and Broughton moved Bessie Smith to the shoulder of the road, and then the doctor tended to the injured singer while Broughton walked to a house to call for an ambulance. But it took Broughton a long time to make the call, and then the ambulance didn't arrive very quickly. Bessie's condition was deteriorating. So the men started moving the fishing tackle out of the back seat and into the trunk, to make room for Bessie in the car.

As they were doing that, a fast-moving car slammed into Hugh Smith's car, which was in the middle of the road. That car's occupants, a white couple who had been out partying, were not seriously injured but were hysterical. As the doctor examined them, the police and an ambulance arrived, followed by a second ambulance (summoned by the truck driver after he drove to Clarksdale). All three patients were driven to Clarksdale hospitals. Bessie Smith was taken to the G. T. Thomas Afro-American Hospital, where she was pronounced dead at 11:30 A.M., of shock, possible internal injuries, and compound bone fractures. She was forty-three.

The story is tragic but straightforward. But it became controversial a month later, when John Hammond, Sr., erroneously wrote in *down beat* magazine that the great singer "was refused treatment because of her color and bled to death while waiting for attention." That indictment of a racist system was so tantalizing that it hung on in popular mythology for years, despite Hammond's admission of error. It even became the essence of a 1959 play, *The Death of Bessie Smith,* by the distinguished playwright Edward Albee. The play reinforced the myth; it includes a scene in which Bessie's companion drives her to a white hospital in Memphis and is repeatedly told by a nurse to sit down and wait, even though he explains that he has a seriously injured woman in his car.

Hugh Smith explained long after the accident that no ambulance driver would have even tried to take a black person to a white hospital—and, at any rate, the black hospital and the white hospital in Clarksdale were less than half a mile from each other. A curious footnote to the story is that Hugh Smith, even though he was a part-time jazz pianist, had never heard of Bessie Smith, and had no idea who the woman was until much later.

The G. T. Thomas Afro-American Hospital opened just before World War I and closed about 1940. A few years later, Z. L. Hill bought the building and turned it into the Riverside Hotel, which she operated until her death in 1997. Among the guests Hill was proudest of were two decidedly non-blues duos: John F. Kennedy, Jr., and a date (in 1991), and a pair of Siamese twins. But years before that she also had housed Ike Turner and his band, Robert Nighthawk, and Sonny Boy Williamson II, who used to come by the hotel to serenade her.

Although it is well past its prime, the Riverside remains open as a no-frills place where rooms can be rented by the night, week, or month. Within walking distance from the festival grounds, it is a popular place to stay during the Sunflower River Blues Festival. For blues fanatics, the building's history, convenient location, and low price override its shabbiness.

- **Stackhouse Records/Rooster Blues Building**
  232 Sunflower Ave.

From 1988 until it closed ten years later, this steamboat-shaped building was the place to go in Clarksdale if you wanted to run into blues musicians, find out what was going on over the weekend, shop for old 78s, new CDs, photos, posters, mojos, or maps, or just hang out. It also housed Rooster Blues record company's office and recording studio. Stackhouse/Rooster was owned and operated by Jim O'Neal, a major blues buff who also founded *Living Blues* magazine (which he has since sold to the University of Mississippi). Lonnie Pitchford's *All Around Man,* Super Chikan's *Blues Come Home to Roost,* Robert "Bilbo" Walker's *Promised Land*, and other great Mississippi blues albums of the 1990s were recorded for O'Neal's Rooster Blues label. Bluesmen Pitchford and Lonnie Shields helped construct the studio.

The store reopened for a while under new management but has closed again.

- **Sarah's Kitchen**
  208 Sunflower Ave., almost at the corner of E. Second St. (but scheduled to move down the block in early 2004)
  (662) 627-3239

A longtime cook for the county jail, Miss Sarah also cooks here at her restaurant, although the place's hours have been irregular lately. If you find Sarah's open, ask about music. There used to be Thursday night blues jams/open mikes and occasional Saturday night special performances. Sarah's still has a blues-laden jukebox and a bulletin board of photos of musicians playing there.

Robert "Bilbo" Walker, a flamboyant Clarksdale-born bluesman who has relocated to Bakersfield, California, usually holds court at Sarah's around festival time. Record producer Jim O'Neal recorded Walker at Sarah's during the 1999 Sunflower festival, for release as a live album.

A mural of John Lee Hooker, Muddy Waters, and Bessie Smith—three famous blues musicians associated with Clarksdale—is on the side of **Carmen's Pawn Shop**, Sunflower Avenue at East Second Street.

- **Second Street**

Muddy Waters sang about this street in his 1949 "Canary Bird":

> *Well, canary bird, when you get to Clarksdale, please fly*
> *   down Second Street*
> *Well, canary bird, when you get to Clarksdale, please fly*
> *   down Second Street*
> *Well, you know I don't want you to stop flying until you take*
> *   the letter out to Stovall for me.*

The street leads to a bridge across the Sunflower River and connects to the highway to Stovall Farms.

- **Hopson Plantation and the Shack-Up Inn**

These sites are on the west side of Highway 49S, right at the city limits (2½ miles south of the Crossroads, immediately south of the 61 bypass), across from the "Welcome to Clarksdale, Home of the Big Frog" sign.

"The farmers run the black folks away when they got them me-chanicals in the fields, those machines to pick cotton," bluesman Honeyboy Edwards noted in his autobiography. The relationship between human hands and the cotton plant began to fall apart in 1941, when the first mechanically planted and harvested cotton crop was made on the Hopson Plantation.

Bluesman Pinetop Perkins, who played piano with Sonny Boy Williamson and Muddy Waters and has continued an active musical life well into his eighties, once lived and worked at Hopson. Another Clarksdale musician, Ike Turner, credits Perkins for teaching him boogie-woogie piano in the 1940s.

Owner James Butler married into the family that has farmed the land since 1832, and has diligently renovated its buildings using antique materials. The main building, used for dances and parties, includes a post office, a barbershop, and a small, very old cotton gin. Butler moved several old sharecropper shacks to his land from elsewhere in the area, renovated them, and installed features the sharecroppers never had, such as plumbing and air conditioning. A copper coil that had been part of a previous tenant's still has become part of the bathroom fixtures in one renovated cabin. Dubbed the Shack-Up Inn, the cabins are available for rent to vacationers. Reservations can be made by calling (662) 624-8329.

Hopson's commissary building is open to the public, even if you are not staying there. It is stuffed with antique signs, farm equipment, and other odd period pieces—although not all from the same period! The commissary has a bar and serves barbecue on Thursday evenings. It hosts live music about once a month and during the Sunflower and King Biscuit festivals.

Stovall

- ## Stovall Farms

To get there: From downtown Clarksdale, head west on First Street, across the bridge over the Sunflower River. Turn right immediately onto Riverside Avenue, then left immediately onto Oakhurst Avenue. It will change names a few times, eventually becoming Stovall Road. Stay on it past a cemetery and out of town. About three miles out, at the corner of Farrell Road, you will see a Stovall Farms sign in an orchard on the left.

The Stovall family took this land over in the 1840s, hung onto it through the Civil War, and still owns it. A member of the family, Howard Stovall (grandson of Muddy Waters's employer), occasionally plays with local blues bands and has served as director of the Blues Foundation, a Memphis-based organization that works to promote and preserve the blues worldwide. (Despite growing up at one of the blues' holy places, however, Stovall says he never heard any blues as a child. He finally met Muddy Waters in 1983, at Yale.) Stovall is one of the owners of Ground Zero nightclub in Clarksdale.

Muddy Waters, born April 4, 1915, in Rolling Fork, moved to the Stovall Plantation with his grandmother in 1918. At a jook joint on the plantation, Waters heard Son House play, and switched from harmonica to guitar. That jook may have been the one at Stovall Road and Highway 1, where a store now stands.

Decades earlier, this plantation was where the Chatmon brothers—Bo (who later would adopt the surname Carter), Lonnie (later one of the Mississippi Sheiks), Sam, and others—sharecropped in 1917–18 before returning to their hometown, Bolton, to go into music more seriously.

Past the sign is an iron fence in front of a big house. That is the spot where folklorist Alan Lomax inquired about a blues singer he had heard of who worked on the plantation—a young man named Muddy Waters. Another local bluesman, David Honeyboy Edwards, had said Waters was the best around. The Stovalls (their descendants still live there) directed Lomax to the sharecropper cabins nearby.

• Muddy Waters Home Site

To get there: From the Stovall Plantation's big house, keep going down the road. Just past the row of brick houses on the left is a dirt road. At the right of that road, on the main road, is where the cabin was. Grass has grown back over the site. Look closely and you may see some signs of the foundation, some depressions the building left in the earth. Look out into the fields and see where Waters worked, driving a tractor for 22½ cents an hour.

Muddy Waters grew up and made his first recordings in a cabin that recently has been dismantled and stored. In about 1918, when Waters was three, his family moved here from Rolling Fork. Waters, his wife, his uncle, and his grandmother all were still living in the cabin in 1941, when Lomax arrived with a portable recording unit. Although Waters thought the folklorist was really an undercover revenuer out to bust him for his moonshining, he couldn't resist the opportunity to record anyway. Using his bottleneck slide on Lomax's Martin guitar, Waters made his recording debut with tunes like "Country Blues" (which he would rename

"Walkin' Blues" when he rerecorded it, on electric guitar, in Chicago) and "I Be's Troubled" (which would become his first big hit, rerecorded and renamed "I Can't Be Satisfied"). One of the songs Waters recorded for Lomax, "Burr Clover Blues," pays tribute to his employer and to a crop raised there (Stovall, who had patented the burr-clover harvester in 1935, asked Waters to compose a song about the crop):

> Man, I told a man way up in Dundee
> Well, "You go out on Mr. Howard Stovall's place, he got all
>   the burr clover you need."
> Well, now, the reason I love that old Stovall's Farm so well
> Well, you know we have plenty money and we never be rais-
>   ing hell.

When asked to identify himself during an interview portion of the recording session, Waters confidently announced, "Name, McKinley Morganfield. Nickname, Muddy Waters. Stovall's famous guitar picker." Hearing his own recordings after Lomax sent them back would inspire Waters to head into town to make the trip north: "When Mr. Lomax played me the record I thought, 'Man, this boy can sing the blues!'"

Originally a one-room cabin of ax-hewn cypress planks, the Waters home had three additional rooms when Waters and his family occupied it in the 1940s. It had become a tin-roofed, tar-papered house much like countless others used by sharecroppers throughout the South. When the rock group ZZ Top visited it in 1983, however, a tornado had just knocked down the addition, leaving only the solid, antebellum original part. The band took some of the original wood that was lying about and had it made into "Muddywood" guitars, including one donated to the Delta Blues Museum.

Souvenir-seeking vandals (despite a sign that read "Please do not deface this sight, we will lay a Big Nasty Mojo on you if you take anything") and the elements were eroding the rest of the house. So, in a move controversial to blues lovers, the Stovall family struck a deal with the House of Blues nightclub chain in 1996 to dismantle the Waters cabin, restore it, and take it on tour. Builders using materials from another sharecropper shack at Stovall Farms restored the house to a half-size replica of its four-room, Muddy-era state. It was displayed at the 1996 Olympics in

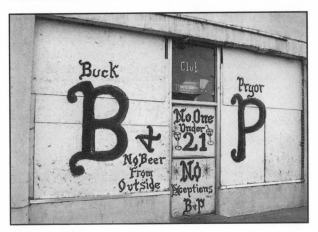

Club on Darby Avenue, Lambert

Atlanta and the 1997 Chicago Blues Festival, then packed away in a New Orleans warehouse. The house has returned to Clarksdale and now stands inside the Delta Blues Museum.

Farrell

About four miles south of Stovall on Highway 1, this community is the one Henry Sims sang about in "Farrell Blues." Sims, who played the fiddle on some of Charley Patton's recordings, took a rare turn at the vocals on this track, and Patton accompanied him:

> *I'm goin' to Farrell, where I can have my fun.*
> *Gon' get me a gal and I can have a run.*

Sims had a knack for playing with great bluesmen. A few years later, Alan Lomax would record him, as Son Simms, playing with Muddy Waters at Stovall.

Lambert

• **The Entertainment Club**
  721 Darby Ave.
  (662) 326-5934

  To get there from Clarksdale, take Highway 6 east to Marks. From Highway 6, head south on Highway 3, through Marks. Lambert is 4 miles south of Highway 6. When you get into the town, you will go by the large Lambert

Auto Parts building on the right. Soon after that is an old gas station on the right. At that intersection (which is Darby Avenue, but lacks a street sign there), turn left. Past the Union Planters Bank is a strip of old storefronts, including B&P Club on the right. The Entertainment Club is in a plain white building, without a sign or visible address, three doorways past the B&P Club. If it is during lesson time, you probably will hear music and see the "J. B. and the Midnighters Delta Blues Education Fund" van parked in front.

After a long career as a blues musician and auto mechanic in Mississippi and Chicago, Johnnie "Mr. Johnnie" Billington settled into a life of teaching children the blues business in the late 1970s. In November 1998, he relocated his blues school here from the Delta Blues Museum in Clarksdale (although one of Billington's former students, Michael "Dr. Mike" James, continues the program there).

As of this writing, the Entertainment Club had not yet become a full-fledged nightclub. A student band performs on Sundays from 8 P.M. to about 9. Visitors are also welcome to observe or participate in the after-school classes, 4 to 6 P.M. Mondays, Tuesdays, Thursdays, and Fridays. Free of charge, Billington trains his students to play guitar, bass, drums, or keyboards. The instruction goes way beyond musical notes, covering how to dress and act like a musician and, especially, how to make money as a musician. Within a few months, good students are accompanying Billington on paying gigs.

chapter 5

THE MID-DELTA

Tutwiler

To get there: Take Highway 49—*not* 49E or 49W—from where those three roads meet with Highway 3. Bear left toward town and follow the guitar-shaped sign to "town center and blues sites." Drive through the downtown to its end, then turn left around behind the buildings. You will see some large murals and the railroad tracks.

Tutwiler is where W. C. Handy had a blues epiphany. While waiting for a train here in 1903, he heard a "lean, loose-jointed Negro" play knife-slide guitar and sing, over and over, "Goin' where the Southern cross the Dog." Handy considered that "the weirdest music I had ever heard." He soon wrote and published some of the first compositions based on the blues and using the word "blues" in the title. One of those was "Yellow Dog Blues," incorporating the verse of his anonymous depot-mate.

One mural depicts Handy's magic moment. Another is about Sonny Boy Williamson II, and includes a large, good map to his grave. Still another proclaims Tutwiler the "Wood Duck Capital of the World."

Tutwiler no longer has a train station. However, there is a

Sonny Boy Williamson II mural, Tutwiler

concrete slab, next to the tracks near the murals, that used to be the foundation of a train depot. That one was newer than the one where Handy waited, which was somewhere in this same area of track.

• **Tutwiler Community Education Center**
301 Hancock St. (the large, modern building on Tutwiler's main street)
(662) 345-8393

The concrete slab has a Tutwiler family quilt painted by the Tutwiler Quilters, a women's cooperative. Their quilts—as well as quilted pot holders, bags, and place mats and blues-themed cards and T-shirts—are available at this center.

• **The Grave of Sonny Boy Williamson II**
To get there: From the murals, cross the tracks and head straight up Second Street, pausing to look at the intricately decorated house and car of Preston Smith at 405 Second Street. Continue up Second Street for 0.4 mile, to an intersection with a gas meter. Turn right and drive 1.5 miles, past some houses. Williamson's grave is on the right, back from the road and in front of the woods.

The great Sonny Boy Williamson II has connections to many places. He was born near Glendora. He lived much of his life, and

Grave of Sonny Boy Williamson II, Tutwiler

became famous, in Helena. He was living in Belzoni when Lillian McMurry encountered him. He recorded in Jackson and Chicago. Toward the end of his life he lived in London, playing with rock musicians and wearing tailored suits and bowler hats. He returned to Helena to die in 1965.

But he is buried near Tutwiler, on a small family plot near a falling-down church. Visitors often leave harmonicas as offerings. The grave remained unmarked until 1980, when Lillian McMurry of Trumpet Records erected a marker that reads:

Aleck Miller
Better known as
Willie "Sonny Boy" Williamson
Born Mar. 11, 1908
Died June 23, 1965
Son of
Jim Miller and Millie Miller
Internationally famous harmonica and vocal, blues artist discovered and
recorded by Trumpet Records, Jackson, Miss., from 1950 to 1955.

The stone has an incorrect date for Williamson's death. He died May 25, 1965. The actual year of his birth is uncertain—1897, 1899, 1901, and 1911 all are possible, as is the date on the stone. Bill Donoghue, a Williamson biographer, picks December 5, 1912, as the most likely birthdate. Williamson's first name is often spelled "Alec" or "Alex," and he went by the name "Rice" Miller.

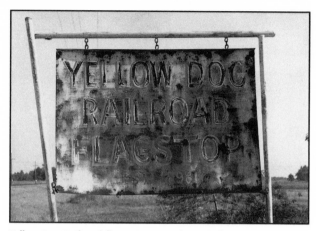

Yellow Dog Railroad flag stop sign, along Highway 49W, south of Tutwiler

There is a double tombstone in front of Williamson's for Mary Ashford and Julie Barner. They are two of his sisters, who both died October 11, 1995, in a fire in the house they shared.

As you drive south of Tutwiler, you may start noticing catfish ponds in the fields along the highways. Farm-raised catfish from these ponds are a big industry for Mississippi. Note the herons and other large birds hanging around for a snack. As the blues line goes:

> *I wish I was a catfish, swimming in the deep blue sea*
> *I'd have all these good-looking women fishing after me.*

On Highway 49W about four miles south of Tutwiler, there is a Yellow Dog flag stop sign, with a little red building near it where people once waited for the train.

Parchman

Mississippi State Pententiary
(662) 745-6611

To get there: Parchman shows up as a dot on highway maps, as if it were a town, but the dot represents just the main entrance and a few buildings. The prison grounds cover forty-six square miles to the west of the entrance. That entrance, with a dramatic-looking gate labeled "Mississippi State Penitentiary" in very large letters, is on the west side of Highway 49W, at the intersection with Highway 32. There is a sign telling you not to stop for photographs—so if you want to shoot a picture of the gate, do it while your car is moving. And yes, the people you see wearing striped outfits, working in the fields, are prisoners. Group tours of the prison may be arranged by calling Linda McIntyre at (662) 745-6611.

From its beginning in 1904 until reform finally came in the 1970s, the main purpose of Mississippi's state prison was not to rehabilitate or even to punish the convicts, but to make money by growing cotton. And it did so, pouring millions into the state treasury. While other state prisons cost the public money, Parchman *made* money for Mississippi. According to most descriptions, it closely resembled an antebellum plantation, with prisoners replacing slaves. (However, it has always housed white inmates and black inmates.)

Because the prisoners worked in organized gangs, as slaves had, Parchman became a kind of preserve for group work songs, which scholars consider an influence on the blues. Folklorists such as John and Alan Lomax visited the prison to document the songs. "What makes it go so better when you singing, you might nigh forget, and the time just pass away," a prisoner named Bama told the Lomaxes. Swinging their axes to chop wood, they sang verses such as these:

> *Big-Leg Rosie with her big-leg drawers*
> *Got me wearin' these striped overalls.*
> *When she walks she reels and rocks behind*
> *Ain't that enough to worry a po' convict's mind?*

A re-creation of a Parchman work song, sung by elderly ex-cons as they chop, appears in Alan Lomax's 1981 documentary, *The Land Where the Blues Began.* The blues is not the same as work songs. But the possibility of going to Parchman hung over the state's black men, including the bluesmen, and sometimes came out in their music. Charley Patton's "A Spoonful Blues," about the power of love over men, includes the line "It's mens on Parchman—doing lifetime—jus' 'bout a" with his slide guitar pronouncing "spoonful" to complete the sentence.

Son House admitted to spending two years in Parchman, from 1928 to 1930, although the details of his case are unknown.

Another inmate/blues singer was Booker T. Washington "Bukka" White, an older cousin of B. B. King. Born in 1909 in Houston, Mississippi, White had recorded a pair of religious songs in 1930—"I Am in the Heavenly Way" and "Promise True and Grand"—and in September 1937 made his big hit, "Shake 'Em on Down."

But the next month, White was indicted for murder. He was convicted on November 8 in Aberdeen and sentenced to life in Parchman. Somehow, however, he was released in 1940—apparently through a pardon from Governor Paul Johnson, according to researcher Gayle Dean Wardlow. The pardon likely was related to White's status as a recording artist. Immediately upon his release, White went to Chicago to record again. He was ready to cut versions of standard and popular blues songs, but producer Lester Melrose put White up in a hotel and gave him two days to write some original songs. "So help me God, I got down to it," White later recalled. He came up with twelve new compositions, including two related to his stay in Parchman.

In "When Can I Change My Clothes?" White dreamed of the day he could get out of the striped prison garb:

> *Never will forget that day when they had me in Parchman jail*
> *Wouldn't no one even come and go my bail*
> *I wonder how long, baby, before I can change my clothes?*

In later verses, White laments that he has to go out and work in the rain and cold wearing only those same flimsy clothes.

In that same 1940 session, White also recorded "Parchman Farm Blues," which opens:

> *Judge give me life this morning down on Parchman Farm*
> *I wouldn't hate it so much but I left my wife and home*

Despite writing these melancholy songs, White told an interviewer in 1963 that he had been treated better inside Parchman than he often was after his release. As a musician, he said, he had avoided much of the hard work in the prison.

By the 1980s, musical talent was still making prison life much easier. David Kimbrough (son of the late Junior Kimbrough), who served time at Parchman, told *Living Blues*: "I got down there and I was out there workin' in the fields, you know, choppin' grass, they had me doin' everything. And so I was singin' and [a guard said], 'You need to get in the Parchman band, man, you don't need to be out here in this field.' . . . Six months later I was in the band. Didn't never have it hard 'cept for the first six months I was there. I was always off the farm there with the band. We was gone every weekend, sometimes whole weeks, you know, livin' in motels . . . You out there workin', you could have your beer or whatever, get you a little sex or whatever you want to do out there, you know."

Kimbrough (then going by the name David Malone) secured a recording contract while he was a prisoner, and recorded a demo at Parchman for his 1994 album *I Got the Dog In Me*. He recorded the released version, however, in an Oxford studio after his parole, with non-inmate musicians.

House in the 1920s, White in the 1930s, and David Kimbrough in the 1980s are the only blues recording artists known to have done felony time in Parchman. Others may have had misdemeanor convictions that landed them there for less than a year.

A song by Mississippi jazz-blues pianist Mose Allison, "Parchman Farm" (covered by British bluesman John Mayall on his 1966 LP *Bluesbreakers with Eric Clapton*) is based on old work-song lyrics:

> *Sittin' over here on Parchman Farm*
> *Ain't ever done no man no harm.*

Allison followed it up with a more sardonic "New Parchman":

> *Sittin' over here on Parchman Farm*
> *The place is loaded with rustic charm*

The late Clarksdale barber-musician Wade Walton, on his out-of-print early-1960s LP *Shake 'Em on Down*, included the talking blues "Parchman Farm." On it, he talks about bringing two white folk-song collectors from California to the prison in 1958. A pistol-packing assistant warden turns them away, addressing Walton:

> *"Boy, you know better than this. If you know like I know*
>   *you'd leave here running right now."*
> *[Thrums a chord on the guitar.] That was me, Wade,*
>   *running.*
> *[The guitar simulates running.]*

> *Oh, Dave and I left Parchman farm. Didn't get no race*
> *relations done. Whoo!*

In 1961, Electro Record Company of Hattiesburg released a single, the instrumental "Harmonica Boogie," by the Confiners "of Mississippi State Penitentiary," the label noted. The group's four members were Parchman prisoners who were let out for public appearances.

Many nonfamous Parchman inmates undoubtedly sang the blues. Writer David Cohn collected verses from women inmates in the 1930s. Most of them were variations on standard blues verses, but this one gives some insight into the tedium of women prisoners' work:

> *You talkin' bout trouble, you don't know what trouble means.*
> *What I call trouble is a Singer sewing machine.*

The 1999 Hollywood film *Life*, directed by Ted Demme, features Eddie Murphy and Martin Lawrence as New York moonshine runners framed for murder while in Mississippi. They are sentenced to life sentences at Parchman that last from the 1930s to the 1990s. Although the movie was set in Mississippi, it was filmed in California. A jook joint scene features songs by Bo Carter and Casey Bill Weldon in the background. Later in the film there is a Bukka White song, with modern instrumental backing dubbed in.

Elvis Presley's dad, Vernon, was convicted in 1938 of forging a check, and was sentenced to three years in Parchman. He served only eight months. But it affected the three-year-old Elvis, who cried because he missed his daddy so. Elvis and his mom, Gladys, often rode the Greyhound, five hours each way, to visit Vernon.

Shelby

To get there: From Highway 61 (which becomes Broadway in Shelby), turn west onto Second Avenue at the town's main intersection.

Notice the old train depot on your left—it is the Shelby Public Library. Built in 1887, the building functioned as a depot

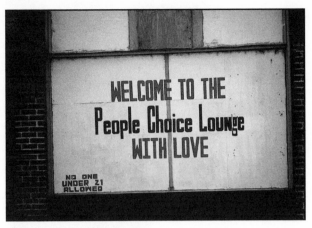

Club on Second Avenue, Shelby

until the 1960s. It became the town library in 1977. At the architect's insistence, the building was left pretty much in its original state. The original station sign and other artifacts are on display inside.

Continue to the second stop sign, at Second Avenue and Lake Street. There are three jook joints there, all painted in typical funky ways: "Welcome to the People Choice Lounge With Love," "The Windy City Blues House," and "Do Drop Inn, Big E's Place, where the good times are."

Windy City occasionally books touring blues acts—look for posters around town.

On Sundays, the Do Drop Inn has become a fairly reliable place to hear live blues. Little Jeno Tucker, a veteran blues singer based in Clarksdale, was a regular performer there until his death on June 13, 2000. Since then, other acts such as the Billy Smiley Band or the Wesley Jefferson Band have been playing.

This is a big club, with a dance floor and a bandstand, but it is dark and friendly enough to still have real jook joint ambiance. There are murals of city scenes and the Playboy bunny logo. It is open Fridays and Saturdays for dancing to a deejay. The live music is Sundays only, and it begins and ends early—about 6 to 10 P.M. (most of the musicians, young graduates of Clarksdale's Delta Blues Education Program, have to be in school the next morning).

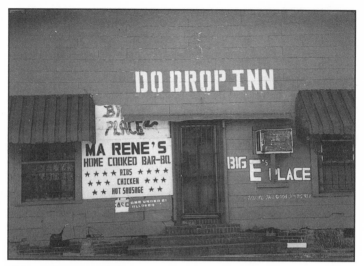

Club on Lake Street, Shelby

- **Between Shelby and Winstonville**

On the east side of Highway 61, about a half mile north of Winstonville, notice the bottletree near the road, in front of a house. An African American folk tradition, a bottletree is a real or artificial tree with bright-colored bottles slipped over its branches. The pretty bottles are supposed to lure evil spirits, which become trapped inside and thus cannot enter the house. Modern southerners, black and white, who display bottletrees usually do so out of respect for the tradition or because they like the way it looks—not because they really believe in spirit-proofing the house.

Mound Bayou

To get there: The town straddles Highway 61. Turn west at the Walk of Faith Church, a brick building before the U.S. post office, and drive two blocks to see the Bank of Mound Bayou, 201 W. Main St., which was built in 1904 at a cost of five thousand dollars. The bank closed in 1922 and has since been the Circle Inn. Currently it is abandoned and for sale. The city is considering buying it and turning it into a museum. Continue west past the bank building for another two blocks to city hall, which has a display inside of several striking sculptures of musicians, done by an unknown artist who left them there and then disappeared. There also is a small museum of nineteenth-century artifacts such as lamps, weapons, dishes, and photographs.

The outside of the building features a wooden relief sculpture of the faces of African American heroes.

This town was founded in 1887 as an all-black community of independent farmers. It thrived in its early years, with its own bank and an oil mill. But when cotton prices and land values fell in the 1920s, the farmers turned back to tenancy. The town has struggled along ever since.

Despite its all-black population, Mound Bayou has never been known as a big blues town. Bill Patton, Charley's father, saved the money he made farming at Dockery's, bought land near Mound Bayou, and opened a store there, according to one relative. Charley often spent time in the town.

Mound Bayou used to host an annual Heritage Festival on July 4, with national and regional blues and R&B acts, but the festival has been discontinued in recent years.

Merigold

- **Winery Rushing**

    To get there: Turn east on Merigold-Drew Road, an unmarked paved road just south of the Merigold town limits. Drive 2.8 miles east and look to the left. You'll see the sign through the fields, on a building about 200 yards north of the road:

    THE WINERY RUSHING
    Bonded Winery Mississippi No. 1
    Est. 1977

If you want to get close to the abandoned metal building, turn onto the dirt road. The fields by the main road contain the grapevines.

This is the town where Charley Patton encountered Bolivar County Deputy Sheriff Tom Rushing (misspelled in the song title), Merigold Town Marshal Tom Day, and a bootlegger named Halloway. Patton's 1929 "Tom Rushen Blues" tells a rather difficult-to-follow story of his run-in with these real-life characters, in which the narrator goes to bed, "hoping I would have my peace," but is shaken awake by Rushing. Halloway also has gone to bed, but Day takes whiskey "from under Halloway's head"— and maybe brings it to the man in prison who sings

> *It takes boozy-booze, Lord, to carry me through*
> *But each day seem like years in the jailhouse when there is*
> *no booze.*

Patton lived in Merigold from about 1924 to 1929, staying with a woman named Sudy. Rushing, who served as deputy sheriff from 1928 to 1932, later insisted he never arrested Patton, although he did hear him play, since the two men's professions brought them to the same places: "I heard him a good bit around Mound Bayou, Cleveland and Merigold. Being the deputy sheriff, we had to systematically watch those places, and we were welcome at any place to go in if we wanted to. In those days we got by with it. I don't know how we did it, but we never had to have a search warrant. We just went ahead and did things our way. The honky tonk is a big room. It's got a little café in connection with it where they would serve hamburgers and coffee and so forth. Then they had a big area where they could dance, and they had the side rooms for monkey business." Rushing said he was proud that Patton wrote and recorded a song about him.

Rushing's family remained in the area and in 1977 opened the Winery Rushing, making wines from Mississippi's native muscadine grapes. It was an ironic business for the descendants of a man whose job was to break stills and arrest the area's moonshiners and bootleggers. The winery closed in 1990, but the building remains.

- **Poor Monkey's Jook Joint**
  (601) 748-2254

  To get there: Driving north on Highway 61, go 1 mile past the Merigold–Mound Bayou turnoff, then turn left onto Pemble Road. Take first left onto a dirt road (which has recently been named Poor Monkey Road) and follow it until you see the club.

Unfortunately, Poor Monkey's does not feature live music, except for occasional special events. Nevertheless, it ranks high as a must-visit jook joint because of its archetypal out-in-the-country location, cobbled-together wood architecture, fun atmosphere and irrepressible owner.

The deejay spins soul-blues exclusively—Marvin Sease, Tyrone Davis, et al. The no-rap policy ensures a well-dressed, over-thirty-five crowd who come to pack the little dance floor, drink, and have fun. As at any jook worthy of the name, there is a pool table off in one corner. The ceiling is low and the place is subdivided into small rooms, giving it a homey feel. Silver streamers decorate the walls. Food is served.

The joint's owner, Willie Seaberry (aka Poor Monkey), clowns, mugs, sits in women's laps, and dances and struts about, making sure you appreciate his sharp suit of clothes. Twenty minutes later, he is parading about again, wearing a different outfit. He changes clothes at least half a dozen times a night.

Thursday is the big night, although recently the club has also been open on Mondays and occasionally on weekends. The music starts about 9 P.M. There is a cover charge.

Cleveland

- **Bolivar County Courthouse**
  Court St. at Bolivar Ave.

  To get there: From the intersection of highways 61 and 8, go west on Highway 8 (Sunflower Road) and turn south at the third light, onto Sharpe Avenue, then right onto Court Street.

A historic marker notes that W. C. Handy played in this building in about 1905. He also had another blues epiphany here, which affected him at least as much as the one he had in Tutwiler. A courthouse dance would definitely have been for whites. This may have been the site of an event Handy describes in his autobiography:

My own enlightenment came in Cleveland, Mississippi. I was leading the orchestra in a dance program when someone sent up an odd request. Would we play some of our "native music," the note asked. This baffled me. The men in this group could not "fake" and "sell it" like minstrel men. They were all musicians who bowed strictly to the authority of printed notes. So, we played for our anonymous fan an old-time Southern melody, a melody more sophisticated than native. A few moments later a second request came up. Would we object if a local colored band played a few dances?

Object! That was funny. What hornblower would object to a time-out and a smoke—on pay? We eased out gracefully as the newcomers entered. They were led by a long-legged chocolate boy and their band consisted of just three pieces, a battered guitar, a mandolin and a worn-out bass.

The music they made was pretty well in keeping with their looks. They struck up one of those over-and-over strains that seem to have no very clear beginning and certainly no ending at all. The strumming attained a disturbing monotony, but on and on it went, a kind of stuff that has long been associated with cane rows and levee camps. Thump-thump-thump went their feet on the floor. Their eyes rolled. Their shoulders swayed. And through it all that little agonizing strain persisted. It was not really annoying or unpleasant. Perhaps "haunting" is a better word, but I commenced to wonder if anybody besides small town rounders and their running mates would go for it.

The answer was not long in coming. A rain of silver dollars began to fall around the outlandish, stomping feet. The dancers went wild. Dollars, quarters, halves—the shower grew heavier and continued so long I strained my neck to get a better look. There before the boys lay more money than my nine musicians were being paid for the entire engagement. Then I saw the beauty of primitive music. They had the stuff the people wanted. It touched the spot. Their music wanted polishing, but it contained the essence. Folks would pay money for it. The old conventional music was well and good and had its place, no denying that, but there was no virtue in being blind when you had good eyes.

Handy "returned to Clarksdale and began immediately to work on this type of music."

Handy does not identify the trio as bluesmen. But that might be because he had as yet no name for the kind of music they played. His description sounds like how a trained musician would have described his first exposure to the blues (or his second—Handy does not make clear whether this was before or after he heard the Tutwiler guitarist).

Some writers have speculated that Charley Patton and Willie Brown may have been part of the trio that influenced Handy. But Patton and Brown would have been only in their early teens at the time, and even though Handy calls the musicians "boys," he doesn't seem to mean that literally. Also, Patton, who probably would have been the leader, was only five feet seven inches when fully grown, so it is doubtful that anyone would have described him as "long-legged."

Furthermore, the guitar-mandolin-bass instrumentation does not match what we know of Patton and Brown—or of other Delta blues musicians, for that matter. This probably was some kind of African American string band (decades later, the Mississippi Sheiks would become one of the few recorded examples of this type of group).

Regardless of who the musicians were, Handy saw that the blues was not only arresting, as he had learned at Tutwiler, but also lucrative. The scene also shows us how popular blues-type music already was in the Delta—even among whites—years before Handy, "the father of the blues," began writing it in sheet music, and decades before it appeared on records.

This courthouse is also where Charley Patton applied for four marriage licenses: Gertrude Lewis on September 12, 1908, Roxie Morrow on November 12, 1918, Bertha Reed on April 6, 1922, and Mattie Parker on June 7, 1924. Patton family members said the singer had eight wives. Those probably were not all legal marriages, however. Being a popular, charismatic entertainer, Charley Patton had no trouble picking up women, whether for marriage or more temporary arrangements. He reportedly often fought with his women, however, and would whack them with his guitar to end the fight.

- **Mississippi Delta Blues Hall of Fame**
  In Delta State University's Charles W. Capps Archives and Museum, Fifth Ave. at Court St.

  To get there: From the Bolivar County Courthouse, proceed west on Court Street to its end, at Fifth Avenue, then turn north. The Capps building is on your right.

For now, this is just a wall of fame temporarily housed at the Capps building. There are plaques for the honorees of the Peavine Awards: Charley Patton, Willie Brown, Tommy Johnson, Robert Lockwood, Jr., Henry Townsend, Robert Johnson, Son Thomas, Muddy Waters, Little Milton, Robert Nighthawk, Houston Stackhouse, Joe Willie Wilkins, Bukka White, Howlin' Wolf, and Ike Turner.

Plans call for the hall eventually to have its own building, with a Delta blues archive as well. The annual Peavine Awards ceremony includes a blues concert. Proceeds from ticket sales benefit a Robert Johnson Memorial Scholarship Fund, for music students at Delta State University. The date of the event is not fixed—information and details are available from the Cleveland-Bolivar County Chamber of Commerce (662-843-2712).

- **Airport Grocery**
  Highway 8
  (662) 843-4817

  To get there: From the Capps building, head north on Fifth Avenue to its end at Highway 8 (Sunflower Road). Turn west and go 1 mile, just past the airport turnoff at Bishop Road, to a wood building on the north side of the street. It is 2½ miles west of the intersection of highways 61 and 8.

Actually a restaurant, not a grocery, this is where Greenville bluesman Willie Foster recorded his CD *Live at Airport Grocery.* There are signed posters by various blues artists on the walls, and recorded blues is usually on the sound system. Live blues shows are held about four times a year. Call for a schedule of upcoming shows.

Rosedale

To many blues fans, the name of this town immediately recalls the following verse:

> *Lord, I'm going to Rosedale, gon' take my rider by my side*
> *We can still barrelhouse, baby, 'cause it's on the riverside.*

Robert Johnson sang those words in his 1937 "Traveling Riverside Blues." The British blues-rock group Cream included the verse in their 1969 cover of a *different* Robert Johnson song, "Cross Road Blues," which they renamed "Crossroads."

Johnson's original also mentions Vicksburg, Friars Point, and Tennessee. He apparently was truly traveling on or alongside the river, hitting the hot spots. In the 1930s and 1940s, riverside towns tended to be wide open, offering liquor, women, and music to riverboat men and others who passed through. Rosedale, a famed bootlegging center, was no exception.

The welcome signs ignore the town's blues-and-booze heritage and dub Rosedale "the Delta City of Brotherly Love." However, a group of locals has recently formed the Crossroads Blues Society, with an annual one-day Crossroads Blues Festival. They also hope to erect a monument to Robert Johnson (already the most-monumented bluesman, with markers in Hazlehurst, Morgan City, and Quito) in the Rosedale courthouse square.

At least one blues-loving Clarksdale resident has groused about Rosedale's appropriation of the term "crossroads," which many tourists associate with a Clarksdale intersection. Rosedale blues fans reply that they never heard Robert Johnson sing about Clarksdale. And Rosedale at least has the Hollywood version of the crossroads nearby, in Beulah.

Bruce Street is the traditional jook joint street in Rosedale, although most of the old buildings are gone. If Robert Johnson actually visited Rosedale, he probably played on this street. But then, Johnson played in the clubs, streets, depots, and private homes of many, many towns, so if you've been traveling around the Delta you've probably already stood on several places where he played.

- ### Great River Road State Park

     To get there: Go west on Highway 8 to its end, at Highway 1. Go south on Highway 1 and turn east at the park entrance.

This is Mississippi's only state park on the Mississippi River. It offers camping, boating, fishing, a playground, and a tower from which to view the river. It also must be one of the few state parks anywhere equipped with a whiskey still. On exhibit outside the park's visitors center, the still has a sign with a recipe (twenty-five pounds of corn, twenty pounds of sugar, six packs of yeast, ten gallons of water) and directions for making your own.

- ### Leo's Market

     1310 S. Main St. (Highway 1 at Highway 8)
     (662) 759-0071

A restaurant that features live music by high-quality blues acts from throughout the Delta the first and third Saturdays of the month. The owner, Leo McGee, organizes the town's blues festival.

- ### Bug's Place and the Blanche K. Bruce Foundation

     515 Bruce Street
     (662) 759-0251

Jessie "Junebug" Brown is the friendly and knowledgeable proprietor of this Bruce Street jook, a good place to have a beer and soak up atmosphere, but unfortunately without live music. Brown is one of the principals in the Blanche K. Bruce Foundation, named for Bruce, an ex-slave who became a U.S. senator in 1874, whom this street is named after. The foundation aims to preserve the culture and improve the lot of the poor in this part of the Delta. It puts on the Highway One Blues Festival, a homey affair in Rosedale, Beulah, and other towns in August.

Beulah

- ## The Crossroads from the Movie *Crossroads*

  To get there: From the intersection of highways 8 and 1 in Rosedale, drive 7.4 miles south on Highway 1, through Beulah, to a dirt road on the east side of the highway. It is 2.1 miles south of Beulah's Main Street or 1.6 miles south of the Beulah town limits. Turn onto the road and go over the tracks to the crossroads. There is a small cemetery next to it.

Of all the hundreds of lonely country crossroads in Mississippi, this is the one chosen by the makers of the 1986 movie *Crossroads* for the scenes in which several bluesmen make or break deals with the devil.

This book does not endorse selling one's soul to the devil to achieve blues mastery, either as a historical or a practical matter. Stay home and practice instead, which is really how the great blues artists achieved their powers. However, if you insist on re-creating the apocryphal ritual, this is a perfect place to do it. Not only do you have a real Mississippi Delta dirt-road crossroads, but you also get a cemetery, some burnt old trees, and the remains of a church at the spot. Dogs on surrounding farms tend to howl at night. It is dark except for the moon and stars. And the Mississippi River is close by, adding its power to the place.

Also, since it was really the movie *Crossroads* that popularized the whole crossroads-devil-blues concept, the movie's crossroads could be considered the "real" one.

Dockery

- ## Dockery Farms

  To get there: From the intersection of Highway 61 and Highway 8 in Cleveland, proceed east on Highway 8. After 6 miles you will come to the Dockery community sign, and after another 0.2 mile you will be at Keith Lane, the entrance to the plantation. The street is named after Keith Dockery.

A state historic marker at the road informs you that the plantation was "Established by Will Dockery in 1895 and operated 1937–1982 by Joe Rice Dockery. Included a post office, commissary and cotton gin. The plantation once employed Charley Patton, a legendary blues musician who inspired such greats as Muddy Waters, Robert Johnson, B. B. King and Elvis Presley."

It is nice that the state of Mississippi recognizes the importance of this site. However, that last sentence is not exactly correct. None of those four learned directly from Patton or, except for Johnson, probably ever heard him. Waters's main influences were Son House, an associate of Patton's, and Robert Johnson; Johnson learned directly from House and Willie Brown, another Patton associate; King's and Presley's connections to Patton are much more remote.

A list of well-known musicians who were strongly influenced or inspired by Patton would include Bukka White, John Lee Hooker and, especially, Howlin' Wolf, who learned directly from Patton at Dockery. But they only show traces of Patton's complex, unique style. Like any great artist, Patton is most important for his own work, not for his influence on others.

While many modern blues fans might overlook Patton's incredible music, one must also be wary of an opposite tendency—to deify Patton as the originator of the blues and Dockery as the birthplace of the blues. It is impossible to specify an exact time or place where the blues began—it seems to have appeared throughout the South within a short period around 1900—or to credit any one musician for its creation.

Patton's family moved to Dockery sometime between 1897 and 1904, just a few years after the plantation's 1895 founding. Charley, who was born in 1891, apprenticed to a guitarist at Dockery named Henry Sloan. Although he often traveled and moved away several times, Patton lived at Dockery on and off for about thirty years. There were many musicians in the surrounding towns and plantations, and Patton was the center of the whole scene.

Dockery's itself was home to up to four hundred families. Patton would entertain them at occasional outdoor concerts such as the one his nephew Tom Cannon remembered for an interviewer: "Just like on a Saturday a whole bunch would get together, and he'd play at Dockery's at the big store. There used to be a big brick store there at Dockery's. He'd sit out there on the store porch. People all from Lula, Cleveland, everywhere. Just like he plays for one of those places, they would charge so much at the door. They'd have it in one of these big buildings, and they'd charge 'em at the door."

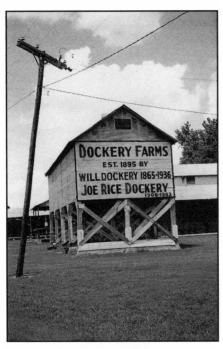

Barn at Dockery Farms, Dockery

Patton and Dockery's other bluesmen—including Willie Brown and Howlin' Wolf—also plied their trade at house parties or off the plantation. It was easy enough to get away—the Pea Vine railroad, a local branch of the Yellow Dog, stopped at the plantation's own depot. Other stops were at Halstead, Boyle, Skene, Victor, Pace, Symonds, Malvina, and Rosedale. The line earned its nickname because of its slow, meandering path. Patton sang about its whistle in "Pea Vine Blues":

I think I heard the Pea Vine whistle blow
Blowed just like my rider gettin' on board.

Some remnants of the Pea Vine tracks are visible along the dirt road across from Dockery's entrance. And back in Cleveland, there is a gift shop on Sharpe Avenue (in the commercial area known as Cotton Row) called Pea Vine Station, in tribute to this historic local railway.

The marvelous music Patton played at Dockery might have been recorded only in sharecroppers' memories had it not been for H. C. Speir, a Jackson music-store owner, who traveled to Dockery (probably following a tip from bluesman Bo Carter) to hear Patton. Speir liked what he heard, and arranged for Patton to record.

Dockery's is mentioned in Patton's 1934 "34 Blues," where he sings, "They run me from Will Dockery's." The song even gives some of the details: "Herman told Papa Charley, 'I don't want you hangin' 'round on my job no more.'" Herman Jett was a white

Dockery overseer who ran Patton off, considering him a loafer. He told Patton to quit interfering with people who were trying to work, and to go get a job.

Countless visitors have photographed the Dockery barn, on which the following is painted simply in red and black on white:

DOCKERY FARMS
Est. 1895 by
Will Dockery
1865–1936
Joe Rice Dockery
1906–1982

A subtler place to pose might be by the small Dockery Farms sign on the old filling station near the road, indicating the office. This is a working plantation and private property, so if you stop, respect the place and the privacy of the people living and working there.

The Dockerys paid no attention to the music of Patton and their other sharecroppers. "We were never the type of plantation owners who invited their help to come in and sing for parties," Keith Dockery, widow of Joe Rice Dockery (founder Will's son), told writer Robert Palmer. "I wish we had realized that these people were so important."

Pops Staples, patriarch of the Staples Singers pop-gospel group, also grew up on Dockery. His beautiful guitar playing is based on the downhome Delta blues.

Drew

Drew and Ruleville, fourteen miles apart on Highway 49W, were heavy blues territory in the 1920s. Charley Patton, Willie Brown, and the other Dockery-based musicians played often in jooks, at house parties, and on corners in these nearby towns. Tommy Johnson moved to Drew as a young man, in the company of an older woman, and developed his Delta-style music here before returning to the Jackson area. Howlin' Wolf lived in the area, farming and learning music, from 1923 to 1933. David Evans's *Big Road Blues* is a scholarly book that focuses on musicians of this area.

Ruleville

This town is the setting of B. F. Jackson's *Black Hometown Movie,* an amateur documentary that caused a sensation in the blues world in 1997–98, when some people thought that the man playing guitar and rack-mounted harmonica in it was Robert Johnson. Experts analyzed the brief, blurry footage to figure out what chords and tuning the musician was using. A Beale Street merchant tried to market the "original" to foreign collectors.

The excitement subsided quickly when someone noticed a poster for a 1941 film on a wall behind the musician. Johnson died in 1938.

The movie is still interesting, however, as probably the only film of a prewar Delta bluesman (he has not been identified, and is probably not anyone famous), although it is unfortunate that his moment on camera is so brief and blurry. It is also a rare document of an afternoon in the black community of a small Mississippi town in the 1940s. Jackson, who was white, made a film called *White Hometown Movie* the same day on the white side of downtown Ruleville. The films are available for viewing at the Southern Media Archive at the University of Mississippi, Oxford (662-915-5851), and at the Mississippi Department of Archives and History, 100 S. State St., Jackson (601-359-6876).

- **Greasy Street**

  To get there: From Highway 49W, turn west on Floyce Street (following the sign for Ruleville Business District) and continue 0.4 mile into town. Go past Main Street and take the next left onto Front Street.

"Greasy Street" is the local nickname for downtown Front Street, Ruleville's traditional jook joint strip. None of the clubs has live music these days, but deejays at the Top 10 Club and the Black Castle mix in a good deal of soul-blues. The Black Castle is the signless metal building at the south end of the row (the new metal building replaces the old wood building, which burned down recently). Saturdays and Sundays are the big nights at those clubs.

Glendora

To get there: From Ruleville, take Highway 8 east to 49E. Glendora is seven miles north.

Aleck "Rice" Miller, the man the world would know as Sonny Boy Williamson II, was born in Glendora probably in 1912. He left home, probably in his teens, after a fight with his father, and never returned.

The tiny town recognizes Sonny Boy with a large painted sign at its entrance, off Highway 49E. It also has a Sonny Boy Williamson Community Center.

On December 5 and 6, 1998 (Sonny Boy's birthday weekend), eighty-seven Glendora children (more than half of all the children in this four-hundred-person town) studied the blues harmonica. They all received harmonicas and two days of instruction by professional harpists including Sugar Blue, Paul deLay, Arthur Williams, "Jumpin'" Johnny Sansone, and Bruce "Sunpie" Barnes. Some of them thought the blues and the harmonica rather square at first, but by the end of the day they were playing blues riffs, gospel tunes, pop melodies. On the second day, even more children attended, and they were teaching one another techniques. A year later, none of them was still playing. The harmonicas were lost. But everyone in the town had become a little more aware of its most famous son and of the blues.

Greenwood & Area

RAILROAD

YAZOO RIVER

Grand Blvd
Poplar
Wolfhall
Main
Fulton

River Rd.

COLUMBUS & GREENVILLE RAILWAY

SOUTHERN

Carrollton

N

⑤
④
③
②
①
⑦
82
82
⑥
⑧
49E

1. Johnson Street
2. Baptist Town
3. Possible site of Robert Johnson's death
4. Leflore County Courthouse
5. to Little Zion Church
6. to Avalon, on Highway 7
7. to Three Forks and Itta Bena
8. Greenwood Blues Heritage Museum

49W
49E
7

Sunflower

L e f l o r e
C o u n t y

Avalon

LITTLE ZION
CHURCH

Itta Bena

82

Greenwood

BLUE LAKE
Quito

Moorhead

ROBERT JOHNSON MONUMENT

Morgan
City
7
49E

49W

Yazoo

In Quito: site of a store once thought
to be the Three Forks where Robert
Johnson was poisoned and a grave
marker for Johnson

chapter 6

THE GREENWOOD AREA

Greenwood

To get there: From Glendora take Highway 49E south to Highway 82. Greenwood is four miles east.

The welcome signs note that Greenwood is the Cotton Capital of the World, and a billboard labels the town "Home of Mississippi's most productive workforce." To blues fans, this town of twenty thousand on the eastern edge of the Delta is where Robert Johnson sang his last song and died so young.

The best prospects for catching live blues in Greenwood these days are occasional events at the Alluvian Hotel, 318 Howard Street, or the Flatland Grill, 101 Professional Plaza, or concerts at the Civic Center, Highway 7 at Carrollton Avenue. The town's annual Balloon Fest, in late June, includes a day of blues and gospel from local and national acts. And there is a soul-blues Cotton Capital Blues Festival the first Saturday of October.

Radio station WGNC, 104.3 FM, mixes a lot of contemporary blues into its programming. WVSD, 91.7 FM, the Mississippi Valley State University station, features blues some evenings. WGRM, 93.9 FM and 1240 AM, is a twenty-four-hour gospel station.

113

High school band marching on Johnson Street, Greenwood

Bluesman Honeyboy Edwards said he first heard Robert Johnson playing in an alley off **Johnson Street** (which is *not* named after the bluesman, but is a pleasant coincidence), near Main, in the fall of 1937. As Edwards recalls in his autobiography, *The World Don't Owe Me Nothing*: "He was playing the blues so good. One woman, she was full of that old corn whiskey, she said, 'Mister, you play me "Terraplane Blues"!' She didn't know she was talking to the man who made it! She said, 'If you play me "Terraplane Blues" I'll give you a dime!' He said, 'Miss, that's my number.' 'Well, you play it then.' He started playing and they knew who he was then. He was playing and trembling and hollering."

Johnson Street is Greenwood's main black business street. Robert Johnson was not the only bluesman to play on its corners for tips. Sonny Boy Williamson II, Elmore James, and Tommy McClennan were among the many other blues singers who played there while they were living in town or passing through.

Johnson Street turns into Carrolton Avenue at the Southern Railroad tracks. On your left, as you head east and cross the tracks, is **Baptist Town**, a poor residential neighborhood dominated by McKinney Chapel M. B. Church, at Young and Short streets near the tracks. Edwards says Johnson died in a room Johnson was renting in a house at Pelican and Young streets. Others say it is more likely that Johnson died on a plantation out in the country, however. His death certificate says he died "outside" Greenwood. At any rate, Johnson lived in Baptist Town for his last months on earth, and played the blues like nobody's business on Johnson Street.

Leflore County Courthouse at Market and Fulton is where a judge decided on October 15, 1998, that Crystal Springs truck driver Claud L. Johnson "is the biological son of Robert L. Johnson and under law is the sole heir." On June 15, 2000, the Mississippi Supreme Court upheld the ruling, rejecting an appeal by Annye Anderson and Robert Harris, a half-sister and grandson of Johnson's half-sister Carrie Harris Thompson.

The court records are public. To view them, turn right as you enter the building, and go into the chancery court clerk's office. Ask for case E-380, Estate of Robert L. Johnson, Deceased, vs. Willis B. Brumfield, Administrator. It fills half of a large drawer.

Claud was born to Virgie Jane Smith on December 16, 1931, in Lincoln County. "R. L. Johnson, laborer" was listed on the birth certificate as his father. Smith said, in a 1992 deposition, that the R. L. Johnson was none other than the bluesman. "Going to home parties, I met him," she said. "He would play there." Smith was seventeen; Johnson was nineteen. He was her first lover. She became pregnant. Johnson came by when Claud was five months old and asked Smith to run away to Tennessee with him, she said. She declined to go. He gave her twenty or thirty dollars, and she never saw him again.

Johnson died, penniless, when Claud was six. There was no point in Claud trying to prove who his father was until after the 1990 release of the Columbia CD set *Robert Johnson: The Complete Recordings*, which began putting money in the Johnson estate.

Besides court proceedings, the files have copies of documents including Johnson's two marriage certificates (to Virginia Travis in Penton on February 17, 1929, and to Callie Craft in Hazlehurst on May 4, 1931) and his death certificate.

- **Three Forks**
  Northeast side of intersection of highways 82 and 49E west of town—*not* the cloverleaf south of town where the highways also meet

The Three Forks Store is the jook joint where, according to testimony from eyewitness Honeyboy Edwards and hearsay from others, Robert Johnson gave his last performance and then wound up crawling on the floor in agony after drinking a bottle of poisoned whiskey. He died within a few days, or perhaps a few weeks. Although no one was ever prosecuted in the case, it seems that Johnson was murdered by the jook joint's owner, who had learned that Johnson was having an affair with the owner's wife. On the back of Johnson's death certificate, a county registrar wrote that Johnson died of syphilis. That idea apparently came from Luther Wade, the owner of Star of the West, the plantation where Johnson died. It is possible that Johnson had syphilis but also was poisoned. Or perhaps it was merely his heavy drinking that night that aggravated the symptoms of the syphilis or helped bring on another condition such as pneumonia. Whether or not Johnson was poisoned, it seems that he did sing his last song at a jook at this site. There is now a church and cemetery here, but they were built after Johnson's death, and after a tornado in the 1940s destroyed the jook where Johnson played. Also, the highway alignments have changed several times since the 1930s, so the intersection was not exactly where it is now.

- **Greenwood Blues Heritage Museum**
  214 Howard St. (but scheduled to move to 222 Howard St.)
  (662) 451-7800

This small museum is open 10 A.M. to 5 P.M. Mondays through Saturdays, or by appointment. It is owned by Steve LaVere who was the main force behind the 1990 CD reissue of Johnson's complete recordings.

The museum is largely about Johnson and his legacy. There is a wall of platinum and gold records for Johnson covers by the Red Hot Chili Peppers, Foghat, the Blues Brothers, Lynyrd Skynyrd, Led Zeppelin, et al. There are official Johnson-related products that were manufactured in recent years—guitar straps, T-shirts, even a six-pack of Crossroads beer. There are parts from Terraplane automobiles, the model Jackson sang about in "Terraplane Blues." Perhaps most interesting are the 1938 aerial maps of the Greenwood area showing the locations relevant to Johnson's death.

There also is a "Memphis Room" full of posters and photographs from the 1960s–'70s blues shows that LaVere was involved with in Memphis. And there are panels of images and information on general blues history with a Delta focus.

The museum is to move into a historic building at 222 Howard after that building is renovated. The new facility is to include a restaurant, a stage for live music, a bakery, and a local-history museum with a re-creation of the WGRM radio studio that was once in the building.

- **Cottonlandia Museum**
  1608 Highway 82W
  (662) 453-0925

This museum has a nice watercolor of Sam Chatmon on display and prints of it for sale. It also has blues videos for viewing on request. Other than that, there isn't much blues-specific content here. But there is much about the context of the blues: cotton-farming equipment, paintings of sharecropper scenes, a dugout canoe used by moonshiners, etc. It is open 9 A.M. to 5 P.M. weekdays and 2 to 5 P.M. Saturdays and Sundays.

- **Malouf Record Shop**
  712 George St.
  (662) 455-9737

This charming, old-fashioned record store in a tin building south of downtown seems like a relic of a bygone era. It sells soul-blues tapes and CDs, local concert tickets, and recorded sermons by Greenwood preachers.

- **Dancing Rabbit Books**
  311 Howard St.
  (662) 453-5995

A small, friendly bookstore, Dancing Rabbit (named for the Treaty of Dancing Rabbit Creek, in which the Choctaws ceded land to the settlers of this area) offers a few hard-to-find blues-related books, CDs, posters, and postcards. It also has some blues-related photography and art on display.

North of Greenwood

- **Robert Johnson's Grave**

  To get there: From Fulton Street in downtown Greenwood, drive north, over a bridge that takes you out of downtown. The street name becomes Grand Boulevard. Continue north, through residential neighborhoods, until you cross a second bridge that takes you over the Tallahatchie River and out of town. From that bridge, continue north 2.3 miles to Little Zion M.B. Church, on the left. There is a Johnson marker in the cemetery next to it, under the big tree toward the back.

Although this was the third place marked as Robert Johnson's grave (see Quito and Morgan City entries in this chapter for the other two), this seems to be the correct one, as there is an eyewitness who confirms the burial.

Rosie Eskridge was twenty-two when her husband, Tom, dug Robert Johnson's grave in the cemetery of this church, to which Eskridge still belongs. She does not remember the exact spot, but she knows it is near the big tree, which the casket sat under while the hole was being dug. Eskridge has never been a fan of Johnson's music or of blues in general, but she knew who the locally prominent singer was. She has not attempted to make money on her story and does not especially relish talking about it, so there is no reason to think she is making it up. Until someone comes forward with other evidence, it seems safe to call this cemetery—although probably not the exact spot where the marker is—Johnson's grave.

Eskridge's story jibes with the now-accepted location of the Three Forks jook joint where Johnson played his final gig, at highways 82 and 49 just outside of Greenwood, instead of in Quito as had been believed earlier. It also jibes with the statement on Johnson's death certificate that he was buried at "Zion Church," although that also can be said of the Morgan City location. There are many churches with "Zion" in their names. Since speaking with Eskridge, Steve LaVere decided this was the correct location of Johnson's grave, and he paid for the marker placed on the site in 2002. LaVere, a longtime Johnson researcher who used to control the rights to Johnson's songs, had identified the Morgan City site as Johnson's grave in the 1980s. (To see a map delineating the geography of the events of Johnson's poisoning, death, and burial, visit LaVere's Greenwood Blues Heritage Museum.)

The stone's inscription includes a reproduction of a Bible-themed note supposedly written by Johnson, along with a quote from his "From Four Until Late" and much commentary.

Given the struggles to correctly identify his grave and the multiple markers, another Johnson quote might be relevant here. In "Me and the Devil Blues," between repetitions of "You may bury my body down by the highway side," the great bluesman inserts a spoken aside: "Babe, I don't care where you bury my body when I'm dead and gone."

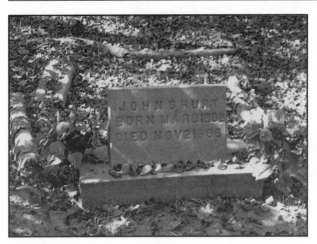

Mississippi John Hurt's grave, Avalon

Avalon

- ### Mississippi John Hurt's Grave

   To get there: From Greenwood take Highway 82 east to Highway 7. Driving north on Highway 7, watch closely for the tiny town of Avalon, which is halfway between Holcomb and Greenwood—it's about 11 miles to either of those towns. In Avalon, turn east onto Highway 41, which has a large sign that says "Auto Electric Rebuilders." After 3.3 miles the road changes from paved to gravel. Continue another 0.4 miles to an uphill dirt road on the left, next to a set of mailboxes (if you get to a mailbox labeled "Hurt" you will think you are at the right place but you have gone a bit too far—go back to the previous mailboxes). Turn onto that road, which winds past a white house and through the woods. The road is rutted but drivable by ordinary sedan, as long as it is dry. Also, be careful if you visit this site during hunting season, which is most of the fall and the winter. (Wearing bright clothes is a good idea.) Drive 1 mile, to a driveway on the right. Park in the driveway and walk about 100 feet farther up the road, to the cemetery entrance on the left. Orange plastic ribbons are tied to the trees around the entrance. Walk in and up the path. Other Hurts are buried in this lovely grove.

Mississippi John Hurt's grave is way in the back. It reads simply:

> *John S Hurt*
> Born Mar 8 1892
> Died Nov 2 1966

There is another stone nearby that you might mistake for Hurt's, but it is that of his son. It reads:

Mr. J. C. Hurt
Born: June 12, 1917
Died: October 12, 1996

Avalon's my hometown, always on my mind
Pretty mamas in Avalon want me there all the time.

New York's a good town, but it's not for mine.
Going back to Avalon, stay where there's pretty mamas all
    the time.
—Mississippi John Hurt, *"Avalon Blues"*

Mississippi John Hurt was born in nearby Teoc and spent most of his life in Avalon, farming and playing music for his own amusement and that of his friends and neighbors. About 1923 he played at a square dance with the white country fiddler Willie Narmour, filling in for Narmour's regular guitarist, Shell Smith. After Narmour and Smith garnered a record contract a few years later, they recommended Hurt to the record company. He traveled to Memphis and New York for two recording sessions in 1928.

Those songs were not big hits at the time, but they had become legendary by the time of the folk revival in the early 1960s. One of them, "Avalon Blues," gave a big clue about his location. Two Washington, D. C., fans headed to Mississippi and found Hurt, seventy years old, still playing and singing the same way he always had. He soon became a star of folk festivals and college stages, and made several new recordings. He returned to Avalon and died a few years later.

Valley

- ## Mississippi John Hurt Museum
  (662) 455-3958 (This is the home number of curator Art Browning; there is no phone at the museum.)

  To get there: From John Hurt's grave, drive back down the hill, past the mail-boxes, and turn left on the main road, continuing in the direction away from Highway 7. Go through a clump of buildings, the Valley community. The road becomes paved as you pass through the town. At the far edge of Val-ley, note Christ Advent Church on the right, and take the left onto the dirt road opposite. From that road, take the first left onto County Road 109. When that road forks, bear to the left, continuing on 109. When you come to a clearing, you will see the museum in the field on your left, before you get to the first house. (There are maps to the museum at Auto Electric Rebuilders on Highway 7 in Avalon, at Cottonlandia Museum in Greenwood, and at Upchurch Store in Teoc.)

Housed in the little shotgun shack that Hurt lived in, this museum contains photos, record jackets, and articles about Hurt, as well as artifacts from his era, including a table that he made. Part of its charm is its remoteness. The house has been moved from its original location a few miles away. Driving to it gives you a feel for the land that produced John Hurt and his music—the Carroll County hills—and might stimulate some ideas about why Hurt's music sounds so different from that of the musicians of the nearby Delta flatlands.

Hurt's granddaughter Mary Frances Hurt Wright, a Chicago schoolteacher, saved his old house from demolition, moved it, and restored it. It opened July 4, 2002, with a dedication ceremony that included a surprise performance by 1960s music star John Sebastian of the Lovin' Spoonful, a group that took its name from a Hurt song. A John Hurt Festival takes place at the site every year on July 4.

Itta Bena

- ## Ralph Lembo's Store
  114 Humphreys St.

  To get there: Go west from Greenwood on Highway 82 to Highway 7. Turn south onto Highway 7, which becomes Main Street in Itta Bena. Humphreys is the northernmost of the two streets that border the grassy strip in the middle of town. Turn east on Humphreys. Lembo's store is on the north side of the street, next to Fred's Express. Recently it was vacant and had a "Mattie's Upholstery" sign above the front window.

The Sicilian-born Ralph Lembo, who lived from 1896 to 1960, peddled dry goods from a cart in Itta Bena before opening this store. Like Jackson's H. C. Speir, Lembo was another white furniture-and-record-store owner who scouted for bluesmen on the side. But while Speir traveled around the state looking for artists, Lembo stayed home in Itta Bena. Probably for that reason, he was not nearly as successful as Speir at finding artists. Lembo did score two big finds: Rubin Lacy and Bukka White, who both auditioned at the store. White described his 1930 audition to an interviewer:

I went on up there and Ralph give me a big glass half full of bonded whiskey. I don't believe I ever had tasted a bonded whiskey. It taste just like syrup to me, it was so good. And I drank the last of it and he caught me licking the glass, just holding it up getting the last drop. And I could feel it commencing building me up. I played "Downtown Women Sic 'Em Dogs On You" and he just had a fit. He said, "Can you stand another half a glass?" I said, "You can fill it up; it ain't gonna hurt." Well, I had sense enough to didn't drink it, I just sipped a little on it 'til I got through, then I killed it. Ooooo, I was the happiest soul going down that highway. You be hearing my foots hitting them rocks like somebody had a sledgehammer hitting on the rock. Man, I was feeling good.

Before Speir tracked down Charley Patton and got him to record, Lembo had talked to Patton, but couldn't make a deal with him.

Lembo also brought Blind Lemon Jefferson, who was already a blues star, to Itta Bena for a performance at Lembo's store in about 1927. Lembo paid Jefferson's train fare from Chicago, and charged people twenty-five cents to attend the Saturday afternoon show. He also booked Jefferson to play at a local high school on the same trip. Both performances were financial failures. And Lembo's attempt to get Jefferson to record while he was in town also fell through.

In about 1930, Lembo heard Walter Vincson and Lonnie Chatmon, who were in Itta Bena to play a white dance. Lembo sent them to Shreveport, Louisiana, to record for Polk Brockman of Okeh Records. At that session they came up with their name—the Mississippi Sheiks.

Vincson said he wrote the Sheiks' big hit, "Sitting on Top of the World," while he and Chatmon were sitting on the street in Itta Bena, rehearsing for a dance—probably on the same visit when Lembo heard them, since they recorded the song at their first session. Chatmon commented, "What kind of song is that?" when he first heard it. But they knew they were onto something good when their tip bucket filled up as they were still working on the song.

Honeyboy Edwards says he lived in the area for a while and sometimes swept Lembo's floor, in hopes of getting a chance to record. The ploy did not work.

Blue Lake

To get there: From downtown Itta Bena, go a few blocks north on Main Street (Highway 7) to an old Gulf gas station on the west side of the street. Turn west there, onto Fitzhugh Street. Follow that street as it goes around a large cotton-gin complex. It becomes gravel for a bit, but stay on it as it becomes paved again and goes through a residential area. After 3.6 miles you will come to a stop sign, just past a cemetery on the right. Turn left and then right at the next street, so you are continuing west. Go 2 miles to a bridge on your left. Drive over the bridge and park.

B. B. King is sometimes said to be from Itta Bena. He actually was born a few miles out of town, on the shore of Blue Lake, near the tiny community called Berclair. At any rate, he stayed in this immediate area only until he was about five. King considers Indianola, where he lived from age thirteen on, his hometown. He plays an annual homecoming concert in Indianola, but he has not forgotten Itta Bena, either. He recently has contributed to the capital campaign at Itta Bena's Mississippi Valley State University, with both cash and a benefit performance.

Blue Lake is a lovely and popular fishing spot. A few houses stand on its banks, but the house King was born in, on the south bank, is no longer there.

Quito

- **Three Forks Store**

    To get there: From Highway 82, take Highway 7 south through Itta Bena, following the signs as the highway zigzags to the right and back to the left. After the second zigzag, continue 2.6 miles south on Highway 7. On the east side of the highway, at the last corner north of the bridge, is a house said to be the building that once was the original Three Forks Store. Since it is now someone's home, respect the privacy of the residents.

Until it fell down a few years ago, this is where a house stood that previously had been a store called "Three Forks." Robert Johnson played his final performance, and was poisoned, in a jook joint called "Three Forks." However, this is not the same "Three Forks." That name is a common one, attached to many places where three roads come together.

This Three Forks store, when it was operating, was at a different location. It was later moved to this spot and turned into a residence. To get to what is said to be its original location: Turn east onto the road just north of this spot, then turn right onto the first gravel road. This intersection was called Three Forks, and there was a store and jook joint here. It is possible that Johnson played

Marker at what might be Robert Johnson's grave, Payne Chapel M. B. Church, Quito

here sometime in his life. But it does not seem to be the place where he played his final gig.

After the building was moved, the *business* also was relocated, to another building that has burned down. The Delta Blues Museum in Clarksdale has the "Three Forks" sign from that burned-down building—not from the Three Forks in Greenwood, which is now believed to be the site where Johnson last sang.

• Robert Johnson's Grave Marker

To get there: From the Three Forks house, continue south on Highway 7 for 0.2 mile, over the bridge and into Quito (there is no sign for the town). Just past the bridge, turn west onto a dirt road across from the big cotton gin with a "HE Hardwick-Etter Ginning Systems" sign. Drive in a block, to the church on the right. Park and walk into the cemetery. Marked with a flat stone, Johnson's grave is in the back, away from the road, near the woods.

In its November–December 1990 issue devoted to Robert Johnson, *Living Blues* magazine identified the cemetery of Payne Chapel M. B. Church, Quito, as Johnson's resting place. The issue even included a photo of the unmarked patch of land, next to a stump, that was supposed to be the grave. The information had come from one of Johnson's ex-girlfriends, who insisted he was in Hell and wouldn't appreciate flowers, much less a tombstone. But a Georgia rock band, the Tombstones, disregarded that advice and showed up soon afterward to place a marker there.

This flat marker is much smaller than the ones at Johnson's other marked graves. It draws its share of offerings, however—especially guitar picks. It is inscribed with a guitar and a treble clef, and reads:

> *Robert Johnson*
> May 8, 1911
> Aug. 16, 1938
> Resting in the blues

The evidence now points to the grave on Money Road, north of Greenwood, as the correct one.

Morgan City

- ## Another Robert Johnson Grave Marker

  To get there: From the Quito grave marker, get back onto Highway 7 and head 3.7 miles south. At a sign on the right that reads "Matthew's Brake Wildlife Preserve," turn east and go to the cemetery by the white church ahead on the left.

After Johnson researcher Steve LaVere found a Three Forks store in Quito, he asked about a "Zion Church"—since that is where Johnson's death certificate says he is buried—and found this one, Mount Zion Missionary Baptist. Going by LaVere's pointer, with financing from Sony Records, which issued the fabulously successful Johnson reissue CD set, a new organization called the Mount Zion Fund erected this marker. The fund has since gone on to coordinate the erection of markers for many other blues artists.

This church was founded in 1909 (although the building was rebuilt in 1983), so it existed during Johnson's day. However, this is not where Johnson is buried. LaVere has admitted that he identified it erroneously and now believes that Johnson is buried at Little Zion Church north of Greenwood.

Even when it was believed that Johnson was buried in this cemetery, no one knew the exact spot. So the monument was placed near the road to fulfill Johnson's line from "Me and the Devil Blues":

> *You may bury my body down by the highway side*
> *So my old evil spirit can catch a Greyhound bus and ride.*

The largest of Johnson's three grave markers, this is an impressive obelisk, lengthily inscribed on all four sides:

1. Born in Hazlehurst, Copiah County, the recording career and brief transit of Robert Johnson left an enormous legacy to American music. Preserved for the ages by Columbia Recording Company, the body of his work is considered to be among the most powerful of its kind, a haunting and lyrical portrait of the human spirit.

2. [The familiar dime-store photo of Johnson, cigarette in mouth, has been replaced on this side after being stolen.] Robert Johnson "King of the Delta Blues Singers." His music struck a chord that continues to resonate. His blues addressed generations he would never know and made poetry of his visions and fears.

Monument at a cemetery where Robert Johnson might be buried, Mount Zion M. B. Church, Morgan City

3. "You may bury my body down by the highway side" . . . This monument erected April 20, 1991 through the generosity of people across America, with profound respect and appreciation for the people and culture of the Mississippi Delta.

4. [A list of all of Johnson's songs.]

Johnson has two or three more grave markers than any other blues artist, and many more words inscribed on the stones. He also gets more gifts left at his graves. Sonny Boy Williamson II's marker, which comes in second, usually has a harmonica or two and some coins. Johnson's draws jewelry, notes scrawled on food-stamp tickets or other kinds of paper, CDs by obscure artists (perhaps left by the artists themselves, hoping that some of Johnson's spirit will penetrate their music), pencils, cigarettes, flowers, beer cans, pretty stones, and of course guitar picks.

Moorhead

- ## Where the Southern Cross the Dog

To get there: From Robert Johnson's graves, head back north on Highway 7 to Highway 82. Turn west and go 13 miles to Highway 3. Turn south into Moorhead. "Home of Grand Ole Opry star Johnny Russell," the signs proclaim. You'll be on Olive Street. At Olive and Southern Avenue, there is a railroad crossing sign. You'll get to the Yellow Dog Cafe and Roberts Country Store, a general store with people sitting on the front porch in an archetypal southern scene. Inside, the store continues the archetype—perhaps a little self-consciously. To the right of the building, on Southern, is the spot where the Southern crosses the Dog. As of this writing, the state historic marker had been removed for renovation.

The intersection of the Southern and the Dog is a perfectly perpendicular crossing, due north-south and east-west. And it sits in a handsome spot. A wood pavilion suitable for picnicking is off to the side. Trees and grass are plentiful. There is a U.S. post office right near the crossing and an old water tower nearby.

The line "I'm going where the Southern cross the Dog," repeated over and over, baffled W. C. Handy when he heard it at the Tutwiler train station in 1903. Many sources infer that the Tutwiler singer was headed for Moorhead. However, that may already have been just a standard blues line. He might actually have been going somewhere else or just hanging out at the depot.

At any rate, some blues singer once coined a line about heading to this spot—the intersection of the Southern (which is still active) and the Yazoo and Mississippi Valley (whose tracks are now part of the Columbus and Greenville line, or C&G). The Yazoo and Mississippi Valley was also known as the Yazoo Delta, and "Yellow Dog" was apparently a reinterpretation of the initials "YD." Writer Paul Oliver talked to some people, however, who maintained that the line was named after an actual yellow dog that used to stand along the track and bark and to others who said it was so named by employees of rival lines, deriding it as a "short dog" or minor line.

Handy used the line in his 1914 composition "Yellow Dog Rag," which he would later rename "Yellow Dog Blues." "My song was made around the line (but not the music) I had heard the guitar player, impassive, sing that night at Tutwiler," Handy explained in his autobiography. Handy's lyrics paint a picture of a happy Southland:

Money don't zactly grow on trees
On cotton stalks it grows with ease.

Charley Patton also sings "I'm goin' where the Southern cross the Dog" in his "Green River Blues." Patton, like the Tutwiler singer, sings the same line three times, without a rhyming answer line. Some people conjecture that Patton *was* the singer Handy heard at Tutwiler. But since Patton probably was born in 1891, he would have been twelve years old when Handy heard the singer, and Handy didn't say it was a boy he heard.

Big Bill Broonzy also sang about the spot in his 1935 "The Southern Blues," which includes a train whistle. Broonzy first wonders aloud whether his baby caught the Southern or the Dog. Then he considers getting a job on the Southern line, to make the money to send for her. Finally he announces:

Said Southern cross the Dog at Moorhead, mama, Lord, and
she keeps on through
I say my baby's gone to Georgia, I believe I'll go to
Georgia too.

Broonzy's song helps explain *why* someone would be determined to get to Moorhead: to get a railroad job or to leave the state.

Greenville & Area

1. The Levee
2. Nelson Street
3. The Flowing Fountain/Nelson Street
4. Walnut Street
5. to Delta Blues Festival site
6. Eugene Powell's grave
7. to Leland

LAKE FERGUSON

Township Line

Broadway

Old Leland Rd.

Nelson St.

Main St.

Washington Ave.

82

Greenville

Holly Ridge

Indianola

Leland

LILLO'S

SON THOMAS' GRAVE

River

River

DELTA BLUES FESTIVAL

454

82

Bourbon

Washington County

Mississippi

Hollandale

Murphy

Sunflower

49W

12

61

Rolling Fork

GREENVILLE TO VICKSBURG

Greenville

The Delta's largest city, Greenville has a long blues heritage centered on its infamous Nelson Street. It also hosts the region's biggest and oldest blues festival. In recent years, spurred by the development of waterfront casinos, Greenville nightlife has heated up. The town has more live music than anywhere else in the Delta. The music scene has moved, however, from authentic-but-decaying Nelson to the newly redeveloped Walnut Street.

Among the must-see Greenville-area blues musicians is Eddie Cusic of Leland, who took a young Little Milton into his band in the 1950s, then later set down his electric guitar to become a powerful solo acoustic singer-guitarist. Electric guitarist T-Model Ford is often on tour but plays his stripped-down, good-times boogies at Nelson Street clubs when he is in the area. Guitarist Little Bill Wallace, a semiretired Greenville blues artist is definitely worth hearing if you get the chance. Guitarist John Horton is a flashy dresser who plays Albert King-style lead with his own group or with others. Then there's Mississippi Slim, an even flashier dresser, sometimes

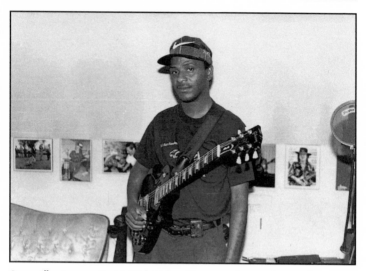

Greenville singer-guitarist "Little" Dave Thompson in recording studio,
October 1999, Greenville

coloring his hair to match his bright red or blue suits. Catch him
singing outside on Walnut Street or at a festival.

Radio station WBAD, 94.3 FM, is the one to listen to in
Greenville. It plays some contemporary blues and gospel, mixed
in with R&B and oldies.

• The Levee

To get there: Driving west on Highway 82, cross Highway 1 and take a
right on Washington Ave. Washington turns back to the left and ends at
the levee. Take a left on Walnut St and go one block; you can drive up on
the levee.

Downtown Greenville (like downtown Helena and many other
spots) is a fine place to walk along the levee. The Mississippi River
levee, the wall of earth that holds the river in its banks, is the
world's largest human creation. A few years ago, a northern newspaper described the levee at Helena as a "natural amphitheater"
for the audience at a blues festival. However, the levee is not natural at all. Men and mules built it over more than a century of hard
work, moving the dirt wheelbarrow by wheelbarrow. The levee-

camp hollers the workers sang were a predecessor of the blues. Later on, levee camps attracted blues singers. On the days when the levee workers were paid, as Honeyboy Edwards explains, "[T]here's prostitutes coming out and whiskey flowing, and I'm right there playing my harp and guitar. I'm going to make enough money to stake a gamble with . . . I knew the paydays, when they paid off up and down them levees, up and down the Mississippi clean to Vicksburg. I didn't work but I knew when they got paid off. I kept that in my book."

There had been small levees along the Mississippi since the 1720s, and the complete, federally funded levee was in place by 1912. The river has overflowed or broken through numerous times, however, with disastrous results. As Kansas Joe and Memphis Minnie sang in their 1929 "When the Levee Breaks" (later covered by the rock group Led Zeppelin):

> *If it keeps on raining, levee's going to break*
> *And all these people have no place to stay.*

The Mississippi River flood of 1927, the worst disaster in U.S. history, happened after the levee burst near Greenville. Floodwater covered twenty-six thousand square miles of the Delta, killing hundreds of people and driving hundreds of thousands from home. Greenville was hit the worst. Many whites, especially the elderly, women, and children, were evacuated. Planters fearful of permanently losing their labor forced the blacks to stay. Thousands camped on the levee, which was the only high ground.

Bessie Smith's "Back Water Blues" was a big hit at the time of the flood. Bessie had somehow had the intuition to write and record it three months *before* the big flood hit. She was inspired by lesser flooding on the Ohio River she had seen while on tour:

> *Then I went and stood upon some high old lonesome hill.*
> *Then I looked down on the house where I used to live.*

> *Back water blues done caused me to pack my things and go*
> *'Cause my house fell down and I can't live there no more.*

A much less famous blues singer, Alice Pearson of Greenville, cut a locally relevant "Greenville Levee Blues":

> *Living on the levee, sleeping on the ground*
> *I will tell everybody that Greenville's a good old town.*

The epic blues about the flood was Charley Patton's 1929 "High Water Everywhere," parts 1 and 2, which covered both sides of a 78. Patton sings and plays at his most impassioned, and reports on a dozen places all over the Delta:

> *Looky here, boys, around Leland tell me river is raging*
> *   high—boy, it's rising over there! Yeah.*
> *I'm going to move over to Greenville, bought our tickets,*
> *   goodbye.*
> *Looky here, the water dug out, Lordy, levee broke, rolled*
> *   most everywhere.*
> *The water at Greenville and Leland, Lord, it done rose*
> *   everywhere.*
> *I would go down to Rosedale, but they tell me there's*
> *   water there.*

The flood formed Lake Ferguson, an oxbow that now separates the city from the river itself. Still, the memory of the flood and a history of riverboat traffic give Greenville a strong connection to the Mississippi. The river's silt even finds its way into Greenville tap water. Its brown color is shocking, but the water won't hurt you. Cheers!

• Nelson Street

Friends back home may have thought you were crazy for wanting to visit Mississippi blues sites, and warned you of dangers they imagine here. But even in Mississippi, even in Greenville, people will warn you not to go to Nelson Street. Even longtime residents of Greenville, even some blues musicians, might caution you against it.

Well, after all those warnings, how could you *not* want to visit Nelson Street? This onetime prime commercial street of Greenville's black community certainly is long past its heyday. And it has not yet entered the rehab stage that community and city officials have been talking about for a long time. Many of its businesses are abandoned, and not much live blues has been heard there lately.

There is life, though. Taverns with colorfully painted fronts house jukeboxes and pool tables. Aspiring boxers duke it out in a ring clearly visible through a big glass window. Murals on Nelson

and its side streets com-
memorate local people or
make antidrug statements.
On Saturday nights Nel-
son becomes a cruising
street for young motorists.
A barbecue vendor is usu-
ally cooking and selling his
wares from a smoke-chug-
ging stand. A shoeshine
vendor might be ready for
business—or for a beer, if
you have one to spare.
People, alone or in little
groups, are just hanging
out. And at any time Nel-
son Street tends to have
plenty of cops driving to
and from the street's po-
lice substation.

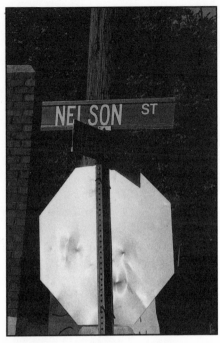

**Mississippi's most infamous and blues-
drenched street: Nelson Street, Greenville**

Nelson Street is worth
a visit so that you can
look at the buildings and
try to imagine what the street was like from the mid-1940s
through the 1970s, when Little Milton, Eddie Cusic, Charley
Booker, Willie Love, Little Bill Wallace, T-Model Ford, and a host
of other top-notch local blues artists, as well as big-name touring acts, played in its clubs. Like Jackson's Farish Street and
Clarksdale's Issaquena Avenue, this is one of the places where the
postwar blues thrived and developed. Willie Love and His Three
Aces, featuring Little Milton on guitar, celebrated the street in
their 1951 "Nelson Street Blues" (a hit on Jackson-based Trumpet Records):

> *Boy, if you ever go to Greenville, please go down on
> Nelson Street*
> *Yeah, walk on the levee and have a lot of fun with most
> everybody you meet.*

The song goes on to suggest that you stop at various Nelson
Street businesses—Tails and Tie Shoeshine Parlor, Deluxe Barber-

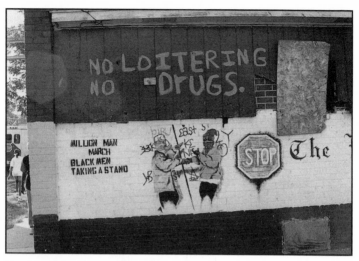

Mural on Nelson Street, Greenville

shop, Sharp Shop ("for a sharp suit of clothes"), Snow White Laundry, and, finally, the Silver Dollar Cafe, "that's right on the corner. You can stop in there now and have just as much fun as you want to."

If you feel safer in crowds, visit during the annual **Little Wynn Nelson Street Festival**, held on the day before the annual Delta Blues Festival (which is on the third Saturday of September). The free festival affords a rare opportunity to see Nelson Street lively and crowded with people walking around, shopping, eating, and listening to music. Fine local blues acts and a headliner play on a stage at one end of the street, while gospel groups play at the other end. Vendors sell hamburgers, fried catfish, and barbecue, as well as yo-yos, shoes, and other goods. Unfortunately, most Nelson Street bars lack live music even at festival time.

- **Perry's Flowing Fountain**
  816 Nelson St.

Perry's flowed on for awhile after original owner Perry Payton died on May 3, 2000, but recently it was closed for good. Payton, who worked as a mortician by day, had been connected to blues history since his youth, when he helped his dad, also a mortician,

Greenville singer Mamie "Galore" Davis, a former Ikette, singing with guitarist John Horton and trumpeter Robert Williams at the 1999 Little Wynn Nelson Street Festival, Greenville

deal with the hundreds of dead from the Natchez Rhythm Club fire. He opened the Flowing Fountain in the 1970s.

The club's largest room was named Annie Mae's Café. That also is the name of Little Milton's 1985 hit, which goes:

> *Annie Mae's Café, you can find one in every town*
> *I go there after hours and drink a little whiskey, before long*
> *somebody's acting a clown.*

Was the Flowing Fountain the original Annie Mae's Café that inspired the song? Payton said so. And as Milton starts his guitar solo, he clearly speaks, "In my hometown they call it the Flowing Fountain." However, in his liner notes to *Greatest Hits,* Milton explains that it's generic: "People always ask, 'Is there such a place?' And I tell them, 'Everywhere I go there's always one.' And that's the truth. The point is, it's a club that stays open late, good food still served and liquor available."

Milton did not write the song, however. That credit goes to George Jackson and Larry Addison. And Jackson told writer Rob Bowman he based the song on an actual Annie Mae's Café where he used to hang out in *Memphis.* At any rate, thanks to Milton's improvised line and the sign on the wall inside, the Flowing Fountain became the real Annie Mae's Café.

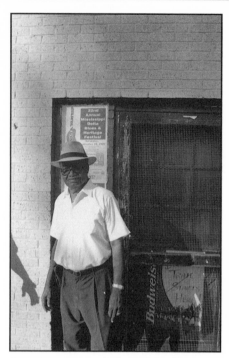

Owner Perry Payton in front of the Flowing Fountain, 816 Nelson Street, Greenville

Roosevelt "Booba" Barnes, king of Greenville blues in the 1980s, worked as a bartender and regular performer at Perry's Flowing Fountain before opening his own club.

- **Playboy Club**
  928 Nelson St.

This club, then owned by the late Booba Barnes, appears in the movie *Deep Blues*. Although he doesn't look too pleased or comfortable, Greenville's mayor at the time, Frank Self, shakes the hand of wild jook-joint owner/musician Barnes and commends him for what he has done for the festival and the town. Narrator Robert Palmer asks Self if the town appreciates Nelson Street's blues history, and the mayor assures him that it does. "We're starting, very busy, to clean up Nelson Street, make it a tourist attraction," he tells Palmer.

After his little chat with the mayor, Barnes launches into his burning signature song, "Heartbroken Man." He wears a red suit and big gold chains. As always, he bugs out his eyes and plays with an intense, nervous sound. He slows the tempo down for the next number but keeps up the intensity, playing with his teeth.

In that song, Booba pays tribute to his city: "In my hometown, where I live—the name of the town, they call it Greenville— it ain't no pity, ain't no shame. My baby left me, I'm a heartbroken man."

A furniture store before it was a nightclub, Barnes's Playboy Club has since become a church, The Vessels of Mercy. It has a bright blue exterior that might seem flashy for a church elsewhere but, amid the gaudy storefronts and murals of Nelson Street, looks austere. The club opened in about 1982 and closed in about 1992 when Barnes, riding a wave of national renown after the movie's release, decided he was a professional and moved to Chicago. Sadly, he didn't get to enjoy his success for long. Barnes died of lung cancer on April 3, 1996, at age fifty-nine.

- **Walnut Street**

Right downtown, near the waterfront and the casinos, Walnut Street has in the past few years become the place to hear live music in Greenville. Because of the street's convenient location and because it does *not* have a seedy reputation, upstart Walnut has bypassed traditional Nelson in quantity and variety of live music.

The Walnut Street Blues Bar, 128 Walnut St. (662-378-2254); One Block East, 240 Washington Ave. (one block east of Walnut) (662-332-3800); and The Sandbar, 129 Walnut St. (662-335-7888); feature live music regularly. Blues is often, but not always, the genre—rock groups also play at these clubs, so call ahead or just walk around until you hear what you're seeking.

Besides providing live music, Walnut Street Blues Bar also functions as a museum of sorts. It has a long wall covered with Greenville blues-related photos, posters, articles, and a few instruments.

Emulating Beale Street (which in turn was emulating Hollywood Boulevard), Walnut Street has begun to feature bronze plaques in the sidewalk in recognition of prominent entertainers with local connections. B. B. King and Boogaloo Ames were the first two so honored, and there are plans for Sam Chatmon and others. Greenville artist Alan Orlicek creates the plaques.

- **The Meeting Place**
  247 South 6th St.
  (662) 335-9123

This friendly neighborhood bar, away from Nelson and Walnut streets, has been featuring live blues on Sunday nights.

- **The Mississippi Delta Blues & Heritage Festival**

This festival began in 1977, operated by Mississippi Action for
Community Education (119 Theobald St., 662-335-3523), a nonprofit community-development corporation that dates from
1967 and lists among its founders the civil rights leader Fannie
Lou Hamer.

Dubbed "the Big One" by its organizers, this is the biggest
blues festival in the Delta and one of the biggest and oldest in the
country. Besides the main stage, there is a smaller "jukehouse"
stage for local acts, as well as a gospel tent. It lasts from noon to 11
P.M. one day, the third Saturday of September; the festival site is at
Highway 1 at Route 454, six miles south of Highway 82.

Held in a big grassy field, this is the kind of festival where
people come in groups and set up camp, bringing chairs, blan-
kets, and awnings and feasting on their own food and drink. In
the festival's early years, attendees would bring in the equipment
and supplies to do their own barbecuing at the site. Grills have
been prohibited, but coolers are still allowed. If you want to
travel light, plenty of barbecue is available for purchase. Bring
repellent for the mosquitoes, and beware of the fire ants when
staking out your turf. Make sure to walk around and check out
all three stages.

Metcalfe

- **Eugene "Sonny Boy Nelson" Powell's Grave**

To get there: Head north out of Greenville on Highway 1. Right after a sign
that says "Metcalfe 1 1/2 mi.," the road forks. Take the right fork, Broadway
Road Extension. Proceed 1 mile to another fork, and again take the right
fork, onto an unmarked paved road. Go 1.1 mile, then turn left onto a dirt
road that crosses a little bridge and leads into a cemetery. The headstones
are flat, so it is difficult to notice Powell's stone until you are right in front of
it. From the road that leads in, about 90 feet before the two scraggly trees,
walk to the left, into the cemetery, for about 90 feet.

The flat stone includes an etched drawing of Powell by Alan
Orlicek. It reads:

> BLUES AIN'T NOTHIN' BUT A WORRY ON YOUR MIND
> [A LINE FROM A FAVORITE SONG]
> Play it a long time 'cause a short while is gonna make me mad
> [a quote from him]

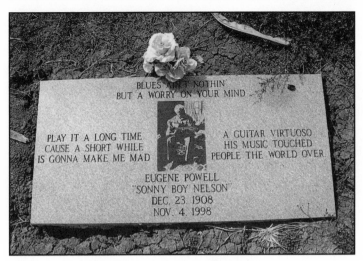

Eugene "Sonny Boy Nelson" Powell's grave, Metcalfe

A guitar virtuoso his music touched people the world over
Eugene Powell
"Sonny Boy Nelson"
Dec. 23, 1908
Nov. 4, 1998

Eugene Powell, who used to play for Parchman inmates as a boy and recorded in 1936 as Sonny Boy Nelson, was one of the last surviving artists from the original blues recording era. After his one recording session, he married Mississippi Matilda—who also cut a few tunes at that session—and led a quiet life, working at John Deere in Hollandale for decades. But in the 1970s, Powell's old friend, bluesman Sam Chatmon, helped him get festival gigs, and the two of them became beloved elder statesmen of the Mississippi blues. Keb'Mo, Lonnie Pitchford, and Alvin Youngblood Hart were among the young musicians who stopped by Eugene Powell's for lessons in the 1990s.

Leland

I said Greenville's smokin', baby, and Leland's burnin',
*   Leland's burnin' down*
Well, I believe I'll retrieve my woman out of Greenville town.

So sang local bluesman Charley Booker in his 1952 recording "No Ridin' Blues." The words proved strangely prophetic (much as Bessie Smith's "Back Water Blues" predicted the 1927 flood). A month *after* "No Ridin' Blues" was issued, a whole block of downtown Leland was destroyed in a blaze that could be seen from miles away and threatened to spread.

Leland's downtown is north of Highway 82. Broad Street takes you into town. There is a jook joint on Main Street called Boss Hall that occasionally features live music.

• Lillo's Italian Restaurant
Highway 82 near the intersection of Highway 61
(662) 686-4401

A plain, dependable old Italian-American restaurant, this may seem an unlikely place to hear the blues. But for many years, until his death February 4, 2002, Lillo's presented Abie "Boogaloo" Ames, a pianist dubbed the "Mozart of the Delta," every Thursday. Backed by a dance band, Boogaloo wore a suit and a bowler hat, sipped whiskey and stroked the keys on standards, swing tunes, boogie-woogie, deep blues, or whatever struck his fancy. He and his disciple, Eden Brent, are the subjects of an award-winning 1999 TV documentary, *Boogaloo and Eden: Sustaining the Sound*. Brent carries on her master's tradition at local festivals and clubs. Lillo's continues to host live music on Thursdays, although rarely blues.

• Leland Blues Murals
To get there: From Highway 82, take the main Leland exit north onto Broad Street. After the second traffic light, take the first left onto Fourth Street. There is a mural on the second building on the right. Continue on Fourth, take the next left onto Main Street, and go one block to the other mural, at Third and Main streets.

In 2000, various local artists and volunteers pitched in to paint these murals of blues singers born within twenty-five miles of Leland. The long list of local talent includes such stars as Jimmy Reed and Little Milton, along with local favorites such as Eddie Cusic, Willie Foster, and James "Son" Thomas.

Among the group are the pale-skinned blues-rockers Johnny and Edgar Winter. The Winter brothers grew up in Beaumont,

Texas, but actually were born in Leland, where their father, John Dawson Winter, Jr., once served as mayor. Johnny Winter included his own "Leland Mississippi Blues" on his 1969 debut album.

- **Highway 61 Blues Museum**
  400 N. Broad St.
  (662) 686-7646

The museum is open 10 A.M. to 5 P.M. Mondays through Saturdays. There is an admission fee.

This museum does not try to tell the whole story of blues in the Delta, or even of the whole length of Highway 61. It focuses on artists from the area within 50 miles of Leland—which turns out to be a remarkable cast of characters. Little Milton, Charley Patton, Jimmy Reed, B.B. King, Albert King, and Johnny Winter are some of them, alongside local favorites Willie Foster, Son Thomas, Abie "Boogaloo" Ames, and others famous and obscure, living and dead. The museum also contains farm implements that city dwellers might have heard of in blues songs but never seen: a crosscut saw and a singletree.

The museum's director, Billy Johnson, presents an annual **Highway 61 Blues Festival** in mid-June, again spotlighting some of the many blues artists with local connections.

- **James "Son" Thomas's Grave**

  To get there: About one mile east of Leland on Highway 82, turn south onto an unmarked road across from a large Phillips 66 gas station. Go ½ mile to the first left, Old Tribbett Road, turn left and go another ½ mile to the intersection with Mark Road, where there is a graveyard in front of a small, new brick church set way back from the road, Greater St. Matthew M. B. Church. Turn into the driveway and look to the left. Thomas's grave is near the front, facing the driveway.

The front of the stone reads:

> James "Son" Thomas
> Oct. 14, 1926–
> June 26, 1993
> World renowned Sculptor and Recording Artist,
> beloved father, grandfather and friend.

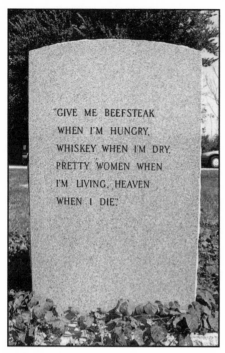

Back side of James "Son" Thomas's grave, near Leland

The back of the stone quotes from Thomas's "Beefsteak Blues":

Give me beefsteak when
    I'm hungry,
Whiskey when I'm dry,
Pretty women when I'm
    living,
Heaven when I die.

Thomas, a gravedigger by trade, was a charismatic local bluesman with a high-pitched voice and an unusual guitar style. He was also a gifted sculptor who specialized in clay skulls. Hailing from Yazoo County, Thomas moved to Leland in 1961, at age forty. A few years later he met the anthropology student William Ferris, from Vicksburg. In film, photography, and words, Ferris documented the blues house parties of Thomas, Poppa Jazz, and other Delta bluesmen in an era when many people thought the blues was already dead. Thomas and Ferris helped each other in their careers: Thomas's music and art gained international renown (he performed for the Reagans at the White House, and appeared on Charles Kuralt's *On the Road*), while Ferris became author of the well-respected *Blues from the Delta* and a professor at the University of Mississippi and founder of the Center for the Study of Southern Culture there (he later served as director of the National Endowment for the Humanities).

Thomas died June 26, 1993, at age sixty-six. One of his sons, Pat Thomas, has vowed to carry on his dad's musical legacy. Although he has not yet caught up to that level of virtuosity (as he readily admits), Pat manages to capture some of the feel, and has inherited the vocal quality. Pat Thomas lives in Leland but performs only occasionally. He usually appears on the acoustic stage of the annual Sunflower Blues Festival in Clarksdale.

Bourbon

A town called Bourbon ought to have a place to get a drink, and this one does. The Bourbon Mall, 105 Dean Road (662-686-4389) is not a shopping mall, but a roadhouse-style restaurant that specializes in steaks and features live music nightly. Often the music is rock or country, but it is blues at least once a week. When you call to check on who is playing, you can also hire a limo from the restaurant's fleet to come and pick you up, which might be a good idea, since it's a remote location—fifteen miles southeast of Leland off Tribbett Road South.

Holly Ridge

- **Graves of Charley Patton, Willie Foster, and Asie Payton**

  To get there: From Highway 82 between Leland and Indianola, take the Holly Ridge turnoff, which is to the north. The town is a mile from the highway. Turn left onto Main Street and look for New Jerusalem M. B. Church, 0.2 mile down on the left. Patton reportedly used to sing at the church. The graveyard is another 0.2 mile past the church, just past Holly Ridge Gin.

Near the road, on the right, is the grave of Asie Reed Payton. An obscure performer, he is one of the few whose headstone (another modern one, financed by his record company) reads "bluesman." A Holly Ridge tractor driver who lived from April 12, 1937, to May 19, 1997, Payton also sang and played the blues. His one and only recording is a posthumous one, the 1999 Fat Possum release *Worried*. It was recorded in two sessions intended as demos in 1994—one live at Junior Kimbrough's jook, the other at a studio.

Charley Patton's grave marker is near the back of the cemetery and on the far left, near the gin. His remains are probably not right at the marker, however—some sources say he lies underneath the gin building. The stone reads:

Charley Patton
April 1891–April 28, 1934
"The Voice of the Delta"
The foremost performer of early Mississippi blues
whose songs became cornerstones of American music.

Charley Patton is buried in the town where he and Bertha Lee lived for most of the last two years of his life, 1933 and 1934. They performed at jooks in the area, and especially in the back of a white-owned store in Holly Ridge, which also was Patton's last residence. The white store owner sometimes accompanied him on fiddle. The store probably was on one of the corners of the main intersection in Holly Ridge.

Near—but not too near—a church and right next to a gin, this seems an appropriate resting place for the great Delta bluesman and sometime gospel singer. The cemetery contains a lot of hand-engraved stones, although Patton's, erected in 1991 (and financed largely by blues-influenced rock musician John Fogerty), is modern and professionally done.

A niece told interviewers that a representative of Vocalion records had come to the site shortly after Patton's death and put up a tombstone. That stone apparently has vanished, however.

Near Patton's is the grave of Greenville-based singer-band-leader-harmonica player Willie Foster, identifying him curiously as a "harmonica parader."

Foster was literally born on a cotton sack when his mother, working in the fields near Leland, lay down to give birth to him on September 19, 1921. Foster bought his first harmonica at the Rexall (now Fred's Xpress) in Leland, paying for the twenty-five-cent instrument gradually over a period of weeks. After serving in the military in World War II, Foster lived and played in various Midwestern cities but found his greatest success after about 1990, when he was living back in the Delta and playing locally, regionally, and sometimes internationally. The loss of first one leg, then the other, did not slow down his musical career. Foster continued to sing, blow harp, and lead the band masterfully from his wheelchair. He had just finished a private-party gig the night he died, May 20, 2001.

Club Chicago, Church Street, Indianola

Indianola

"Welcome to Indianola, Home of B. B. King," this town's signs proclaim. They feature a picture of King, a cotton boll, and a factory. There is a B. B. King Road west of downtown, on one side of a big cotton gin.

King was born September 16, 1925, on the bank of Blue Lake near Berclair, outside of Itta Bena. When he was about five years old, he moved with his mother to Kilmichael, in the hill country east of the Delta. In 1935, after his mother's death, his dad took him south to Lexington, on the edge of the Delta. In the fall of 1938, young B. B. got on his bicycle and rode back to the Delta, to Indianola, to live with relatives and work in the cottonfields. He has claimed the town as his home ever since, and the town has returned the favor, considering him its son. He titled a 1970 album *Indianola Mississippi Seeds*.

Indianola has connections to other blues greats: according to his death certificate, Charley Patton died on April 28, 1934, at 350 Heathman Street (a house that is no longer standing), and master string bender Albert King (no relation to B. B.), was born April 25, 1923, in Indianola, but moved to Forrest City, Arkansas, as a child.

From Highway 82, Catchings Street takes you south into downtown Indianola. The black section is south of that, across the tracks. Church Street is the street for little jooks, liquor stores, and a few downhome restaurants. There are some colorful buildings and some colorful characters hanging out and drinking in front of them. But there has not been any live music on Church Street recently. Even Mary Price's famous Keyhole Club—a green building without a sign—has dropped its live music lately.

Church Street's clubs once presented acts such as Louis Jordan, Count Basie, Pete Johnson, Jay McShann's band featuring Charlie Parker, and Sonny Boy Williamson II. As a teenager, B. B. King would lurk outside the clubs to get a listen and a peek inside. After a while, he got the idea to bring his guitar along and sit on a curb singing gospel music for tips. "I was this skinny kid with his own corner on Church Street in Indianola, my hopes in the hat by my side," he wrote.

A $10 million museum devoted to B. B. King is planned for downtown Indianola. King and his management have endorsed the project. The state legislature has approved a special county tax to support its operation. High-stakes fund-raising also is under way. The museum is scheduled for opening in late 2005.

• B. B. King's Footprints, Handprints, and Signature

B. B. King used to sing for tips at this spot, on the east side of Church Street just south of Second Street, as a teenager. He started off singing church songs and received smiles and blessings from passers-by. When he tried the blues, however, people responded with cash. He noted the difference and decided to focus on the blues.

On June 5, 1986, King placed his footprints, handprints, and signature in the sidewalk where he used to sing. Recently, a large photo of King has been added to the site along with a historical marker. On a wall a block west of this corner there is a King mural by Lawrence Quinn of Jackson.

• Club Ebony
404 Hanna Ave.
(662) 887-9915

The Ebony is not a little jook joint, but a large, well-kept-up nightclub/restaurant in a residential area. It has been in business

since 1948. Current owner Mary Shepard bought it in 1974 from
B. B. King's former mother-in-law, Ruby Edwards (King met his second wife, Sue Carol Hall, at the club). King still plays at the Ebony
once a year, right after his free outdoor homecoming concert.

Besides the annual B. B. King performance, the Ebony presents
occasional shows by big-name soul-blues acts such as Denise
LaSalle, Little Milton, or Willie Clayton. There is live music from
local bands on Sunday nights.

• B. B. King Homecoming

King comes back to Indianola to play a free outdoor concert
each year on the first Friday in June (unless June 1 is a Saturday, in
which case the concert is May 31) at B. B. King Park on Roosevelt
Street. He has done that since 1968, in memory of the slain civil
rights leader Medgar Evers. "It helps heal some hurt," King wrote.
"It helps to see thousands of little black and white kids playing together, to see the big crowds so happy to hear blues that feels good
to everyone."

When King skipped the homecoming for two years, Club
Ebony owner Mary Shepard set him straight. "I said, 'Mr. King,
this is your home. You need to come back home,'" she says.

• 308 Blues Club and Café
308 Depot Ave.
(662) 887-7800

The 308 is a large club that opened in November 2003. It presents live blues on Fridays and Saturdays, by blues acts from
throughout the Delta. It also serves downhome food such as barbecue, catfish, plate lunches, and salmon-and-rice breakfasts.

• Gin Mill Galleries
109 Pershing St.
(662) 887-3209

This art gallery and furniture studio is in an old cotton gin
building in downtown Indianola. The Gin Mill carries some local
blues CDs and photographs of blues artists and Delta scenes by
gallery owner Thomas Bingham and others.

Belzoni

To get there: From Indianola, go south on Highway 49W. Belzoni is 23 miles from Indianola.

Belzoni is the town where Lillian McMurry tracked down Sonny Boy Williamson II, who was living in a shack here, and asked him to record for her Trumpet label. When a teenage Elmore James moved to Belzoni in the 1930s with his parents, Sonny Boy and Robert Johnson both were prominent local musicians, and both influenced James's music. Sonny Boy and Elmore were still in town around 1947, doing radio advertising (the Talaho Show) for a local drugstore and playing in the area, sometimes with Arthur "Big Boy" Crudup, who also lived around here. Sonny Boy met his wife, Mattie Gordon, while living in Belzoni.

Contemporary bluesman Paul "Wine" Jones also hails from Belzoni, where he works as a welder at a catfish farm.

• The Old Jailhouse

To get there: Go south of downtown on Hayden Street. It is in the 100 block, past the courthouse (which has a new jail behind it) and just before the library, on the left.

No longer in use, the old county jailhouse Charley Patton sang about is still standing (although it is condemned and falling apart). Patton was familiar with the inside of this building. He sang about it in his 1934 "High Sheriff Blues":

> *Get in trouble in Belzoni, ain't no use to screamin' and cryin'*
> *Mr. Webb will take you back to Belzoni jailhouse flyin'.*

This song has the same tune and accompaniment as Patton's 1929 "Tom Rushen Blues," which describes a jailing in Merigold. However, "High Sheriff" is more autobiographical. Patton really was jailed in Belzoni. An Officer Webb arrested both Patton and his wife, Bertha Lee, in a disturbance at a house party where they were playing. W. R. Calaway of American Record Company bailed them out and brought them to New York to record for what would be the last time. "High Sheriff Blues" is one of the songs Patton recorded at that final session.

- **Catfish and Buffalo Fish Festivals**

Mississippi's two favorite fishes are both honored with annual festivals on the first Saturday of April (unless Easter falls in the first weekend of April, in which case the festivals are moved to the second Saturday).

The World Catfish Festival, which started in 1976, is a mass corporate-sponsored event that includes the crowning of the Catfish Queen and a catfish-eating contest. The 2000 festival included entertainment from Greenville's Willie Foster—the first time blues was on the program.

The African-American Heritage Buffalo Fish Festival, which debuted in 1996, is a much smaller, more downhome event. It usually features a performance by soul-blues star Denise LaSalle, who is a Belzoni native.

- **Kozy Korner**
  109 George Lee St.
  (662) 247-9942

From Highway 7, continue south into town. The highway becomes Hayden Street. At Hayden and Jackson streets (where city hall is), turn right and go a few blocks west to George Lee. Kozy Korner is the very long building. The back is the family's living quarters; the front is a good-sized jook joint, open since 1971, where singer-guitarist Jim Yarbor used to play the blues. He suffered a stroke and doesn't play anymore, although he usually hangs out in the bar, which is run by his wife, Mary, and other relatives. The friendly cafe has a blues-laden jukebox, pool tables, homecooked food, and plenty of atmosphere.

Hollandale

To get there: From Belzoni, take Highway 12 west. Hollandale is 21 miles at the intersection of Highway 12 and Highway 61.

This town had a lively blues scene around 1936, including Bo Carter, who that year organized a group of musicians—Eugene "Sonny Boy Nelson" Powell, Mississippi Matilda, and Robert Hill—to go record in New Orleans. Hacksaw Harney and Willie "Brother" Harris also lived in town, as well as others who never recorded.

Sexy Lady Club, Blue Front, Hollandale

"Bo Chatmon put me on to the first record I ever made, in 1936," Powell told an interviewer decades later. "He said I wasn't doing nothing but wasting music, said, 'I'm gonna put you on record.' That was Bo Carter, Sam Chatmon's brother. So them were the first ones I ever made in my whole life. Sonny Boy Nelson with Mississippi Matilda and Robert Hill in 1936. It was down in New Orleans. I liked it down there, you know, country boy, had my wife with me, nothing to worry about, was giving her a good time, I felt good. I thought I was something, doing something I hadn't never done—I thought I was more than I was! I put out three records for ninety dollars, and that was some money then."

Houston Stackhouse told an interviewer he remembered a day in Hollandale about 1930 when Robert Nighthawk, with another guitarist and a pianist, was playing at a black-oriented drugstore while Bo Carter and Lonnie Chatmon played at a white drugstore.

Summerfest is a wonderful free blues festival, held the Friday and Saturday before Memorial Day at Hollandale City Park. Information on it is available by calling 662-827-5545.

The **Rainbow Inn** on Old Highway 61 south of town is a clean and friendly jook joint but does not have live music.

- **Blue Front**

Highway 12 becomes Washington Street. Take that across the tracks to a row of dilapidated storefronts along the track, on South Simmons Street. Known as Blue Front, this was the black entertainment and dining district for decades. Some jooks still operate there, although none has live music.

• Sam Chatmon's Grave

To get there: From Highway 61, turn west on Highway 12 into Hollandale. At the stop sign, turn right onto East Avenue South. At the four-way stop, turn left onto East Washington and then right on Morgan. Follow Morgan as it zig-zags, across Dr. Martin Luther King Jr. Drive, and ends at Sanders Memorial Garden. Turn right into the cemetery. The grave is on the left, at the third tree.

The stone reads:

SITTING ON TOP OF
THE WORLD
Sam Chatmon
Jan. 10, 1899
Feb. 2, 1983
Considered to be among the most important
figures in American music,
his contribution helped create the lyrical art form of the blues.
Performed with the Mississippi Sheiks and the Chatmon Brothers.
A beloved friend and true gentleman.

Across the drive from the fourth tree is the grave of Chatmon's wife, Elma Lue Chatmon, April 10, 1911, to March 18, 1996.

Born in Bolton, Sam Chatmon lived in Hollandale from the 1940s on. He was an active musician in the 1930s, pretty much re-tired from music in the forties and fifties, then became active again from the 1960s on, probably reaching his greatest glory in his old age.

His tombstone proclaims him "among the most important figures in American music." But in his youth, Sam Chatmon was not even the most illustrious musician in his own family. Of ex-slave fiddler Henderson Chatmon's thirteen children, the big names were Bo Carter, a blues star of the 1930s with such hits as "Please Warm My Weiner," and Lonnie Chatmon, vio-linist with the Mississippi Sheiks of "Sitting On Top of the World" fame.

Sam Chatmon played on only a few recordings of the im-mensely popular Sheiks, who were mainly a duo composed of Lon-nie and singer-guitarist Walter Vincson. However, he probably often joined in on their live performances. Chatmon distinguished himself from his musical siblings by outliving all of them and

Leland bluesman Eddie Cusic playing in front of drawings of Sam Chatmon, at the dedication of Chatmon's grave marker, March 1998, Hollandale

bringing traces of the old black-string-band and smutty-blues traditions into the late twentieth century. He was a funny entertainer and fine musician who played at festivals and clubs across the country in his later years.

Sam Chatmon worked in the **cotton compress** that is part of the complex of buildings around the cotton gin on Morgan Street near Washington. He lived at **818 Sherman Street**, which is still standing. Respect the privacy of the house's current tenants if you go to look at it.

Murphy

For real fans of the movie *Crossroads*: Take Highway 12 east from Hollandale and go ten miles to Sunflower Road, which is just before a bridge across the Sunflower River. Turn right on Sunflower and go about five miles south to Murphy Road (noting Torrey Wood & Son, a rare surviving wood cotton gin that just happens to be named "Wood," on the left on your way). At the intersection there is an abandoned white building with a wooden porch. In the 1986 Walter Hill film *Crossroads,* this is the building where Willie Brown (played by Joe Seneca) and young hotshot Eugene Martone (Ralph Macchio) escape from the rain and meet the runaway girl Frances (Jami Gertz).

Panther Burn

To get there: Panther Burn is 8 miles south of Hollandale on Highway 61.

A scene in the movie *Blues Brothers 2000* is set in Panther Burn, although obviously it was not filmed there. The movie shows Spanish moss hanging from all the trees along the highway, something you don't see in this nontropical Delta town.

The real Panther Burn does have a Ray Charles Road, however.

Rolling Fork

To get there: From Panther Burn go south on Highway 61 for 13 miles.

Muddy Waters was born in this town on April 4, 1915, but moved to his grandmother's house near Clarksdale before he was three. Still, Rolling Fork is proud of its native bluesman. A monument stands on the south side of the courthouse square, on China Street by the gazebo. It reads:

IN HONOR OF MUDDY WATERS
Muddy Waters, master of the blues, was born McKinley Morganfield in 1915 near Rolling Fork. His special technique and interpretation powerfully influenced the development of Delta blues music.

For a while, the town also had signs on Highway 61 welcoming visitors to the home of Muddy Waters. Some visitors stole the signs, however, and there are no plans to replace them.

Waters sang about his hometown in his 1953 cover of Big Joe Williams's 1935 "Baby, Please Don't Go":

You got me way down here
Down by Rolling Fork
You treat me like a dog
Baby, please don't go

Vicksburg

To get there: Go south on Highway 61.

Second only to Gettysburg as a major Civil War site (the battlefield is preserved as Vicksburg National Military Park, 3201 Clay St., 601-636-0583), this charming river town also figures in blues history. By the traditional definition, Vicksburg is the southern tip of the Delta, as Memphis is the northern tip. Songwriter-bassist Willie Dixon was born and raised here. Like many others, Dixon fell under the spell of Little Brother Montgomery.

"Vicksburg—where I run upon Little Brother," Skip James says in his introduction to his own version of "Vicksburg Blues," on his 1965 recording *Skip's Piano Blues*. Montgomery, perhaps the greatest of all blues pianists, made his lovely tribute to Vicksburg his signature tune:

> *I got the Vicksburg blues and I'll sing 'em anywhere I please*
> *Now the reason I sing 'em—to give my poor heart some ease.*

A slow-slow blues with a slip-sliding bass line, Montgomery's "Vicksburg Blues" quickly became a piece every Delta blues pianist was required to play. Guitarists, too, developed versions of it—including Howlin' Wolf's "44 Blues" and Skip James's "Special Rider Blues."

A Louisiana native, Montgomery was a regular in Vicksburg joints in the 1920s, relocated to Jackson in the 1930s, and then became part of the electric Chicago blues scene in the 1950s.

There is a **little jook joint,** without live music, at 1200 Pearl Street, and another at Grove and Walnut streets.

- **Bottleneck Blues Bar**
  Ameristar Casino
  4646 Washington St.
  (800) 700-7770

Yes, it's a casino bar with slot machines, big-screen TVs, and all. But it's decorated jook-joint style and often features good blues or R&B acts.

- **Slipper's Inn**
  2416 Pearl St.
  (601) 636-9887

Slipper's Inn, a thirty-year-old jook, was the set of the jook joint in "Warming by the Devil's Fire," director Charles Burnett's segment of the 2003 PBS *The Blues* series. Other scenes from that film also were shot in Vicksburg. Slipper's does not offer live music but has some blues on the jukebox. It is open until 10 P.M. weekdays and until midnight Fridays and Saturdays.

- **Willie Dixon Way**
  This small street connects South and Veto streets between Washington and Mulberry streets. It is near the Vicksburg Convention Center, 1600 Mulberry St.

This street was dedicated in 2002 to Willie Dixon, blues composer extraordinaire, who also produced, arranged, sang, and played bass. Born in 1915 in Vicksburg, Dixon was already selling songs to local bands in his teens, besides singing in a gospel group, working as a carpenter, and boxing. By the late 1930s, he had moved to Chicago. He began working with the Chess brothers in the late 1940s and soon became their mainstay songwriter/arranger/producer/bassist. Dixon worked on sessions with Muddy Waters, Howlin' Wolf, Little Walter, Chuck Berry, Robert Nighthawk, Lowell Fulsom, Bo Diddley, Otis Rush, and others. Among his hundreds of compositions are the classics "Hoochie Coochie Man," "I Just Want to Make Love to You," "Spoonful," "Back Door Man," "Little Red Rooster," "My Babe," "Bring It On Home," "Evil," "I Ain't Superstitious," "Mellow Down Easy," "The Seventh Son," "You Shook Me," "Pretty Thing," "I Can't Quit You Baby," "You Need Love" (covered by Led Zeppelin as "Whole Lotta Love"), and "Wang Dang Doodle." Dixon died in 1992 in Chicago and is buried there. The city of Vicksburg dedicated this street in his honor in 2002.

- **Margaret's Grocery and Market**
  4535 N. Washington St.
  (601) 638-1163

Margaret's Grocery and Market is a handbuilt religious shrine. Although not directly related to the blues, this is a fantastic work of African American folk architecture.

Jackson

1. The Old Capitol Museum/State Street
2. Queen of Hearts/Ann Banks Street at MLK
3. Mr. B's/Gallatin & Porter Street
4. Farish Street:
   Speir Phonograph Company, Field's Cafe,
   Record Mart, and the Alamo Theater
5. Ishmon Bracey's grave
6. King Edward Hotel/Capitol & Mill Street
7. Subway Lounge/West Pearl Street
8. Malaco Records/West Northside Drive

chapter 8

THE JACKSON AREA

Jackson

I liked Jackson better than I did either Memphis or New Orleans. Blues was more popular. Anytime you go to Jackson, they's be telling us, "Put me down there where they chunkin' tin cans." They mean just play 'em as low as you can get to 'em, then. Where they going to chunk tin cans, that's in the alley. You don't find no tin cans in the street. "Put 'em in the alley," that's what they holler for.
—Sam Chatmon

The state capital, being outside the Delta, does not conjure up "blues" in the popular imagination the way other Mississippi locations do. Even those on the Library of Congress field-recording trips largely ignored Jackson, presuming that it was too urban to have real folk singers.

But, as Sam Chatmon observed, the town actually has a strong blues tradition, one that goes back a long way and continues today. Being a big city, it has always attracted musicians. Chatmon reported seeing Memphis Minnie playing on the streets of Jackson in about 1910, when she was in her early teens and already a hot guitarist. Skip James met Lightnin' Hopkins, a

Blues exhibit at Old Capitol Museum, Jackson

Texan whose fame would not come until after the war, in Jackson in 1930. James said Hopkins, then a teenager, spent a week in Jackson, during which time the two mainly gambled, but James also gave Hopkins a few guitar pointers.

Jackson radio station WMPR, FM 90.1, plays soul-blues much of the time, with some gospel programming. The Jubilee! Jam (601-969-2008), held in mid-May on outdoor stages downtown, features various music and arts, including the blues.

- **Old Capitol Museum**
  State Street at Capitol Street
  (601) 359-6920

The museum is open 8 A.M. to 5 P.M. Mondays through Fridays, 9:30 A.M. to 4:30 P.M. Saturdays, and 12:30 to 4:30 P.M. Sundays. Admission is free.

This three-floor museum of Mississippi history contains only a small blues exhibit, in the twentieth-century room on the first floor. Besides a resonator guitar and photographs, the exhibit includes some unique artifacts: a record cutter and label-printing block from Trumpet Records, along with a microphone of the type Trumpet used. There also are copies of some Trumpet hits:

Elmore James's 78 "Dust My Broom" and Willie Love and his Three Aces' 45 "Nelson Street Blues."

Near the blues exhibit are other items that might be of interest to blues fans. One is a model of the first mechanical cotton picker, with a 1936 *New York Times* article explaining that the machine, invented by Texan brothers John and Mack Rust, would deprive nine million people of work (the brothers planned to devote the profits to the rehabilitation of those displaced workers). And a railroad exhibit has a photo of blues-yodeling country singer Jimmie Rodgers and a piece of Yazoo and Mississippi Valley (aka Yellow Dog) track.

King Edward Hotel, where the Mississippi Sheiks, Bo Carter, and other "race record" artists recorded in 1930, Pearl and Mill streets, Jackson

- **King Edward Hotel**
  Pearl St. and Mill St.

The King Edward is long abandoned but continues to tower over downtown Jackson, its original sign still on top. Like the Peabody in Memphis and other grand downtown hotels in southern cities, the King Edward was the site of field-recording trips by northern record companies.

The Okeh label set up a studio at the King Edward December 15–19, 1930, and recorded the Mississippi Sheiks, the Mississippi Mud Steppers (Walter Vincson of the Mississippi Sheiks, with Charlie McCoy—among their recordings is an instrumental "Jackson Stomp"), Bo Carter, Walter Jacobs (Vincson again, in an alias), Charlie McCoy, Slim Duckett and Pig Norwood, Elder

Curry, Caldwell Bracey, the Campbell College Quartet, and Elder Charlie Beck.

Decades later, blind and impoverished, Bo Carter was living in a Memphis roominghouse when he recalled that session at the King Edward for British writer Paul Oliver: "Tell ya, we was the Mississippi Sheiks and when we went to make the records in Jackson, Mississippi, the feller wanted to show us how to stop and start the records. Try to tell us when we got to begin and how we got to end. And you know, I started not to make 'em! I started not to make 'em 'cause he wasn't no musicianer, so how could he tell me how to stop and start the song? We was the Sheiks, the Mississippi Sheiks, and you know we was famous."

There are tentative plans to restore the King Edward as a hotel and telecommunications center. In the meantime, it is an illegal haven for homeless people and a party site for college students.

• Pascagoula Street

This is the street where bluesman Bo Carter reportedly lived in the 1920s. A native of Bolton, twenty miles to the east, Carter became a national blues star in the 1930s with such songs as "Banana in Your Fruit Basket" and "My Pencil Won't Write No More."

Carter was a central figure in the Jackson blues scene of the 1920s and early 1930s, which also included his brothers Sam, Harry, and Lonnie Chatmon; Walter Vincson (Lonnie's partner in the Mississippi Sheiks); and brothers Charlie and Joe McCoy (Joe became "Kansas Joe" when he recorded with his wife, Memphis Minnie). All these musicians collaborated occasionally on recordings and probably more often in live performances. Some of them also worked with Tommy Johnson, who was living in the city.

Pascagoula Street is one block south of Pearl Street, which is the traditional border between black neighborhoods and white ones. The part of Pascagoula west of Terry Road, near Varnado Alley, is a poor neighborhood with character that may date from the 1920s.

Although the nonpoetic word "Pascagoula" didn't make it into any of his songs, Carter did sing an "East Jackson Blues" in 1928:

> *When you come to East Jackson, man, and don't find me there*
> *You can bet your bottom dollar that I'm walking the road*
> *somewhere.*

- **Former Residence of Tommy Johnson, Skip James, Elmore James, and Other Bluesmen**
  905 Ann Banks St.

Tommy Johnson was born in Terry, a town about fifteen miles south of Jackson, in about 1896. He moved to Drew, in the Delta, as a young man and learned from Charley Patton and his associates at Dockery. But he developed a style that differed from theirs: a delicate, precise guitar-picking to back up his vibrato-filled, yodel-like vocals that delighted audiences throughout the state.

Johnson continued to travel to the Delta during picking season but was based in Jackson or Crystal Springs for the rest of his life—a startlingly long life, considering his taste for "canned heat" (Sterno), shoe polish, or anything else that would get him high, as well as plenty of regular whiskey when he could get it. Johnson's drinking was legendary even among blues singers, who are not known as a teetotaling bunch. He immortalized his own habits in the song "Canned Heat Blues" (a 1960s blues-rock group took the title for its name):

> *Crying mama, mama, mama, crying, canned heat is*
>   *killing me*
> *Believe to my soul, Lord, it's going kill me dead.*

The house at 905 Ann Banks is where Tommy Johnson stayed when he was in town. It was the longtime home of Johnny Temple, who lived there until his death in 1968. Other blues artists who stayed at the house include Joe and Charlie McCoy, Skip James, and Elmore James, who was rooming there with Temple just before James's death in 1963.

After that dizzying lineup of blues-star residents, the house is vacant as of this writing but still in fairly good shape. And it remains in earshot of the blues—one empty lot separates it from a great jook joint, the Queen of Hearts.

- **Queen of Hearts**
  2243 Martin Luther King, Jr., Dr. (at Ann Banks St.)
  (601) 352-5730

The club is open nightly; live music is generally on Sundays only. The building dates from about 1900, and people have been playing the blues in it at least since 1972. "Big Bad Smitty and I

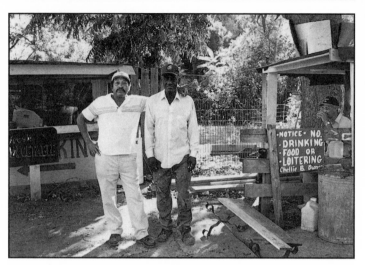

Owner Chellie B. Lewis (left) and drummer Charlie Jenkins outside the Queen of Hearts jook joint, 2243 Martin Luther King, Jr., Drive, Jackson

started the blues in Jackson," says club owner Chellie B. Lewis. "The blues had gone." The Queen of Hearts also hosted Jackson's first blues festival, in 1978, according to Lewis.

"This club is for you, but if you came to clown you can just turn around," reads the inscription on the mirror behind the club's tiny stage. Singer-harpist Sam Myers, who has since left Jackson to join Dallas-based Anson Funderburgh and the Rockets, used to play regularly at the Queen of Hearts. So did Big Bad Smitty, who moved to St. Louis and then died in 2002.

The energetic King Edward, who wears a bowler hat and sometimes plays guitar with it, has been playing at the Queen of Hearts since its early days, and still does. He puts on a fierce performance whether there are five or fifty people in the club. Other singers stop in to sing a few or just to socialize. The music usually doesn't start until after midnight—and sometimes not at all. Relax, have a drink, and be patient, or take up a collection to motivate the band.

• Farish Street

The traditional black business street, Farish Street is to Jackson what Beale Street is to Memphis and Nelson Street is to Greenville. As centers of black commerce and activity, these streets also naturally became focal points for the blues. In the 1950s, Willie Love told Lillian McMurry, Farish Street had a church with moonshine stored under it and a restaurant with liquor flowing from a water faucet.

Farish has fallen into decline and decay. However, it seems to be on the verge of rejuvenation. The city has declared the area a historic district, purchased about half the buildings in the 200 and 300 blocks, and hired Performa, Inc.—the same company that restored Memphis's Beale Street—to turn it into an entertainment district. In the meantime, there are quite a few active businesses remaining among the abandoned buildings—restaurants, bars, a barbershop, and a newly renovated theater.

The Louisiana-born piano great Little Brother Montgomery, who spent a lot of time in Jackson, recorded "Farish Street Jive," a spirited instrumental, in 1936. (Montgomery apparently liked place-name songs. He also cut "Vicksburg Blues" and "Shreveport Farewell.") "Farish Street Rag," another instrumental, was recorded by the New Orleans Nehi Boys.

The **Farish Street Festival** (601-960-2383), held on a Saturday in September, presents music on outdoor stages on the street. It features big-name soul-blues acts.

- **Speir Phonograph Co.**
  225 N. Farish St.

  To get there: The building is still standing, although it is boarded up and gutted. It lacks a street number, but it is just south of an alley and across the street from number 230. There is a "Brown Furniture Co." sign toward the south end of the building. Speir's company was in the northern third, under the word "company" in ghostly old paint. He later moved his business to 111 and 118 N. Farish, buildings that have been demolished and replaced by the McCoy Federal Building.

Henry C. Speir, a white store owner, was one of the most influential nonmusicians in blues history. Besides running his store in Jackson, Speir traveled the South as a talent scout from the mid-1920s to the mid-1930s, finding blues artists for record companies. He would drive hundreds of miles to hear a singer he had heard about, then ask him to play. As Speir told writer Gayle Dean Wardlow, if he liked an artist he would say, "You sound pretty good. You know, I make records; if you will keep practicing and get your songs together real good and come to Jackson in a few days, I see that you get on records." An artist who took him up on the offer received travel reimbursement and spending money, along with fifty dollars per recorded side. Speir reportedly received a hundred and fifty dollars from the record company for each session of at least four songs.

Charley Patton, Skip James, and Willie Brown were among Speir's discoveries and the ones he considered the finest musicians. Among the other blues artists he worked with were the Mississippi Sheiks, Bo Carter, Son House, Will Shade, Robert Wilkins, Tommy Johnson, William Harris, the Mississippi Jook Band, Ishmon Bracey, Kokomo Arnold, Jim Jackson, Blind Joe Reynolds, Geechie Wiley, Elvie Thomas, and Isaiah Nettles. He also discovered and recorded many jazz, sacred, and hillbilly artists.

To pass the audition, an artist had to have at least four original songs. One whom Speir rejected was the bluesy hillbilly singer Jimmie Rodgers. Speir told Rodgers to go back home to Meridian and work up some more material.

Speir established his music store in 1925, specifically to sell records to the black community. He used talent scouting as a way to increase the store's business. There was a small recording machine upstairs for auditions and for vanity recordings, which anyone could make for five dollars.

By 1929 Speir had moved the store to 111 N. Farish, where an often-reproduced photograph was taken of him, another man, and a young woman standing in the narrow store. Among the artists who auditioned there was Robert Johnson, in 1936. Speir passed Johnson's name on to Ernie Oertle, an ARC records salesman, who took Johnson to San Antonio to record.

In 1930, according to Wardlow, Speir was offered the whole Paramount Record Company for twenty-five thousand dollars, including the costs of moving it from Grafton, Wisconsin, to Jackson. Speir turned down the offer because he did not have the money and was unable to raise it through the chamber of commerce.

About 1937, Speir left Farish Street and moved his business to West Capitol Street. In 1944, in the wake of a nationwide musicians' strike, Speir decided the record business was dead. He closed his music store and opened a furniture store in a white neighborhood in northern Jackson. Speir died in 1972.

- **Ace Records**
  241 N. Farish

  To get there: Ace Records is two buildings north of Speir Phonograph (Ross Furniture is between the two). The last door before the corner was the entrance to Ace.

Producer Johnny Vincent started Ace in 1955 to record New Orleans artists Earl King, Huey "Piano" Smith, and Bobby Marchan. King's "Those Lonely, Lonely Nights" was the label's first big hit, recorded at the Trumpet studio on Farish Street. "The piano was a little bit out of tune" for the "Lonely Nights" session, King told an interviewer. "But the guitar was out of tune and we had better takes than [the one] that was in tune." Blues artists Johnny Littlejohn and Willie Clayton also recorded here.

In the 1990s, Vincent relocated to Pearl, a Jackson suburb, where he operated the pop-blues label Avanti (135 Fairmont Plaza, 601-939-6868). Avanti artist Rue Davis recorded "Farish Street Blues," a tribute to the street's beloved businesses, but it remains unreleased. Vincent died on February 4, 2000, at age seventy-four.

- **Record Mart (and Trumpet Record Company and Diamond Recording Studio)**
  309 N. Farish St.

  To get there: The bricked-up middle door of this building, which also includes Big Al's Recovery Room, was the entrance to Record Mart.

This building was once a furniture store; its function began to change in 1949 when the owner's wife, Lillian McMurry, found Wynonie Harris's "All She Wants to Do Is Rock" in the store and put it on the turntable. "It was the most unusual, sincere and solid sound I'd ever heard. I'd never heard anything with such rhythm and freedom," McMurry, who was white, recalled later. It was her first exposure to black music.

McMurry started ordering blues and gospel records and selling them from her husband's store. She put speakers outside to attract customers. She sponsored a blues radio show and sold records by mail order. The record department soon took over the store. She founded the Trumpet label and began recording music—gospel groups at first. After hearing about the live radio broadcasts done by Sonny Boy Williamson II, McMurry tracked him down and persuaded him to make his first recordings. Sonny Boy brought in Joe Willie Wilkins, Elmore James, and Willie Love for his January 4, 1951, session, which included "Eyesight to the Blind," Trumpet's first hit. The recording studio for those songs and many other early Trumpet records was at **Scott Radio Service**, 128 N. Gallatin St. That building has been demolished and replaced by a parking lot.

Williamson remained close to McMurry throughout his life. She produced most of his hits, bailed him out of jail, and paid for his tombstone after he died. On one occasion, McMurry allegedly ran Williamson out of her studio at gunpoint—using his gun, which she had made him turn over when he entered—for cursing. He returned and apologized a few weeks later.

In 1953, Williamson recorded "309"—the street address of his record company. A kind of musical calling card, it also includes two phone numbers for McMurry:

> To get in touch with my manager, please call 5-4121
> She can always tell you that Sonny Boy is out on the run.

Besides playing with Williamson, Elmore James made his first recording, "Dust My Broom," under his own name for McMurry, then left her label.

Big Joe Williams, the Crawford-born country bluesman who had been recording since 1935, showed up at Trumpet in 1951 and recorded for McMurry. An even older bluesman—Bo Carter, who had recorded more than a hundred sides for other labels between 1928 and 1941—also sought to revive his career at Trumpet Records, but was turned away. As McMurry told an interviewer: "He was friends of Sonny Boy, Willie Love, and Joe Willie Wilkins and a nice old fellow, light-skinned like [his brother] Sam Chatmon . . . Anyway, Bo Carter couldn't sing anymore; Bo was half blind, his voice broken completely. I'd audition him and tried to be kind and turn him down gently. Sonny Boy and Willie always helped get Bo gone without hurting his feelings. Today, some of those auditions would be collectors' items for just the blues collectors but Diamond Record Co. could not sell them then."

Trumpet folded in 1954, and McMurry's next label, Globe Records, didn't make out. But McMurry continued to make sure her artists got their royalties when other labels rereleased their material. She died March 28, 1999, at age seventy-seven, in Jackson.

McMurry installed a recording studio in the building in 1953, calling it Diamond Recording Studio. Sonny Boy and Jerry "Boogie" McCain both recorded at the studio here at 309. Earlier recordings were made at other Jackson locations or out of town—Williamson's "309," for example, was recorded in Houston.

Later, this building served as the offices of the *Jackson Advocate*, an outspoken African American newspaper. The paper moved its offices one street west to 438 Mill Street after the Farish Street building was firebombed in 1997.

- **Peaches Café**
  327 N. Farish St.
  (601) 354-9267

This locally beloved soul food restaurant has been open since 1961 and is still owned and operated by its founder, Willora "Peaches" Ephram, with help from her son Roderick. On Thursdays, veteran blues guitarist Jesse Robinson plays for lunchtime diners, 11 A.M. to 2 P.M. On weekend nights Peaches becomes a jook joint–like neighborhood hangout with grooving to the blues from the jukebox and, occasionally, live music. Beer is served weekend nights (BYOB liquor).

Alamo Theater
333 N. Farish St.
(601) 352-3365

This is a grand old theater that once hosted movies, vaudeville shows, touring jazz acts, and a weekly talent contest. Pianist Otis Spann, a Belzoni native who moved to Jackson at an early age, won the Alamo's talent contest at age eight, in 1938, and became a regular part of the stage show. Dorothy Moore of "Misty Blue" fame, a native Jacksonian, also was a frequent winner of the contests.

The current Alamo was built in the 1950s (replacing an earlier Alamo) and restored in 1996, with support from the city and various agencies. Its façade and sign have been returned to their original glory, but the interior is simple and modern. People have not

The Alamo Theater and other buildings on Farish Street, Jackson

yet started flocking to the post-restoration Alamo's occasional shows, which feature blues, jazz, classical music, or plays. A plan to bring back the talent contests has not yet been realized.

- **Big Apple Inn**
  509 N. Farish St.
  (601) 354-9371

Sonny Boy Williamson II and his wife, Mattie, lived in the upstairs apartment in this building during the years he was recording at Trumpet. Their address was 507½ N. Farish. Williamson associates such as Willie Love and Elmore James also stayed in the apartment. Gene Lee, owner of the restaurant downstairs, used to go fishing with Sonny Boy. "We'd get on our bicycles and ride to the Pearl River, push our bicycles over the tracks," Lee says. "With our cane poles. We never caught any fish. It was relaxation for him, after playing all night."

Later, that apartment became the state NAACP headquarters, and civil rights leader Medgar Evers worked there as state field secretary. He was murdered in 1963 at age thirty-six.

The Big Apple is known to regulars as Big John's, after original owner Juan "Big John" Mora, Lee's grandfather. And it is famous for a downhome dish that Big John invented: pig-ear sandwiches. The ears are boiled and served on a biscuit-size roll, dressed with coleslaw, mustard, and hot sauce. Whenever he's in town, B. B. King is among the musicians, politicians, and regular folks who stop by for a bagful. Bobby "Blue" Bland, who also enjoys them, calls them "listener sandwiches." Smoke-sausage, hamburger, hot dog, and bologna sandwiches also are available, as well as hot tamales.

- **Birdland**
  538 Farish St.
  (601) 352-5124

This bar was once the Crystal Palace, which brought in touring jazz and R&B acts. The old name is still visible in fading paint on the brick wall on the building's south side.

- **Edward Lee Hotel**
  144 Church St. (in the first block west of Farish St.)

This was the hotel where touring black musicians usually stayed when they came to Jackson for gigs at the Alamo or Crystal Palace. Framed by empty lots, the large brick building is abandoned and falling down. Unfortunately, its sign has recently disappeared.

North of Church on Farish is a row of old **shotgun houses** recently purchased by the city, restored and repainted. Long before the restoration, bluesman Willie Love lived in one of these homes. Bluesman Hacksaw Harney lived at 722 Farish and posed in front of his home for a photo by Steve LaVere that has become a postcard.

- **Ishmon Bracey's Grave**
  To get there: Heading west on Highway 80 between Terry Road and Ellis Avenue, turn right at the Jim Hill High School sign, onto the frontage road. Continue west on the frontage road, around Wright Music Company and past the school. You will wind up heading north on Hattiesburg Street. The large cemetery occupies both sides of the street. Take the northernmost entrance into the part on the east side of the street.

Bracey's grave is about halfway back, in the middle of a row. It is one of the few cross-shaped stones in the cemetery. It reads:

REST IN PEACE
Rev. Ishmon Bracey
Born Jan. 9th, 1901
Died Feb. 12, 1970

Born in Byram, Ishmon (sometimes spelled "Ishman") Bracey lived in Jackson from the 1920s on, singing and playing guitar in a simple, straightforward style. H. C. Speir approached him while he was playing on Mill Street in Jackson in 1927 ("I thought he was the law," Bracey recalled of that encounter). Bracey recorded a few sides for Speir but never reached the legendary status of some of his peers. One distinctive aspect of his recordings is the addition of a pianist and clarinetist, along with Bracey's voice and guitar—unusual instrumentation for a Mississippi blues record of the 1920s.

Bracey played the blues until he turned to religion in 1951. He still didn't mind talking about the blues after that, telling interviewers about his old pal Tommy Johnson.

Bracey's grave is interesting because the stone is a fairly old one erected by his family soon after his death, rather than a large new one provided by fans or a record company, as are many blues artists' stones. The site is easily accessible and right in the city.

- **Subway Lounge**
  Basement of the Summers Hotel, 619 W. Pearl St. (near Minerva St.)
  (601) 352-6812

The Summers Hotel was, for decades, one of the few hotels in Jackson open to blacks. Retired schoolteacher and part-time singer Jimmy King opened the Subway Lounge in the old hotel's basement in 1966, running it first as a jazz club and switching to blues around 1986.

It was a classic after-hours, literally underground nightspot. The place didn't even open until after midnight, and the live music went on until at least 4 A.M. After the bar closed at 1 A.M., you could go buy beer and, if you were hungry, "blues dogs" from the house next door. Many musicians stopped by after gigs to hang out or sit in.

The Subway and its musicians were celebrated in the 2003 Starz! TV documentary *Last of the Mississippi Jukes*. The film also deals with the history of the building and the efforts to save the building from demolition or collapse.

But alas, even a movie was not enough to save the Subway. It closed later the same year, after flood damage made the building even more hazardous and more expensive to repair. Most of it has collapsed, but part of the front remains. King hopes to open a new Subway Lounge on Farish Street.

- **Poindexter Park Inn**
  803 Deer Park Street
  (601) 944-1392

This bed-and-breakfast is run by former city councilwoman Marcia Weaver, a blues enthusiast and manager of Jackson singer Dorothy Moore of "Misty Blue" fame. Weaver is familiar with the history and current state of blues in her city, and has a small library of blues-related books at the inn. A restored historic building in a rundown neighborhood, Poindexter Park Inn is very convenient to the Subway Lounge.

- **930 Blues Café**
  930 N. Congress St.
  (601) 948-3344

This cozy nightclub is up a narrow flight of stairs in a historic house and is decorated jook-joint style. It offers live blues nightly, generally of the high-energy electric variety (although unfortunately the place is too small to allow much dance space). There are house bands during the week and regional or national acts on Fridays and Saturdays. The downstairs is a restaurant that serves hearty lunches with a limited menu available at night.

- **E&E Restaurant**
  2605 Robinson St.
  (601) 354-0801

This restaurant is owned by Charles Evers, brother of slain civil rights leader Medgar Evers. It offers dancing to recorded blues, and occasionally to live music, on Sunday nights.

- **Hal & Mal's Restaurant and Brewery**
  200 S. Commerce St.
  (601) 948-0888

Blues is occasionally on the bill at this downtown restaurant/brewpub/nightclub, but not as often as rock, jazz, and bluegrass. The wall decorations include signed photos of various artists, including Albert King. Jack Owens's mailbox and the sunglasses Elvis Presley wore in the Rose Bowl parade are also on the premises. The women's bathroom has a Ma Rainey theme, while the men's is devoted to Elvis.

- **George Street Grocery**
  416 George St.
  (601) 969-3753

This is another downtown club that sometimes offers blues, but also presents rock and other genres. George Street is where Texas-based Anson Funderburgh and the Rockets were playing in 1982 when Jackson singer-harpist Sam Myers sat in with them for the first time. Myers became a full-time member of the group a few years later. A blues jam begins at 9 P.M. on Tuesdays. Check the listings in Thursday's *Clarion-Ledger* for the week's blues offerings at this and other Jackson clubs.

- **Malaco Records**
  3023 W. Northside Drive
  (601) 982-4522

Tommy Couch and Wolf Stephenson got into the music business by booking bands for fraternity parties when both were pharmacy students at the University of Mississippi in the early 1960s. After graduating, they moved to Jackson and continued booking bands and promoting concerts, using an office they rented from Ace Records.

Soon they tried their hands at recording. Johnny Vincent of Ace told them about the Northside Drive building, part of which he was renting as a warehouse. They rented the other half as a studio, and they are still there.

Fred McDowell's 1967 album *I Do Not Play No Rock 'n' Roll* was recorded at Malaco and released on Capitol. Besides that one venture into deep blues, and a few experiments with disco, funk, pop, and country, Malaco has focused on soul, soul-blues, and, in recent years, gospel. Denise LaSalle, Shirley Brown, Latimore, and Bobby Rush are among the company's soul-blues mainstays.

Two Malaco releases are the blues anthems that rekindled blues interest among black listeners in the 1980s: Z. Z. Hill's 1982 "Down Home Blues" and Little Milton's 1984 "The Blues Is All Right." The company also has had three top ten pop hits, all recorded here: King Floyd's "Groove Me" in 1970–71, Jean Knight's "Mr. Big Stuff" in 1971, and Dorothy Moore's "Misty Blue" in 1976.

Malaco gives tours by appointment only.

- **Red Hot & Blue**

    1625 E. County Line Rd.
    (601) 956-3313 (and a branch at 5530 Highway 80, Pearl, 601-664-0098)

This suburban strip-mall barbecue restaurant was founded by Malaco Records co-owner Tommy Couch, who has since sold it. Its walls are covered with signed posters, photos, and other memorabilia from blues artists, and not only from Malaco artists. On display is a giant multimedia painting of bluesman "Son" Thomas by Patterson-Barnes. There are blues jams Monday nights, blues acts on weekends, and recorded blues on the stereo every day.

Vaughan

- **Casey Jones Museum**

    10901 Vaughan Rd.
    (662) 673-9864

    To get there: Take Interstate 55 to exit 133, about 30 miles north of Jackson. Follow the signs to the museum, 1 mile from the exit.

The museum is open 8 A.M. to 4 P.M. Mondays, Tuesdays, Thursdays, and Fridays, 8 A.M. to noon Wednesdays and Saturdays. There is an admission charge.

There were hundreds of train crashes, many of them fatal, in 1900. But one of them, which happened outside Vaughan on April 30, is still famous today, with dozens of songs and three museums dedicated to it (the others are in Water Valley, Mississippi, and Jackson, Tennessee).

The wreck that killed Casey Jones was not especially newsworthy or deadly (only one person, Jones, was killed). We remember it today only because Wallace "Wash" Saunders, a black engine wiper, wrote "The Ballad of Casey Jones" for his dead friend, a thirty-six-year-old white engineer. A traveling engineer heard Saunders sing the song and gave it to his brother, a vaudeville entertainer. Copyrighted by Frank and Bert Leighton, the song became a hit (on sheet music, in those days before record-

The Casey Jones Museum, Vaughan

ing) immediately. Legend has it that Saunders sold it for a pint of gin—but he may not have received even that.

The wreck has been commemorated musically in many more songs, of all genres, in the years since. (One non-blues version and a movie place the wreck in California, for some reason.) In 1928, bluesman Furry Lewis made it a poignant two-part epic, "Kassie Jones," recasting the accident as a family tragedy:

> *This morning I heard someone was dying, Mrs. Kassie's*
> *   children on the doorstep crying:*
> *"Mama, Mama, I can't keep from crying. Papa got killed on*
> *   the Southern line.*
> *On the Southern line. Papa got killed on the Southern line."*

Mississippi John Hurt also interpreted the accident in song. Titled "Talking Casey," Hurt atypically uses a slide on the number, using it to mimic the sounds of the train, the sheep that get on the track, and Jones cursing at them.

The museum contains maps, sheet music, model trains, train equipment, photos, drawings, and paintings. The actual bell from the ill-fated train is there. And you hear a taped rendition of the original ballad. The museum building is the former Pickens Sta-

Detail from Elmore James's grave marker, Ebenezer

tion, which was moved from a nearby town to replace the original Vaughan Station, both of which were built about 1900.

Why Jones couldn't stop the train remains unclear.

Ebenezer

• **Graves of Elmore James and Lonnie Pitchford**

To get there: From Highway 55, take exit 146 (Highway 14, Goodman, Ebenezer). Take Highway 14 west for 1.3 miles, until it makes a T intersection with Highway 17. That T is in the town of Richland, where Elmore James was born (he was not born in the larger Richland just south of Jackson). Head north on Highway 17 for 2.6 miles, to Newport Road. Turn left on Newport Road and drive 3.9 miles to New Port M.B. Church, a red brick building on your left.

Park at the church and walk behind and to the right of it, into the cemetery. Elmore James is buried about a hundred feet back, midway between the church and the right-hand edge of the cemetery. His stone is striking. It is black, with a three-dimensional metal sculpture of him coming from the front of it. The front reads:

Elmore James
"King of the Slide Guitar"
January 27, 1918
May 24, 1963

The reverse says:

> Born in Holmes County, Mississippi, Elmore James electrified the rural Delta blues with his unique slide guitar style. Creating a powerful legacy that will remain forever in American music. "The sky is crying . . . look at the tears roll down the street."

Lonnie Pitchford's grave is about thirty feet farther back. His gravestone has built-in pegs for a playable string, although the string is usually missing.

The legend on Elmore James's headstone is no exaggeration. He really is responsible for the electric slide-guitar sound, which has become familiar in blues, rock, even pop and country. Apparently being the brother of a radio technician gave James the idea and the know-how to amplify his acoustic guitar. He also is the songwriter of such classics as "It Hurts Me, Too," "Shake Your Moneymaker" and "The Sky Is Crying," a line from which is on his tombstone.

A native of nearby Lexington, Lonnie Pitchford was born on October 8, 1955, and died on November 8, 1998. He was, for his age, startlingly well versed in the blues of earlier eras. He was also a remarkably good musician, regardless of age. Pitchford first gained fame as a master of the one-string guitar, which he would build onstage and then play. He also was a master of the six-string guitar in its acoustic and electric versions, and was an especially adept interpreter of Robert Johnson material (which he learned directly from Robert Lockwood, Jr., who was Johnson's only pupil). Pitchford made only one full album, *All Around Man*, during his too-short life. He also appears in the documentary *Deep Blues* and on its soundtrack, on a few concert compilations, and on a John Mellencamp album.

Bentonia

The tiny town of Bentonia (population 518) looms disproportionately large in blues history and legend. It is the hometown of Skip James, who recorded such classics as "Devil Got My Woman," "I'm So Glad," and "22-20 Blues" in 1930. It is hard to avoid the word "haunting" when discussing James's music, which features his falsetto singing and minor-key guitar playing or quirky piano. After a long period away from music, James did some more recording and performing during the 1960s blues-folk revival. He died on October 3, 1969, and is buried in Philadelphia, Pennsylvania.

Skip James had seemed to be a unique artist, but it turned out there was another Bentonia man, Jack Owens, about the same age who played in the same style. It is unclear which of the two origi-nated the style, or whether they are part of a Bentonia "school" that predates them. Although Owens did not record until the 1960s, he had been playing at house parties and jooks in his area for many years. In his last decades he recorded several albums, ap-peared in the movie *Deep Blues*, and performed at festivals, always accompanied by Bentonia harpist Bud Spires.

- ## Blue Front Cafe
  108 E. Railroad Ave.
  (601) 755-2278

  To get there: From Highway 49, take either Bentonia exit and head into town. Cross the tracks and look for the Blue Front Cafe, which has a big sign, next to a ramshackle old grocery building.

Owner-musician Jimmy Holmes keeps the Bentonia blues tra-dition alive in this jook joint that dates at least from 1948. It often features live music on Sunday afternoons, and sometimes on other days. The live music is more frequent during the cold months, when a wood-burning stove warms up the place.

There is a giant poster of Jack Owens, who used to play here, on the wall. Owens's longtime musical partner, harpist Bud Spires, still lives in the area and stops in sometimes. The regular band is the Blue Front Boys, featuring Holmes on guitar and Sonny Reedus on bass. They usually play electric-band blues, but both Holmes and Reedus are familiar with the James-Owens solo style and "cross-note" tuning.

In 1995, Jack Owens and Bud Spires played the blues in a na-tional TV commercial, for Levi's, filmed at the Blue Front.

- ## Jack Owens's Grave
  To get there: From downtown Bentonia, take Cannon Road (Highway 433) northeast for 4.4 miles, then turn right at Scotland Road (there is a sign pointing you toward Scotland). You will go past Old Liberty M. B. Church, where Owens's funeral was held. Continue to the cemetery, up a dirt drive

into the woods on the right, 3.0 miles from the turn onto Scotland Road. There is a small "Day Cemetery" sign. Park at the end of the drive and walk in toward the right and almost to the back.

The grave is marked by a double stone for Owens and his wife, Mrs. Mable Owens. A guitar is inscribed between them. His half reads:

> *Mr. L. F. Nelson*
> (Jack Owens)
> Sunrise Nov. 17, 1904
> Sunset Feb. 9, 1997

Owens's sister, Marie Owens, is buried nearby.

Jack Owens was a farmer who for a while ran a jook house as a side business; music was never the main thing in his life. But after folklorists David Evans and Alan Lomax discovered and documented his music, Owens's reputation expanded beyond the Bentonia area, where he lived all of his life. He played at festivals, did a few tours, and appeared in the documentaries *Land Where the Blues Began* and *Deep Blues* along with Spires.

"The Devil" or "Must Have Been the Devil" was Owens's signature tune, one he would play for a long time. Skip James called his version "Devil Got My Woman." This piece crops up in the repertoires of singers from outside Bentonia: Robert Johnson's "Hellhound on My Trail" and Bo Carter's "Old Devil" are both related to it.

Yazoo City

This town has lent its euphonious name to Yazoo Records, a reissue company that has brought the music of old blues 78s to new generations via LPs and then CDs. The Yazoo River forms the east border of the Delta, as the Mississippi does to the west. (The name "Yazoo" comes from an extinct Indian tribe).

A **Yazoo Historical Blues Museum** is planned for inside the Triangle Cultural Center, 332 N. Main St., 662–746-2273. The center puts on a Yazoo Blues Festival the last Saturday of June, next to the building.

Crystal Springs

Tommy Johnson, the crooning singer of such blues master-pieces as "Cool Drink of Water," "Canned Heat Blues," and the much-covered "Big Road Blues," was born in nearby Terry and grew up in Crystal Springs. Johnson lived from 1896 to 1956 but recorded only a handful of songs, in about 1929. He is buried on private property in Crystal Springs.

There is a grave marker for Johnson inside the **Crystal Springs Public Library**, 200 S. Jackson St., 601-892-3205. The library is open 9 A.M. to 5 P.M. Mondays through Saturdays. Efforts are on-going to allow public access to the abandoned cemetery where Johnson is buried and to place the marker there.

With his brothers Ledell and Mager, Tommy Johnson used to play in front of **Thaxton's** drugstore, 112 E. Georgetown St., in the mid-1920s. The building is still there, now occupied by Optical One. Look up to find the "Thaxton's" in raised brick on the front of the building.

Hazlehurst

Robert Johnson, "the King of the Delta Blues," was born out-side the Delta, in this town on Highway 51 south of Jackson, on May 8, 1911. He left Hazlehurst when he was a baby, being taken first to Memphis and then to Robinsonville (in the Delta), where he spent his childhood and teen years and began playing music.

But Hazlehurst was still to play a role in Johnson's personal and musical life. Around 1930, he came back to look for his real father, Noah Johnson. It is unknown whether that search was successful. But Robert Johnson, a young widower, got remarried in Hazle-hurst, to an older woman named Calletta Craft. He also appren-ticed with an unrecorded bluesman named Ike Zinnerman. And he practiced a lot. When Johnson returned to the Delta a few years later, the improvement in his playing astounded everyone to the point that some wondered if he had made a deal with the devil.

• **Robert Johnson's Birthplace**

Robert Johnson was born on a farm just north of Hazlehurst. The spot is where Interstate 55 and Highway 28 intersect today, making it the easiest blues-heritage spot to visit—driving north on I-55 you go across Johnson's front yard. The actual house he was born in has been moved to a secret location, local sources say. The house might eventually be restored as a Johnson museum.

• Robert Johnson Monument

Hazlehurst's town square is loaded with markers and monuments. One historical marker commemorates Mrs. Annie Coleman Peyton, a Hazlehurst citizen who led the effort to establish Mississippi State College for Women (now Mississippi University for Women), the country's first state-supported college for women, in 1884. A small stone monument acknowledges the Illinois Central Railroad. There are monuments to the veterans of several wars and a marker for the town itself, which was named for the chief engineer of the first railway connecting Jackson and New Orleans, the last spike of which was driven in Hazlehurst in 1858. And the newest monument, tombstone-like, recognizes the town's most famous citizen, Robert Johnson. The inscription is taken verbatim from the Johnson memorial in Morgan City. Memorial bricks in front of the monument include one for H. C. Speir, Sr., the Jackson record store owner and talent scout who recommended Johnson to Vocalion Records.

That big building on the square is the **Copiah County Courthouse**, where Johnson married Calletta Craft on May 4, 1931. Johnson used to play on the courthouse steps on Saturday afternoons.

Renfroe Valley

• J. B. Lenoir's Grave

To get there: From the intersection of highways 84 and 27 in Monticello, head south on Highway 27 for 15 miles to Price Road. Price is on the left only; Dummy Line Road is opposite it. There is a sign reading "Sauls Valley Baptist Church, 5 mi." at the intersection, on the left. Turn left, onto Price Road, and drive 1.7 miles to Salem M.B. Church, on the left. The Lenoir grave is near the middle of the small cemetery.

J. B. Lenoir (pronounced "Lenore") was part of the Chicago blues scene of the 1950s–'60s. Although he never made it big or even was able to support himself through music, he had a distinctive style that touched many who heard it. Many of Lenoir's songs are overtly political, although his best-known number is the nonpolitical "Talk to Your Daughter." He sang in a high, womanly voice, accompanying himself with infectious rhythms on the acoustic guitar.

In the early 1960s Lenoir traveled to England as part of the American Folk Blues Festival. He befriended and impressed British bluesman John Mayall, who wrote two songs about him, "The Death of J. B. Lenoir" and "I'm Gonna Fight for You J. B." Lenoir died in 1967, at age thirty-eight, due to injuries from a car accident.

Lenoir is the subject of a film made by Steve and Ronnog Seaberg, intended for Swedish television. It didn't air, however, until 2003, as part of Wim Wenders's "The Soul of a Man" episode on PBS's *The Blues* series. Wenders had become a fan of Lenoir's after hearing Mayall's songs.

Lenoir is buried in the community where he was born. The grave has a double stone for J. B. and his wife Ella L. Craft, identified as "father" and "mother." It bears a photo of J. B. in his trademark zebra-striped coat. There are an engraved guitar and some musical notes and the inscription, "Let the works we've done speak for us."

Varnado, La.

- **Birdie's Roadhouse**
  26646 Highway 21
  (985) 732-4032

  To get there: From J. B. Lenoir's grave, take Highway 27 north back to Monticello, then Highway 587 south. Highway 587 will become Highway 35 and then, at the Louisiana border, will become Highway 21. The club is on the right, about 7 miles south of the state border.

This club is a little off the blues path, but if you are visiting J. B. Lenoir's grave late on a Friday or Saturday afternoon, you might want to swing down to Birdie's—about an hour's drive. It is also about an hour from New Orleans; about 2½ hours from Jackson.

Birdie's looks as if it's been there forever, the proverbial little shack out in the sticks, near the prison. But it just opened in 2000, in a 1936 double-shotgun house that was moved to the site and renovated as a jook joint-ish club. It has a great blues jukebox (J. B. Lenoir, Frank Frost, Robert Nighthawk), live music 10 P.M. to 2 A.M. Fridays and 8 P.M. to midnight Saturdays. Thursday is open-mike night. Beer only is served, BYOB liquor (there are compartments in the wall where regulars lock up their bottles).

Port Gibson

- **F. S. Wolcott's Rabbit Foot Minstrel Show Headquarters**
  Carroll St. and Market St.

  To get there: From Highway 61, continue south into town and turn right at the stoplight where the Exxon station is (Carroll Street, although there is no street sign). Go two blocks to the corner of Market Street (again unmarked). Titles for Cash is the business occupying the building that Wolcott once owned and used as headquarters for the minstrel show. The performers sometimes rehearsed on the field in front of the building.

From about 1900 to the 1940s, the Rabbit Foot Minstrels were one of the country's two most popular minstrel shows (the other was Silas Green from New Orleans). Wolcott, a white man, ran the black entertainment revue from his hometown of Port Gibson. Touring nationally by train (and later by bus), a minstrel show would come to town and perform under a large tent. The show featured comedians, wrestlers, jugglers, animal acts—and blues singers.

Among the many singers who toured with Rabbit Foot are Ma Rainey, Bertha "Chippie" Hill, Bessie Smith, Jim Jackson, Big Joe Williams, Louis Jordan, Jim Seals (father of Son Seals), Maxwell Street Jimmy Davis, Rufus Thomas, Chico Chism, Diamond Teeth Mary, and Brownie McGee.

It was while touring with Rabbit Foot in 1902 that Ma Rainey heard a young Missouri woman singing a "strange and poignant" song that awakened Rainey to the blues—an experience similar to W. C. Handy's blues awakening in Mississippi a few years later. It was also while she was with Rabbit Foot, in 1914, that Rainey met and coached the young Bessie Smith, who joined the troupe that year.

Natchez

Jackson on a high hill, Natchez just below
I ever get back home, I won't be back no more.
—Charley Patton, "Screamin' and Hollerin' the Blues"

Before the Civil War, Natchez and Vicksburg were the state's only towns with sidewalks, brick buildings, or paved streets. Natchez, the oldest settlement on the Mississippi River and the first cotton capital, was once home to half of America's millionaires. It still has hundreds of antebellum structures, which it shows off during fall and spring pilgrimages. Like Charleston, South Carolina, or Savannah, Georgia, Natchez is an Old South town.

It also shows some New Orleans flavor in its architecture, atmosphere, and music. One

Natchez bluesman Little Poochie performing in 1999, downtown Natchez

unusual Natchez blues band, Hezekiah and the House Rockers, included a trombonist. That band has broken up, but its leader, singer-harpist-drummer Hezekiah Early, still lives in the area, often playing and recording with slide guitarist Elmo Williams.

Bluff City Blues, a three-piece band featuring the great Little Poochie on vocals and guitar, is a more orthodox Natchez blues act.

The town's annual **Blues on the Bluff Festival** (601-446-9351) takes place in mid-April in Natchez Memorial Park.

A historical marker notes the site of **Forks of the Road** slave market, on the left as you come into town from the north on Highway 61. This was the South's second-largest slave market in the nineteenth century.

- **Site of the Natchez Rhythm Club Fire**

  To get there: Highway 61 becomes St. Catherine Street. Just north of Martin Luther King Street, past the large brick Holy Family Church on the left, there is a fork in the road and a barnlike, signless car wash on the right, which is where the Natchez Rhythm Club stood.

The Natchez Rhythm Club burned to the ground on April 23, 1940, killing two hundred sixty of the five hundred people inside. The death rate was so high because the windows had been boarded up to prevent people outside from enjoying the show without paying the cover. That left only one exit. Among the dead were Walter Barnes and most of his orchestra, a popular jazz group who were playing that night. To deal with the bodies, African American morticians were called in from miles around, including a young Perry Payton of Greenville, who was helping his mortician father. Payton later established his own funeral home business and the Flowing Fountain nightclub in Greenville.

In the immediate wake of the fire, blues singers Gene Gilmore and Leonard "Baby Doo" Caston recorded songs about it, which were released back-to-back on one single. Caston played piano on both tracks, and Robert Lee McCoy accompanied both on harmonica. Caston's "The Death of Walter Barnes" included these lines:

> *Now, it was just about midnight, just about twelve o'clock*
> *Poor Walter played his theme song, the dance hall began*
>   *to rock.*

> *The peoples all was dancin', enjoyin' their lives so high*
> *Just in a short while, the dance hall was full of fire.*

Gilmore's "The Natchez Fire" was equally somber:

> *Lord, it was late one Tuesday night, people had come from*
>   *miles around*
> *They was enjoying their lives when that Rhythm Club*
>   *went down.*

> *Lord, it was sad and misery when the hearses began to roll*
> *It was over two hundred dead and gone, Lord, and they can't*
>   *come here no more.*

Sixteen years after the fire, Howlin' Wolf recorded his tribute, "The Natchez Burning." A slow, spooky number that is different from anything else he recorded, the song personalizes the tragedy:

> *Did you ever hear about the burning that happened way*
>   *down in Natchez Mississippi town?*

The whole building got to burning, there was my baby laying on the ground.

• Monuments to the Rhythm Club Dead and to Richard Wright

Although there is no marker at the site of the tragedy, there is a monument to the Rhythm Club dead at the riverfront, Broadway and State Street. Donated by the Natchez Social and Civic Club of Chicago, the monument lists the names of those who lost their lives in the fire.

About a hundred feet north of that monument is a historical marker for novelist Richard Wright, who was born in Natchez in 1908. Wright wrote the introduction to *Blues Fell This Morning: Meaning in the Blues*, the 1960 book by British writer Paul Oliver.

Biscuits and Blues
315 Main St.
(601) 446-9922

This restaurant-nightclub has blues acts most Sunday nights. It is part of a small chain that also has restaurants in San Francisco, California, and St. Paul, Minnesota.

chapter 9

EAST MISSISSIPPI

Although it is on the opposite side of the state, the area between Meridian and Tupelo resembles the Delta in some places, with soybeans and sometimes cotton growing on flat prairies. A handful of great musicians come from this region. And the residents of this area seem to recognize their musicians as heroes, with monuments and other tributes. (Refer to map in Chapter 1.)

Columbus-based WMUW, 88.5 FM, broadcasts the blues from noon to 3 P.M. on Sundays.

Meridian

This rough, funky old town has railroad tracks everywhere and a cool-looking (but not lively) art deco downtown. Although it is the third-largest city in Mississippi, Meridian has never had much of a blues scene. It is, however, the hometown of a major figure in American music—Jimmie Rodgers, the Singing Brakeman, the Blue Yodeler, the Father of Country Music. (This is not the same person as Jimmy Rogers, the Delta-born blues guitarist who worked with Muddy Waters in Chicago.)

Meridian also was home base of blues researcher/writer Gayle

Dean Wardlow while he was working on the books *King of the Delta Blues* and *Chasin' that Devil Music* and his many articles. Wardlow has moved to Mississippi's Gulf Coast.

- **Jimmie Rodgers Museum**
  1725 Jimmie Rodgers Dr.
  (601) 485-1808

  To get there: Enter Highland Park at 39th Avenue and 16th Street and follow the signs around to the museum. Look for the full-size train outside the building.

Like Elvis Presley, Jimmie Rodgers is one of the few white singers regularly identified as a blues singer by black blues singers and blues fans. And this for a man who is also credited as being the father of country music! If there is any doubt, Rodgers's music proves that, from the beginning, country-western itself was based strongly on the blues.

Rodgers, who recorded in the late 1920s and early 1930s, was a contemporary of the first generation of recorded bluesmen. He certainly met and heard blues singers in his work and travels on the railroad. Rodgers used stock blues verses and chord progressions in his songs, many of which have "blue" or "blues" in their titles. Even his trademark yodel may have been influenced by African American field hollers.

In his autobiography, B. B. King lists as one of his early influences Rodgers, "a yodeler who happened to be white, but who sang songs like 'Blues, How Do You Do?' They called him the Singing Brakeman and I sang along with him." Howlin' Wolf admired Rodgers, and may have based his wolf howl on Rodgers's yodel. Leadbelly liked to sing Rodgers songs, including the yodels. Even Robert Johnson would play a Jimmie Rodgers tune when requested, according to his pal and fellow bluesman Johnny Shines, who did the same.

The Rodgers museum is supposed to move soon into the complex of buildings around the refurbished Union Station downtown. Besides being more centrally located, that site will be appropriate for a museum dedicated to a man who worked on the railroads for years. In the meantime, it is in a replica of a depot building in a city park, with an old train next to it.

The museum contains Rodgers's awards (including a Handy Award and places in the Rock 'n' Roll Hall of Fame and the Nashville Songwriters Hall of Fame), letters, and records. Also on display are musical instruments, including the Martin guitar with his name inlaid in the fretboard and "Thanks" on the back, which Rogers holds in his best-known "thumbs-up" photo; a denim jacket worn by Rodgers and a dress worn by Mrs. Rodgers; handwritten sheet music by Elsie McWilliams, Rodgers's sister-in-law and cowriter; and a 1920 windup Victrola that record company executive Ralph Peer gave McWilliams.

● **Jimmie Rodgers's Grave**
Oak Grove Cemetery

To get there: From Interstate 20, take exit 154A (Butler-South). Turn left at the first light, then right at the first road, behind the McDonald's. You will be on Azalea Drive. Turn left on Oak Grove Drive. The cemetery is on the right, just past Oak Grove Baptist Church. From the cemetery entrance road, Rodgers's grave is to the left, two rows from the road.

Several members of the extended Rodgers family are buried in the same broad gravel-filled plot. A large stone is inscribed simply "Rodgers" on one side, with "Carrie" and "Jimmie" on the other. Rodgers and his second wife, Carrie, also have small individual markers. His reads:

"JIMMIE"
James Charles Rodgers
Sept. 8, 1897
May 26. 1933
America's blue yodeler

The one next to him reads:

Carrie Cecil Williamson
Wife of
Jimmie Rodgers
Aug. 8, 1902
Nov. 28, 1967
First lady of country music

Their daughters, Carrie Anita Rodgers Court and June Rebecca, also are buried here. So are Elsie W. McWilliams and her husband, Edwin R. "Dick" McWilliams.

- **Peavey Visitors Center**
  Montgomery Industrial Park, Marion-Russell Road off Highway 45 bypass
  (601) 483-5365

  To get there: From the exit, turn right and go 1 mile to the visitors' center.

The center is open 10 A.M.–4 P.M. weekdays, 1–4 P.M. weekends. Admission is free.

This company was started in 1965 by Hartley Peavey, a Meridian youth who liked to tinker with old radio and TV parts in his parents' basement. It grew phenomenally, and now employs two thousand people in two dozen buildings around Meridian and a few more elsewhere.

Aaron Neville and Steve Cropper are the only blues-related artists (among the rock and country-western players) showcased as Peavey instrument users in the visitors' center. But many lesser-known blues players use equipment, especially amps and PA systems, made by Peavey, which is the world's largest amp manufacturer.

The visitors' center is a museum that tells the company's story with replicas of the workbenches Peavey himself used over the years, equipment he or the company built, and artifacts and photos from various events, including President George Bush's visit to Peavey in 1990.

Thanks to an employee who is a blues fan, there is a small exhibit of 78s by Muddy Waters, Howlin' Wolf, Fats Domino, T-Bone Walker, and John Lee Hooker, along with B. B. King posters.

The fun part is the music room, where visitors of any age or musical inclination may wail away on microphones, drums, guitar, bass, or keyboards, amplified as loud as you please. In case you don't want to accompany yourself, there's even a karaoke machine.

Crawford

- **Welcome Sign**

  Big Joe Williams's hometown honors him as a "blues legend" on its welcome signs on Highway 45A, although he shares the sign with two other Crawford natives—NFL star Jerry Rice and NBA star Clarence Weatherspoon.

Jook joint, Crawford

- **Big Joe Williams's Grave**

  To get there: From Highway 45 Alt heading south into Crawford, go under the underpass and take the first right onto Main Street. Stay on that street for 4.4 miles, going past a group of brick buildings, including the Silver Fox Lounge. Farther up, on the left, you will pass city hall. Continue through town to Bethesda Road, where the Bethesda Baptist Church sign is. Turn left onto Bethesda, a gravel road. Continue straight, past the church, and bear to the right at the fork. Keep driving through the pastures and past a few houses. The grave is 1.6 miles from the turn onto Bethesda, on the right, across from house number 3162. It is near the road, in a pasture that does not look like a cemetery (although there are a few more graves farther back from the road), behind a barbed-wire fence.

The marker reads:

Joe Lee "Big Joe" Williams
1903–1982
"King of the Nine-String Guitar"
Big Joe sustained the longest recording career of any Mississippi
bluesman, spanning seven decades (1929–1982). He was a true
American Original.

Big Joe probably deserves the award for longest *continuous* blues career. Other blues artists of the 1920s and 1930s were "rediscovered" and began performing and recording again in the 1960s. But there was no need to rediscover Williams. He began playing and rambling at about age twelve and just kept on playing, touring, and recording until he died in 1982. He was part of the prewar blues era, the postwar era, the blues revival, and all the slack periods around those. (Despite what it says on his tombstone, however, experts believe that Williams's recording career began in 1935—even though he said that he had played on some earlier recordings.)

Williams was a thirty-four-year-old, seasoned musician on May 5, 1937, when he teamed up with Sonny Boy Williamson I and Robert Nighthawk for the session that launched the recording careers of Williamson and Nighthawk. Such Williams records as "Baby Please Don't Go" and "49 Highway Blues" directly influenced Muddy Waters and Howlin' Wolf. In the 1960s, living in the basement of a Chicago record store, Williams became a mentor to young white bluesmen including Charlie Musselwhite and Mike Bloomfield.

Another remarkable aspect of Williams's career is his invention and use of the nine-string guitar, which he made by installing three extra tuning pegs across the top of the headstock of a six-string and doubling three strings.

In his last years, Williams returned to Crawford and lived in a trailer, although he continued to tour or record when someone made him an offer. He died in a hospital in nearby Macon, Mississippi.

West Point

This town claims Howlin' Wolf as a native son, although he actually was born a ways out in the country, in a community called White Station or simply Whites. It is unusual and commendable, however, for a Mississippi town to make a big deal about its blues heritage, so let's not quibble here.

Wolf lived near West Point as a child, but left in his teens and moved to the Delta. If he was looking for blues teachers, he went to the right place: he learned guitar from Charley Patton and harmonica from Sonny Boy Williamson II. Although he sang and played all of his life, Wolf would not make his name or his living as an artist until he was over forty, in 1951, when he walked into

Sam Phillips's recording studio in Memphis.

But even in the 1960s, when he was an established blues star living in Chicago, Howlin' Wolf would come back to the West Point area twice a year or so to hunt, a hobby that some say was more important to him than music.

Howlin' Wolf statue, downtown West Point

- **Howlin' Wolf Statue**

To get there: Coming into town from the north on Highway 45 Alt, follow the signs into downtown, turning east on West Main (Highway 50). Just past the downtown area, turn right toward the park. Look for the windmill. The statue is next to it.

Wolf's likeness stands in a park near the center of town. Made of black granite, it's a flat statue, like a cutout cookie, with the details etched in. It reads:

A memorial to the blues legend
HOWLIN' WOLF
Chester A. Burnett
June 10, 1910–January 10, 1976
Native of White Station, Clay County, MS
Rock and Roll Hall of Fame, Blues Hall of Fame, West Point, Miss.,
Hall of Fame
Given by Howlin' Wolf Blues Society of West Point MS Inc.
August 29, 1997

Erected during the 1997 Howlin' Wolf Blues Festival, the statue is based on a photo by Memphis photographer Ernest Withers, which was donated by Wolf's widow, Lillian.

- ## Howlin' Wolf Memorial Blues Festival

The town's active blues society also presents this annual one-day, single-stage festival on the Friday of Labor Day weekend, the day before the town's Prairie Arts Festival. It is held indoors at the Civic, Sixth Street near Main.

Its out-of-the-way location has kept this festival from developing into the big draw that Delta festivals have become. West Point residents don't seem to care, and turn out to have a great time at their festival. Each year's headliner must have a connection to Howlin' Wolf. (More information is available at 662-494-2921.)

- ## Anthony's
116 Main St.
(662) 494-0316

This big restaurant is decorated faux-jook-joint style. It features blues on the first Saturday night of each month.

- ## Cottrell Street

Across the tracks from downtown, Cottrell Street is West Point's traditional black business street. **Bill's**, 318 Cottrell, is a little club where Wolf allegedly used to play when he returned to visit in the 1960s and 1970s. It no longer features live music. Across the street from 446 Cottrell is a onetime club that the city has purchased. The building is available for lease so that the blues society can turn it into a Howlin' Wolf museum, as soon as the society raises the money to restore and operate it.

- ## Mural

On the side of Lyon Insurance Agency, 325 Commerce St. (at Westbrook St.), a mural depicts the history of West Point. Painted by visiting Italian artist Joe Vitrano and local artist Terry Craig during the 1998 festival, it includes an image of Howlin' Wolf playing guitar.

- ## Betty Jean's

Alabama bluesman Willie King, an award-winning recording artist, has been playing Sunday nights at this jook joint outside

Prairie Point, Mississippi. To get there from West Point (about an hour's drive), take Highway 45 ALT south and about 8 miles south of Brooksville (and just before Macon), turn east onto Prairie Point Road. Go another 10 miles to Sandyland Road, then turn left and go 3 miles to an unmarked dirt road by a church. Turn right and proceed a little way to the club.

Whites (White Station)

To get there: From downtown West Point, go east on East Main, then left on Eshman Avenue. Go about three miles, then right on Hazelwood Road, then half a mile to White Station Road. Turn left and into the community.

This community, where Wolf actually grew up, is a few miles outside West Point. There isn't really anything to see, but some houses date from the days when Wolf—"Bigfoot Chester"—was a child. The house he lived in with his family is long gone; it stood on the now-wooded lot just before the store and barbecue pit. Many years later, Wolf still came back to White Station annually to visit relatives and friends and to hunt and fish.

"He used to sit and play on the porch while I was cooking biscuits," said Miss Annie Eggerson, the widow of Wolf's first cousin. "He sure could eat some chicken."

Aberdeen

Bluesman Booker T. Washington "Bukka" White was born in Houston, Mississippi, and grew up in the Delta. But he also lived for a while in Aberdeen, just thirty miles from his hometown. He apparently got involved there in the shooting that landed him in Parchman for almost three years. Upon his release, White went to Chicago and recorded twelve songs, including "Aberdeen Mississippi Blues," which contains this verse:

> *Aberdeen's my home but the mens don't want me around*
> *They know I'll take these women, take them out of town*

White settled in Memphis after the recording session. But he still had a relative working in the Aberdeen post office in 1963, when a letter arrived there addressed to "Bukka White, Old Blues Singer, c/o General Delivery, Aberdeen, Miss." The letter was from

California blues fans John Fahey and Ed Denson, who took the song as a clue to White's whereabouts. The relative forwarded the letter to White, who responded to Fahey and Denson, leading to White's "rediscovery" and a new performing and recording career that lasted until his death in 1977.

Tupelo

All right, so Elvis Presley was not a bluesman. He was blues-drenched, however, not only in his choice of material (Big Mama Thornton's "Hound Dog," Arthur Crudup's "That's All Right," and Junior Parker's "Mystery Train," for example) but in his style of singing, acting, and dressing (before Elvis started shopping there, Lansky's in Memphis catered almost strictly to hip-dressed blacks). His music and style, in turn, immensely affected dozens of other performers and millions of regular folks, helping bring the blues lifestyle out into mainstream America.

Also, Elvis Presley—or Jimmie Rodgers, depending on the person's age—is often the only white singer mentioned by black blues singers as one of the blues singers they admire. Yes, real blues singers often consider the King of Rock 'n' Roll and the Father of Country Music *blues* singers. It is interesting that both Presley and Rodgers were from Mississippi.

- **Elvis Presley's Birthplace**
  306 Elvis Presley Dr.
  (662) 841-1245

At a total cost of $180, Vernon Presley built a two-room shot-gun shack next to his parents' house to prepare for the birth of his only child. Vernon and Gladys Presley moved into it in December 1934, and Elvis was born January 8, 1935. The bank that had lent Vernon the $180 soon repossessed the house. The Presleys lived in several other houses in Tupelo until 1948, when the family moved to Memphis. Most of their other Tupelo residences were near the birthplace; it is a neighborhood where you still see people sitting on the front porches of simple wooden houses.

The birthplace house is furnished in period goods that are *not* originals from when the Presleys lived there, such as a washboard

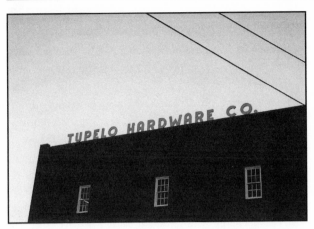

Tupelo Hardware Company, the store where Elvis Presley bought his first guitar, Tupelo

and tub, pots, and framed pictures. The roof and ceiling have been replaced. The fireplace is original. It costs a dollar to enter the house and takes about a minute to see it.

On the birthplace grounds there is a small museum/gift shop, with an additional admission fee.

One building on the grounds that can be entered free of charge is the Elvis Presley Memorial Chapel, built in 1979 from fans' donations. It includes a pulpit from the First Assembly of God Church, which the Presleys attended in Elvis's early childhood, and a Bible that belonged to Elvis.

- **Tupelo Fairgrounds**
  To get there: The fairgrounds are just off East Main Street, near Highway 45.

At age ten, Elvis gave what was probably his first performance in front of an audience. He sang (unaccompanied and into a microphone) "Old Shep" to several hundred people at the annual Mississippi-Alabama Fair and Dairy Show at the Tupelo fairgrounds. It was a contest sponsored by a radio station on Children's Day at the fair, October 3, 1945. Elvis did not win.

- **Tupelo Hardware Company**
  114 W. Main St.
  (662) 842-4637

Charming inside and out, Tupelo Hardware Company is where Elvis Presley bought his first guitar. An old-fashioned, three-story hardware store right on Main Street, it still carries cast-iron cookware, knives, and other such non-hardware items. It no longer stocks guitars or guns, but it did in January 1946 when Elvis and his mother came in to buy one or the other. Fortunately, they decided on the guitar.

Forrest L. Bobo, the clerk who sold them the guitar for $7.75, wrote a letter about the transaction in 1979. The letter is on display along with an old guitar case and a few Elvis-related books. You can buy a yardstick with the name of the store and the words "Where Elvis bought his first guitar," a plastic guitar keychain with the same legend, or a T-shirt. Other than that, it's just a regular and very complete hardware store, with high wood shelves, a tin ceiling and other features that haven't changed since that fateful day. It's open 7 A.M. to 5:30 P.M. weekdays and 7 A.M. to noon Saturdays.

- **McDonald's**
  372 S. Gloster St. (just south of Main St.)
  (662) 844-5505

Fit for a king, this restaurant looks from the outside like an ordinary McDonald's but is full of Elvisiana. There are etchings of Elvis in the glass wall behind the ordering area and a case full of record albums, books, mugs, and knickknacks. The walls are covered with framed photos, articles, quotations, and other interesting writings.

North Mississippi Hills

1. Chulahoma, Junior Kimbrough's Jook Joint
2. Chewalla Rib Shack
3. Othar Turner's place
4. Fred McDowell's grave
5. Gus Cannon's grave
6. Joe Callicott's grave

Memphis

Nesbit
Hernando

Holly Springs

Senatobia

Como
Sardis

Oxford

Lambert

Clarksdale

Water Valley

chapter 10

NORTH MISSISSIPPI HILL COUNTRY

The great folklorist Alan Lomax described what he heard in North Mississippi in the 1940s and 1950s as "an early phase of African-American music—not only that, but a clear revival of African tradition, kept alive in the Mississippi backwoods . . . we have found instruments, musical styles, and dancing that link the black South to the black Caribbean and, no question of it, to the dance of Africa as well."

In the hills, Lomax found such oddities as panpipes (also known as quills), fife-and-drum bands that used handmade cane fifes, and wall-mounted one-string guitars made from broom wire and played with a slide. He also found a hypnotic, grooving type of blues epitomized by Mississippi Fred McDowell.

Fifty years later, the North Mississippi hill sound, as played by R. L. Burnside, the late Junior Kimbrough, and their children and grandchildren, is alive and well and world-renowned. The late music journalist Robert Palmer referred to this sound as "North Mississippi slash-and-drone trance-blues." Veteran jook joint musicians Kimbrough and Burnside, both of whom learned from McDowell in their youth, enjoyed international popularity in the wake of the 1990 documentary *Deep Blues* and their successful (in blues terms, anyway) recordings on the Fat Possum label based in Oxford, Mississippi.

Oxford

Although it is close to both the Delta and the hill country, Oxford does not have much of a local blues heritage—R. L. Burnside, born in nearby College Hill (but long since moved to Holly Springs), is the only recorded bluesman native to the area. But the presence of the University of Mississippi makes Oxford more inclined toward the study and commercialization of the blues than other Mississippi communities.

WMAV, 90.3 FM, hosts a blues program from 10 P.M. to midnight Saturdays that is also broadcast by other NPR affiliates throughout the state.

- **University of Mississippi**
  (662) 915-7211

Known locally as "Ole Miss," this campus is where thousands of armed whites fought to try to keep out the first black student, James Meredith, in 1962. The mob killed two journalists and wounded dozens of U.S. marshals. President John F. Kennedy sent in federal troops to secure Meredith's education and maintain the peace. Nina Simone and Bob Dylan both wrote protest songs about the incident. Bluesman J. B. Lenoir made a 1966 recording, "Shot on James Meredith," about the later, nonfatal, shooting of Meredith in a protest march away from the campus. One of the few politically outspoken blues singers, Lenoir also had written and recorded the 1965 "Down in Mississippi" (later covered by Pops Staples).

Meredith himself is a blues fan who fondly describes a Jackson jook joint performance by "Elmo"—Elmore James—in his memoir, *Three Years in Mississippi.* And Meredith opened a 1998 lecture at the university by dancing to James recordings. He explained that he had listened to the blues for hours every day during his struggle to enter the university, and that the music gave him the strength to continue.

B. B. King, who also donated his records to the university's Blues Archive, recorded a 1980 album here, *Live "Now Appearing" at Ole Miss.*

The University of Mississippi has an indirect connection to the blues dating from 1885, when Will Dockery graduated from it. Ten years later, Dockery would found the Delta plantation where Charley Patton developed his music.

The university radio station, WUMS, 92.1 FM (662-915-5395), sometimes hosts blues programs, most often on Sundays.

- **The University of Mississippi Blues Archive**
  In Department of Archives and Special Collections, third floor of
  J. D. Williams Library
  (662) 915-7753

The room is open from 8 A.M. to 5 P.M. Mondays through Fridays.

At first glance, the Blues Archive looks disappointingly dull. One small display case, an array of posters, and a small rack of records are the only obvious things to look at. But its main functions are preservation and research. The joys of this room go not to the casual looker but to the person who, having obtained the staff's help in gathering items, takes at least a few hours to sit and listen to recordings, read books and magazines, watch videos, or flip through photographs.

Since most of the collection is locked up and the catalog is incomplete, one should ask for staff help immediately upon entering. Nearly any blues-related item you might want is here—if they can find it! Patience and perseverance will pay off.

Among the archive's thirty-three thousand recordings is a complete set of Document reissues—which means that every prewar blues recording is available. The postwar holdings are not so complete. B. B. King donated his collection of seven thousand records in 1982. That list itself is interesting to browse through for clues about influences on him. The video holdings include documentaries like *Deep Blues* and *The Land Where the Blues Began*, as well as privately made tapes of Mississippi artists and some curiosities like Othar Turner and Jessie Mae Hemphill's appearance on *Mister Rogers' Neighborhood*.

- **Living Blues Offices**
  Third floor, Hill Hall, University of Mississippi
  (662) 232-5742

As its name implies, *Living Blues* looks not just at old blues records but also at the living practitioners of the form. Another of its policies, which has sparked some controversy, is to write features only about African American artists (although it reviews records by blues-related artists of any color). A third important part of its philosophy is that an artist's musical quality is what matters, not how many records he or she sells.

Those policies distinguish *Living Blues* from other blues magazines and make it important to serious fans, scholars, and artists. Its consistently good writing, photography, and editing also help that image.

Jim O'Neal and Amy van Singel started the magazine in Chicago in 1970. They moved part of its operations to Oxford in 1983 and had sold it entirely by 1986. It is now part of the university's Center for the Study of Southern Culture.

The magazine's small staff works in a worn-out old building in an out-of-the-way corner of the campus. There isn't much to see there, but no one minds if you stop by for a quick visit. Subscriptions, T-shirts, and some back issues are available for purchase. If you want to read old issues, visit the Blues Archive.

- **University Museums**
  University Avenue at Fifth Street
  (662) 232-7673

The museum is open 10 A.M.–4:30 P.M. Tuesdays through Saturdays and 1–4 P.M. Sundays. Admission is free. Its folk art room, past the main exhibit area, contains four clay sculptures of animals by James "Son" Thomas of Leland, a bluesman who was also highly regarded as a folk artist. William Ferris, author of *Blues from the Delta*, donated the sculptures while he was professor of southern studies and anthropology at the university.

- **Nightclubs**

Half of Oxford's twenty thousand residents are college students, so there are several nightclubs that cater to them. **The Long Shot** (1107 Jackson Ave., 662-236-7063), **Proud Larry's** (211 S. Lamar Blvd., 662-236-0050), and the **Gin** (Harrison St. [no street number], 662-234-0024), all close to the town square, mix blues acts into their schedules. Check the weekly *Oxford Town* for listings of who is playing where.

Water Valley

- ## Fat Possum Records
  904 N. Main St.
  (662) 473-9994

Fat Possum, the self-proclaimed bad boys of the blues business, have moved from their original digs at 603 S. 16th St., Oxford, to this suburban location. Owners Bruce Watson and
Matthew Johnson try to maintain their company's image by being
hostile to the public and the press. But they have been known to
be nice to visitors who show up at the door, sometimes even selling them merchandise. (A better place to shop for Fat Possum
merchandise is at **Off Square Books**, 1110 Van Buren, Oxford.)

Founded in the 1990s, Fat Possum found its niche in selling
Mississippi blues to suburban white youths nationally. To accom-
plish that, it often plays up its artists' jail records, gun enthusiasm
and non-conformity and tries to cast blues as a variety of punk
music. Sometimes it even pairs bluesmen with punkers, as on *A
Ass Pocket of Whiskey*, on which R. L. Burnside plays with the Jon
Spencer Blues Explosion. But despite such commercialism, and its
branching out into other genres, Fat Possum has released a lot of
fine blues albums. Among those are the works of Burnside, Junior
Kimbrough, Cedell Davis, Paul "Wine" Jones, and T-Model Ford,
the award-winning comeback CD by Solomon Burke, and reissues
of earlier artists such as Fred McDowell and Robert Pete Williams.

The Water Valley Casey Jones Railroad Museum
South Main St.
(662) 473-3828

To get there: From the intersection of highways 6 and 7 in Oxford, take Highway 7 south. Continue on it for 17.2 miles, making sure to stay on 7 when
the road forks. When you see the sign for Water Valley, follow it and drive
1.7 miles from the highway to Main Street. Turn right (south) onto Main
Street and go 0.8 mile to the museum, a gray building with a red caboose
behind it.

Open from 2 to 4 P.M. Thursdays through Saturdays (admission is free; donations are accepted), the museum is in the original
Water Valley Depot, which was Casey Jones's base of operations
from 1888 to 1900, when he died in a crash near Vaughan, Missis-

sippi (where there is also a Casey Jones museum). Fatal railroad accidents were common in those days, but this one has become famous because of the song written about it by Wallace "Wash" Saunders, a black engine wiper and friend of Jones's. The song became a vaudeville number and a huge sheet-music hit. Several blues artists, including Furry Lewis and Mississippi John Hurt, have recorded versions of it.

This small, well-tended museum has plenty of photos and artifacts relating to railroad history, and a whistle that might have belonged to Jones. The curators, brothers J. K. and Bruce Gurner and J.K.'s son Jack, know a lot about the Jones incident and are happy to talk about it with visitors.

Abbeville

- **Shaw's Disco 9000**
  Highway 310
  (662) 551-1758

  To get there: From the intersection of highways 7 and 310, turn west on 310 and go about 50 yards, to the second turn-off on the right.

This jook features live blues or R&B on Sundays, continuing the tradition of the burned-down, beloved Junior Kimbrough's in nearby Chulahoma.

Holly Springs

For a town of only seven thousand, Holly Springs is an interesting place. A great jook joint used to be nearby (it recently burned down; there are hopes that it will reopen), and the town has a weird record store and a bizarre Elvis museum. It also boasts two radio stations that sometimes play blues: WKRA, 92.7 FM, "Key 93," a commercial station that slips blues into its regular programming and has a blues show on Saturday mornings, and Rust College's noncommercial WURC, 88.1 FM.

- **Aikei Pro's Records Shop**
  125 N. Center St.
  (no phone)

Aikei Pro's is just a block and a half off the town square, yet it is invisible and unknown even to many downtown Holly Springs merchants. So don't bother asking anyone how to get there. Just walk or drive north from the Holly Springs town square, on Center Street. Keep going until you see the store on the right. It has a big wooden sign and a tin roof, and people are hanging out in front. There is also a row of old bicycles for sale.

The owner, Aikei Pro (born David Caldwell, he renamed himself a Japanicized "Walker Bros.," he explains, as if that clears things up), might be hanging out in front of the store. Or he might be inside. If you arrive during

You can buy almost anything at Aikei Pro's Records Shop, Holly Springs

regular business hours and find the doors locked, knock loudly. Or ask one of the people out front to help you find or rouse Aikei Pro.

When you enter, you'll think you're in a storage room or a workshop; disassembled car radios and stereo components lie in stacks all over the floor. But no, this awesomely cluttered space is the main room of a unique retail establishment. Records are everywhere—in piles, on racks, in piles on racks, under radios, behind radios. There are well-worn used records, old records still in their wrappers, empty record sleeves, sleeves with two or three records inside, 45s, cassettes, eight-tracks. There even are a few CDs, although Aikei Pro explains that he hasn't yet bought into the CD craze. "CDs can get old and scratched, and then you can't play them anymore," he explains. "A record, no matter how old it is, you can clean it up and it plays good as new."

Aikei Pro was a good friend of the late Junior Kimbrough, who often would hang out at the record store. Aikei Pro also is a serious fan of the music of Kimbrough and other North Mississippi blues artists. He collects books and articles about the area's blues tradition, and somehow finds them in the store, immediately, when he wants to show them to someone. Like most record store owners, Aikei Pro will talk about music for hours.

And talking with him is easier than shopping in his store. To really look through the records, you have to climb over or around the heaps of radios, move piles of records to get to other piles, carefully pick through precarious stacks. It is rather like archaeological digging, and the payoffs can be equally exciting. There are blues and gospel records, including ones by local performers. But you also might find Chet Atkins, El Chicano, or the Fat Boys amidst Leadbelly, Eddie Shaw, or Ray Charles. Of course, the records are not in alphabetical order. They are just piled all over the place. Prices are not marked.

Besides records, you also might find the pair of cowboy boots or roller skates you've been seeking, a peacock clock, a set of guitar strings, or an old issue of *Living Blues*. Don't forget to check out the bicycles outside. And if your car radio needs repair or replacement, this is the place.

- **Club 93**
  Highway 7 North (a block north of the square, on the west side of the street)

This big nightclub regularly presents shows by touring soul-blues acts like Marvin Sease, Bobby Rush, Barbara Carr, and Denise LaSalle. On other nights, a deejay spins tunes.

- **Graceland Too**
  200 E. Gholson Ave. at Randolph St.

Located in a residential area near the town square, this museum is in an old two-story white wooden house with a white cinder-block fence and stone lions in front. "Yes We're Open," the sign says. And it's true. They are open twenty-four hours a day, seven days a week (keep knocking if you get no answer, or come back in ten minutes and try again).

Owner Paul McLeod, with his slicked-back hair, sideburns, and paunch, doesn't really look like Elvis, but he somehow reminds you of him. His son, Elvis Aron Presley McLeod, comes even closer. These two men devote themselves to Elvis full time.

Besides giving tours, they scan newspapers and monitor TV broadcasts just in case there is any reference to Elvis. If there is, they file it.

The house is full of records, books, clothing, photos, and artifacts with *some* connection, often tangential, to Elvis. The amazing part is not the collection but the level of human obsession. You may come to laugh but leave with a tear in your eye, touched by Paul McLeod's tremendous passion for his subject. Admission, which includes a tour, comes with a money-back guarantee. On your third visit, McLeod takes your picture in an Elvis-type jacket. The photo goes on the wall, and you become a lifetime member with free admission privileges.

- **Rust College**
  150 Rust Ave.
  (662) 252-8000

Established in 1866, this is the state's oldest historically black college and one of the five oldest in the nation. The Rust College Quartet made some fine religious "race" recordings in the 1920s, and the college still has a top-notch student gospel choir. The Northeast Mississippi Blues and Gospel Music Folk Festival, organized by Sylvester Oliver, an ethnomusicologist and Rust professor, was a favorite festival of many blues cognoscenti in the 1980s through the mid-1990s (unfortunately, it has not been held lately, but there is some talk of resuming it). The school's radio station, WURC, 88.1 FM (662-252-5881), includes gospel, jazz, and occasionally blues in its programming.

- **Chewalla Rib Shack (the original Junior Kimbrough's jook joint)**
  East of Holly Springs

  To get there: From the Holly Springs town square, drive east on Van Dorn. At the next traffic light, turn left onto Randolph. Proceed north to the first blinking traffic light, and turn right onto Salem Road, which is Highway 4. Continue on that out of town. After 1.3 miles the road splits. Bear to the right, following the sign for Chewalla Lake. You will be on Higdon Road. About 3 miles from the split, on the right, you will come to 2644 Higdon Road, a big, modern log house. Chewalla Rib Shack is the small, red-stained, very old log cabin just past it. There is no sign.

Chewalla Rib Shack is the original Junior Kimbrough's jook joint. Don't go there hungry—the kitchen has been closed for years, along with the rest of the building. Its value is historic. For a few years in the early nineties, this one-room shack was the home of the blues.

The Chewalla Rib Shack's history began much earlier, however—in about the 1820s, when someone picked up an ax and hewed rough logs from cypress, then fitted them together, Lincoln Logs-style, to build a six-room house near Byhalia.

About 160 years later, Sammy Greer, a counselor and football coach at Holly Springs High School, was on a fishing trip when he came across the remains of that house in the woods. With the property owner's permission, Greer began dismantling the house and hauling it off to his place near Holly Springs. "Every time I knocked off a log, a snake was sitting there," he says. "I killed thirty-six snakes while I was taking it apart. They ran me off one day."

But he persevered and salvaged enough of the logs to reconstruct a smaller version of the house. The corners of the logs still fit together snugly. Greer lived in the log cabin for a few years in the 1980s before turning it into a grocery store. Then he met bluesman Junior Kimbrough, who had been hosting all-day-and-all-night drinking-and-dancing sessions Sundays at his own home. Kimbrough wanted to move the sessions somewhere. Greer wanted to cook and sell barbecue. The two men teamed up to create the Chewalla Rib Shack, Kimbrough's first actual jook joint. The place opened in June 1990. But first, Kimbrough advised Greer on interior design. "I had it decorated with antiques, real nice," Greer says. "Junior, he said to clear it. 'That ain't gonna work with the type of people we're going to be getting in here.'"

The place was successful immediately. "They'd be jam-packed like sardines in a can," Greer says. People would arrive early in the day, driving in from miles away, and drink and socialize on the grounds until the musicians arrived. Since the shack was so small, many people would remain outside all evening, digging on the music. Those who had too much to drink were welcome to lie down and sleep it off on the grounds, or in one of the two tiny "cathouses" in the back and to the left. Kimbrough himself lived for a while in the cathouse on the right. "The law was not going to bother you. I was the police here," Greer explains. "We never had any problems. We'd go all night, selling beer and food and bootleg whiskey."

In the 1991 documentary *Deep Blues*, Jessie Mae Hemphill

performs two solo numbers at Chewalla Rib Shack. Junior Kimbrough, who hadn't yet made an album, also plays there in the film. "If you want to hear him, you have to go jookin'," Robert Palmer, the narrator, advises.

After a few years, Greer became tired of the jook joint business. Kimbrough moved his jook to a bigger location in Chulahoma, where his son Kinney carries on the tradition today.

The Chewalla Rib Shack remains standing, as it probably would even if a tornado hit. A tragedy befell the antique cypress structure a few years ago, however. Greer had been renting it out, and one day he came home to a smiling tenant and a red-stained shack. "He said, 'Look—I stained the logs for you. Doesn't it look nice?'" Greer recalls. "I fell down on my knees and said, 'Oh, my God! You ruined my shack!' I ran him out the same day." Greer has since spent hundreds of dollars and hours bleaching and sandblasting, but a red stain remains on Marshall County's original house of blues.

The house is on private property and is guarded by a dog, so look at it from the street, unless you have permission to get closer. There are tentative plans to reopen it as a take-out restaurant.

Chulahoma

- ## Junior Kimbrough's Jook Joint

  To get there: From the intersection of highways 78 and 7 on the south edge of Holly Springs, drive south on 7, 1½ miles, to Highway 4, then west on 4 for 10 miles. Junior's was just past Muse Road, on the north side of the road.

Until a fire destroyed it on April 6, 2000, Junior's was perhaps the wildest blues spot in the world. A 130-year-old building, it had served as a horse stable, a general store, a cocktail lounge, and perhaps as a church at various times before David "Junior" Kimbrough took it over and turned it into a jook joint in the early 1990s (he relocated here from the Chewalla Rib Shack east of Holly Springs).

Every Sunday night during those years, people danced to Kimbrough's "cotton patch blues"—a hypnotic, groove-based style. "My songs, they have just the one chord, there's none of that fancy stuff you hear now, with lots of chords in one song," Kimbrough once told an interviewer. "If I find another chord I leave it for another song."

After Kimbrough died on January 17, 1998, at age sixty-seven, his music and his jook joint lived on. Two of his sons—drummer/jook joint manager Kinney and singer-guitarist David (who recorded a 1994 album, *I Got the Dog in Me*, as David Malone)—kept it going strong, with help from relatives, neighbors, and visitors. Among those neighbors was R. L. Burnside,who often played here.

An arson-caused fire destroyed the building, which was uninsured, along with the musical instruments, sound system, and many priceless mementos, including the late Johnny Hughes's paintings on the wood rafters. The fire also closed the business. But the Kimbrough family and friends were raising funds and making plans to rebuild it on the same site or nearby and to reopen at a temporary spot in the meantime. (Information is available at 662-564-1000.)

Hudsonville

• Junior Kimbrough's Grave

To get there: From Holly Springs, drive 10 miles north on Highway 7. One mile past Bolden's Grocery, turn left on Clear Creek Road. Go 1 mile, then left on Kimbrough Church Road for 1/3 mile. You will see a small graveyard on the left. Pull in on the dirt road and park. Walk straight in, away from Kimbrough Church Road and about 20 yards to the left.

Junior Kimbrough, the patriarch of Holly Springs blues, is buried in a small country cemetery, with his brother Felix and Felix's wife, Irene, lying next to him. The front of Kimbrough's headstone reads:

MEET ME IN THE CITY
In Memory of legendary
Bluesman
David "Junior" Kimbrough
July 28, 1930
Jan. 17, 1998

The back reads:

"Junior Kimbrough is
The beginning and
end of all music."

"Meet Me in the City" is the title of one of Kimbrough's songs. The quotation on the back is by Charlie Feathers, a white rocka-

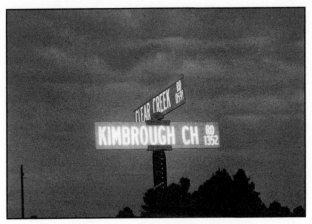

Street sign near Junior Kimbrough's grave, Hudsonville

billy artist who grew up in this area and admitted being greatly influenced by Kimbrough. The headstone was erected in February 1999, about a year after Kimbrough's death, with funds raised from his fans in Oxford. Visitors often leave bottles of beer in tribute.

Como

- ## Fred McDowell's Grave

  To get there: From Interstate 55 take exit 257, the Como exit, and proceed west on Highway 310, through Como, for 4.5 miles, to Hammond Hill Road. Go north three miles to the intersection of Hammond Hill and Tate-Panola Road. Hammond Hill M. B. Church is on the northeast corner; the church cemetery is on the northwest corner. Park in the church parking lot and walk across the street to the cemetery. Walk over the knoll and into the small, crowded cemetery, which is surrounded by fields. McDowell's grave is in the middle of a row toward the back.

About three feet tall, the stone has a photo of the blues singer and the inscription:

"MISSISSIPPI FRED"
McDowell
Jan. 12, 1904–July 3, 1972

Below the date is the Masonic symbol, reflecting McDowell's proud status as a high-level member of that organization. Under that is another inscription:

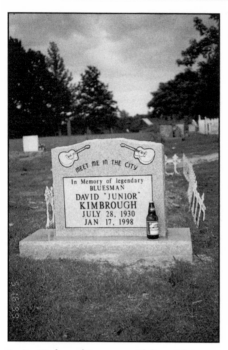

Ester Mae McDowell
1906–1980

Despite their identical middle names, Ester Mae is not the same person as Annie Mae McDowell, the wife who accompanied McDowell on his gospel recordings. Toward the end of his life, McDowell left Annie Mae for Ester Mae. He had no children with either wife, but Annie Mae's children are the heirs to whatever royalties his recordings and songs continue to generate.

Junior Kimbrough's grave, with beer left in tribute, Hudsonville

McDowell adapted the old spiritual "You Got to Move" to his style. His version was, in turn, covered by the Rolling Stones, making it by far the best-known song in McDowell's repertoire. His estate collected royalties on the Stones' cover, which appeared on their hit album *Sticky Fingers* in 1972, the year of McDowell's death. The back of his gravestone bears a verse from the song:

> *You may be high,*
> *You may be low,*
> *You may be rich, child*
> *You may be poor*
> *But when the Lord*
> *Gets ready*
> *You got to move*

Fred McDowell was born in 1906 in Rossville, Tennessee. He took up guitar at about age twenty and moved to Memphis in the late 1920s, but somehow was not among the many bluesmen recorded in that era. He moved to Hudsonville, Mississippi, in

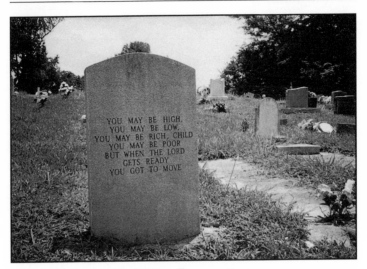

Back side of Mississippi Fred McDowell's grave, Como

about 1940 and to Como in the 1950s. He played strictly locally until 1959, when Alan Lomax stopped by and recorded him. A few years later, Chris Strachwitz of Arhoolie Records also recorded McDowell, and his career took off.

In the 1960s, McDowell performed at colleges and festivals throughout the United States and Europe. But he continued to live in a trailer in Como, where fans and aspiring musicians—including Bonnie Raitt, who based her slide style on his—would stop by to visit and listen to him play. And, despite his international success, McDowell continued to work at the Stuckey's store and gas station that stood on the southeast corner of Highway 310 and Interstate 55. His agent, Dick Waterman, once asked him why he kept the job.

"All my friends are here, so you know I'm going to be here," McDowell told him. "There's nothing for me to do at that trailer all day. And if a car comes in and needs gas, I might as well go fill it up. I'm going to be here anyway. They give me thirty-two dollars a week, and I'm just *stealing* that money, Dick." Stuckey's also served as an office for McDowell, who did not have a telephone at home. The other employees got used to receiving calls from people with strange accents: "We got Paris, France, on the phone, Fred."

Gravel Springs

- ## Othar Turner's Picnics
  (662) 562-7606

  To get there: Take Interstate 55 to the Como exit (number 257) and proceed east, away from the town of Como, on Highway 310. After 2½ miles, turn north onto Hunter Chapel Road. The road's name changes to Gravel Springs Road when you cross the county line. Keep going, 4 miles total, over a narrow wood bridge and past Hunter Chapel on your right, until you get to the first stop sign, O. B. McClinton Road. Turn right and drive about half a mile, until you see a lot of parked cars and hear music. Park on the road and walk onto the farm, on the south side of the road. (This is a private residence. Please don't drop in anytime except on the picnic weekend.)

Of the many astounding discoveries of Alan Lomax's long and illustrious career—including making the first recordings of Muddy Waters and Fred McDowell—Lomax considers the discovery of the African American fife-and-drum tradition his major accomplishment.

The origins of this music remain obscure. It sounds nothing like the martial fife-and-drum sound associated with colonial New England. And the fife used by black southerners is not carved from wood, but cut from natural cane. The cane is hollowed out, and the finger holes are burned in, with a hot poker. The player blows the fife flute-style, creating a soaring sound that can be heard over the drums for miles around. Two snare drummers and a bass drummer keep the swinging beat.

The music is associated with summer picnics, held on farms in the North Mississippi hills. Animals are butchered and barbecued; beer and moonshine are served; the fife and drums play; and the people dance, drawn to the festivities by the sound of the music. "And I didn't want to miss nothing," recalled John Bowden, who was born in the area in 1903 and played fife until the 1970s. "I hear a drum hit, and, man, I just, *whew,* I'd have a fit."

Lomax discovered fife-and-drum music at one of these picnics, hosted by Sid Hemphill in 1942 (Hemphill's granddaughter, Jessie Mae Hemphill, played drum in fife-and-drum groups and also was a fine blues singer-guitarist until her retirement in the mid-1990s). The picnics were common in those days. Now the tradition remains in the hands of one remarkable family.

The head of the family who carries on the tradition was Othar Turner, who died February 26, 2003, at the age of ninety-four. He made and played a mean fife (or "fice," as he pronounced it), sang the blues and spirituals, and led the world's premier fife-and-drum ensemble, the Rising Star Fife and Drum Band. Turner was also, in the 1980s, perhaps the unlikeliest-ever guest on the television program *Mister Rogers' Neighborhood.* Drummers Abe Young and Jessie Mae Hemphill accompanied him on the show.

The group usually included at least one of Turner's children and one of his grandchildren. Throughout his later years, Turner showed no sign of imminent retirement, but there was another talented fife player waiting in the wings—his granddaughter Sharda Thomas, born in 1990, who has mastered the physically demanding instrument and also has the poise, confidence, and charisma to lead the band and charm the listeners.

Besides doing farm work and playing music, Turner also threw great picnics at his farm. Despite Turner's death, the family still holds the annual picnics on the last weekend of August. They feature live music from the family band, which alternates sets with electric blues jams by local musicians or perhaps a disc jockey. Home-raised goat and pig barbecue is served, along with coleslaw and cold beer or soft drinks to wash it down.

The picnics last all weekend, starting on Friday night, picking up again Saturday afternoon and going way into the night, and then again on Sunday. Admission is free, and food and drink are sold at very reasonable prices.

People stand around and talk with friends, drink, eat, dance, and laugh. As the night goes on, the dancing becomes wilder. The fife-and-drum musicians move slowly around the lot as they play, and the dancers follow them, gyrating in response and spurring on the musicians to keep the beat going. These are community events, held so that the neighbors can have fun. Visitors from outside are welcome. But don't expect things to happen when you want them to. This is a picnic, not a concert. And you are a guest, not a customer. Relax, be friendly, have fun, and ask permission before sticking a camera in someone's face.

Sardis

- ## Sardis Courthouse
  215 Pocahontas St. (Pocahontas is parallel to and just across the railroad tracks from Main St.)

Sardis no longer has a county jail. Prisoners are taken to the jail at the other county seat, Batesville. But before this building was built in 1972, the site had an old courthouse dating from the early 1900s, with a jail behind it.

That jail is where Robert Lockwood, Jr., and Sonny Boy Williamson II were sentenced to twenty-one days for vagrancy in about 1935. As Lockwood later told writer Robert Palmer, they were locked up on a Friday:

> On Saturday, we went up on the second floor and raised the jailhouse windows and started playing. In a matter of minutes, the jailhouse was surrounded with people. There was a little fence down there, about as big as the one on the side of my yard, and the people started throwing nickels and dimes and quarters over that fence. The trusty went out there and picked the money up, and we knew he didn't bring it all to us. We knew *he* got fat, but when he turned it in to us, we had made four hundred dollars. That day. The next night, the high sheriff and the deputy sheriff came and asked us did we want to go out and make some money. Sid and Ed was their names. And for the next twenty-one days, they took us out to serenade for the whites, every night but Sunday. They'd take up the money for us, pass the hat, make the people not put nothin' less than a dollar in it. And then they'd take us back and put us in jail. Now, mind you, they was bustin' places for corn whiskey right and left, and they gave us a whole gallon of that. We had girls comin' to the jailhouse and spendin' the night. We was eatin' from a hotel down the street. So it really wasn't like bein' in no jailhouse. But it was terrible 'cause it was against our will.

The town still has a historic downtown, reminiscent of what it must have looked like when Lockwood and Sonny Boy were there playing the jailhouse blues.

Hernando-Nesbit

- ## Gus Cannon's Grave

  To get there: From Interstate 55, take exit 284, Nesbit Road–N. Hernando. Go west onto Pleasant Hill Road. Drive 0.2 mile to Highway 51 and turn right. One mile up the road, on the left, there is a large cemetery between two churches, across from the Place Pub. The first church is Oak Grove M. B., 2541 N. Highway 51. Cannon is buried about halfway back from the road and a quarter of the way in from the right.

He has two stones—one upright and one flat. The upright one has an engraved drawing of a jug over a banjo and says:

Gus Cannon 1874–1979
Baby Let Your Mind Roll On
Composer—songwriter—jug band pioneer
Pride of Memphis—Beale Street Balladeer

The small flat stone, right in front of the large upright one, reads:

Gus Cannon
September, 1875
Oct. 15, 1979
May he rest in peace.

Note that the two stones disagree on the year of Cannon's birth—and both might be way off. Most sources list September 12, 1885, as the date of his birth. Whichever date is correct, Gus Cannon was one of the oldest blues singers to record. His main instrument, the banjo, predates the guitar in African American musical tradition. Cannon also played the jug, on a rack around his neck. With the incredible harpist Noah Lewis and guitarist Ashley Thompson, Cannon formed Cannon's Jug Stompers. They were a premier jug band of the 1920s, with such hits as "Walk Right In" and "Viola Lee Blues."

• Joe Callicott's Grave

To get there: Callicott's grave is near Interstate 55's exit 284, the same exit as Gus Cannon's grave, but they are on opposite sides of the interstate. To get to Callicott's, head east on Pleasant Hill Road for 3.2 miles, to Getwell Road, and turn left. Go 0.4 mile to Mount Olive C. M. E. Church, on the left. Park at the church and go up the sidewalk that leads into the small cemetery north of it. Walk straight in from where the sidewalk ends. Callicott's grave is almost at the far side.

The stone reads:

JESUS ON MY BOND
Mississippi
Joe
Callicott
1899–1969
An original medicine show 'songster' who played through
the vast Delta from 1918 until his death
Recorded for Arhoolie Records

Handmade grave marker in cemetery where bluesman Joe Callicott is buried, Mount Olive C. M. E. Church, Pleasant Hill

This cemetery has quite a few hand-carved or hand-painted stones that you might find interesting. Callicott's headstone, however, like those of many blues singers, was professionally inscribed, and is bigger and more modern than most of those around it. This is not because blues artists' families have the means for such extravagance, but because the stones are usually erected by fans or record companies, often long after the musician's death.

"Mississippi" Joe Callicott was born in Nesbit, lived there most of his life, and is buried there. Callicott was friends with Frank Stokes and Garfield Akers, fellow North Mississippi bluesmen. He recorded "Traveling Mama Blues" and "Fare Thee Well Blues" in 1930—his only recording session until 1967, a few years before his death, when folklorist George Mitchell tracked him down in Nesbit and recorded him. One of Callicott's songs from the later session, which he called "Love My Baby Blues," has been covered by Ry Cooder as "France Chance." Callicott's complete recorded works are available on *Mississippi Delta Blues, Vol. 2, "Blow My Blues Away."*

RECOMMENDED READING

Albertson, Chris. *Bessie.* New York: Stein and Day, 1972.

Booth, Stanley. *Rythm Oil: A Journey through the Music of the American South.* New York: Pantheon Books, 1991.

Bowman, Rob. Booklet in *Malaco Records: The Last Soul Company* (CD box set). Jackson, Miss.: Malaco Records, 1999.

———. *Soulsville, U.S.A.: The Story of Stax Records.* New York: Schirmer Books, 1997.

Broonzy, William. *Big Bill Blues: William Broonzy's Story as Told to Yannick Bruynoghe.* New York: Da Capo Press, 1992.

Calt, Stephen. *I'd Rather Be the Devil: Skip James and the Blues.* New York: Da Capo Press, 1994.

Calt, Stephen, and Gayle Dean Wardlow. *King of the Delta Blues: The Life and Music of Charlie Patton.* Newton, N.J.: Rock Chapel Press, 1988.

Charters, Samuel. *The Blues Makers.* New York: Da Capo Press, 1991.

Danchin, Sebastian. *'Blues Boy': The Life and Music of B. B. King.* Jackson: University Press of Mississippi, 1998.

Davis, Francis. *The History of the Blues: The Roots, the Music, the People from Charley Patton to Robert Cray.* New York: Hyperion, 1995.

Doughty, Junior. "Junior's Juke Joint." Web site. www.deltablues.net

Edwards, Honeyboy (as told to Janis Martinson and Michael Robert Frank). *The World Don't Owe Me Nothing: The Life and Times of Delta Bluesman Honeyboy Edwards.* Chicago: Chicago Review Press, 1997.

Erlewine, Michael, Vladimir Bogdanov, Chris Woodstra, and Cub Koda, eds. *AMG All Music Guide to the Blues: The Experts' Guide to the Best Blues Recordings*. San Francisco: Miller Freeman Books, 1996.

Evans, David. *Big Road Blues: Tradition and Creativity in the Folk Blues*. Berkeley: University of California Press, 1982.

Ferris, William. *Blues from the Delta*. New York: Da Capo Press, 1984.

Garon, Paul, and Beth Garon. *Woman with Guitar: Memphis Minnie's Blues*. New York: Da Capo Press, 1992.

Guralnick, Peter. *Last Train to Memphis: The Rise of Elvis Presley*. Boston: Little, Brown and Co., 1994.

———. *Searching for Robert Johnson*. New York: E. P. Dutton, 1989.

Handy, W. C. *Father of the Blues: An Autobiography*. New York: Da Capo Press, 1941.

King, B. B., with David Ritz. *Blues All Around Me: The Autobiography of B. B. King*. New York: Avon Books, 1996.

LaVere, Stephen C. Liner notes to *Robert Johnson: The Complete Recordings*. New York: Columbia Records, 1990.

Levine, Lawrence W. *Black Culture and Black Consciousness: Afro-American Folk Thought from Slavery to Freedom*. New York: Oxford University Press, 1977.

Lomax, Alan. *The Land Where the Blues Began*. New York: Pantheon Books, 1993.

McKee, Margaret, and Fred Chisenhall. *Beale Black & Blue*. Baton Rouge: Louisiana State University Press, 1981.

Mitchell, George. *Blow My Blues Away*. Baton Rouge: Louisiana State University Press, 1971.

Oliver, Paul. *Blues Fell This Morning: Meaning in the Blues*. New York: Cambridge University Press, 1960.

———. *Conversation with the Blues*. New York: Cambridge University Press, 1965.

———. *The Story of the Blues*. Boston: Northeastern University Press, 1969.

Oshinsky, David M. *"Worse than Slavery": Parchman Farm and the Ordeal of Jim Crow Justice*. New York: Free Press, 1996.

Palmer, Robert. *Deep Blues*. New York: Penguin, 1981.

Peabody, Charles. "Notes on Negro Music." *Journal of American Folk-Lore* 16 (1903): 148–52.

Raichelson, Richard M. *Beale Street Talks: A Walking Tour Down the Home of the Blues*. Memphis: Arcadia Records, 1994.

Ryan, Marc. *Trumpet Records: An Illustrated History with Discography*. Milford, N. H.: Big Nickel Productions, 1992.

Thompson, Robert Farris. *Flash of the Spirit: African and Afro-American Art and Philosophy*. New York: Vintage Books, 1984.

Tooze, Sandra B. *Muddy Waters: The Mojo Man*. Toronto: ECW Press, 1997.

Trynka, Paul. *Portrait of the Blues*. New York: Da Capo Press, 1996.

Wardlow, Gayle Dean. *Chasin' That Devil Music: Searching for the Blues*. San Francisco: Miller Freeman, 1998.

Wilson, Charles Reagan, and William Ferris. *Encyclopedia of Southern Culture*. Chapel Hill: University of North Carolina Press, 1989.

RECOMMENDED LISTENING

To get in the mood for your trip, to listen to as you drive down Highway 61, and to bring back memories when you get home, here are some recordings to get you started in the Mississippi blues. The albums on this list include great music by most of the artists discussed in this book. All are available on CD and highly recommended by the author.

Cannon's Jug Stompers, *Cannon's Jug Stompers (1927–1930)*. Herwin 208. One of the rare banjo players in the blues (sometimes he even used a slide on it), Gus Cannon worked with the extraordinary harpist Noah Lewis and other musicians to create these charming, often beautiful songs that they stomped out on the streets of Memphis.

Bo Carter, *Greatest Hits, 1930–1940*. Yazoo 1014. The prolific but now-underappreciated Carter was one of the dominant bluesmen of the 1930s, combining dazzling and unusual guitar work with erotically teasing lyrics. This collection includes a few tunes by the Mississippi Sheiks, a string band that Carter belonged to part time.

John Lee Hooker, *The Legendary Modern Recordings 1948– 1954*. Virgin 39658. Hooker, a Clarksdale native, has probably made more recordings and more money than any other bluesman. This is the one to get for a full dose of that heavy, foot-stomping, solo electric-guitar boogie. It's a sound imitated by many, but no one else does it like this.

Mississippi John Hurt, *Avalon Blues: The Complete 1928 Okeh Recordings.* Sony 64986. "Well sir, I just make it sound like I think it should," is how Hurt once explained his prodigious, unique talents to an interviewer. Although he remained a fine performer right up to his death in 1966, these recordings (cleaned up sonically) are the ones that established his warm, folksy style and deceptively intricate guitar playing.

Robert Johnson, *King of the Delta Blues Singers.* Columbia/Legacy CK 65746. Sixteen tracks by the late-1930s artist whose life, myth, and music epitomize the blues for many people. This clean-sounding collection leaves out the back-to-back alternate tracks that make some other Johnson sets laborious to listen to.

Frank Frost, *Jelly Roll Blues.* Paula 20. In the mid-1960s, when everyone thought the blues' heart had moved to Chicago, out came this laid-back but thoroughly modern set from Helena, Arkansas bluesman Frost—with the great, rarely recorded Arthur Williams on harp.

Skip James, *Complete Early Recordings.* Yazoo 2009. The eerie, otherworldly sounds of this enigmatic Bentonia singer-guitarist-pianist are something everyone needs to hear. James recorded again in the 1960s, but these 1931 recordings are his most brilliant. Some of the tracks are quite scratchy, but the music is masterful.

Paul "Wine" Jones, *Mule.* Epitaph 80305. This album of powerful, 1990s electric jook-joint blues has a raw, unfinished quality that only adds to its appeal. As they used to suggest on 1960s rock albums—play this record at maximum volume!

Junior Kimbrough, *All Night Long.* Fat Possum 1002. With his son Kinney on drums and neighbor Garry Burnside (son of bluesman R. L.) on bass, Junior Kimbrough's first album, which he didn't make until he was in his 60s, captures the feel of this North Mississippi bluesman's hypnotic, deceptively simple sound.

Albert King, *King of the Blues Guitar.* Atlantic 8213–2. This one has King backed by Booker T and the MGs and the Memphis Horns—the Stax sound at its bluesiest. The CD includes all of King's classic LP *Born Under a Bad Sign,* plus all of his Stax singles.

B. B. King, *Great Moments with B. B. King.* MCA MCAD–4124. There is a baffling array of B. B. King CDs available, but this compilation of his 1960s work is a good one to start with. It includes a live version of his "Gambler's Blues," which kicks off with a long, burning guitar solo that might be his best ever.

Fred and Annie Mae McDowell, *My Home Is in the Delta.* Testament 2208 Fred McDowell's rock-solid North Mississippi sound continues to resonate through his influence on R. L. Burnside, Junior Kimbrough, Bonnie Raitt, and others, as well as through his own large catalog of powerful recordings. This haunting collection, with his wife helping on vocals, offers blues and spirituals.

Memphis Jug Band, *Memphis Jug Band.* Yazoo 1067. On the verge of chaos but somehow always right, this great jug band featured funny lyrics, snappy vocal interplay, harp and kazoo solos soaring over the guitars, and, anchoring it all, that booming jug bass line.

Memphis Minnie, *Bumble Bee.* Indigo 2005. A good sampling by this prolific, influential but often underrated guitar virtuoso and hip blueswoman who was one of the dominant blues artists of the 1930s. "When the Levee Breaks," "Black Rat Swing," and the dazzling instrumental "Let's Go to Town" are among the many classic tracks here.

Little Milton, *Greatest Hits.* Malaco 7477. Milton Campbell had made some wild music for Sun in the 1950s, but the 1960s' Chess tracks on this album capture the period when he had found his own voice and was turning out exquisite work such as "Annie Mae's Café," "The Blues Is Alright" and "Walking the Backstreets and Crying." One of the blues' finest electric guitarists and singers, Milton for some reason has yet to "cross over" to white American and foreign audiences the way his old buddy B. B. King has.

Little Brother Montgomery, *Complete Recorded Works (1930–1936).* Document 5109. This Louisiana singer-pianist became a Chicago blues fixture from the 1940s on. Before that, he spent a lot of time in Mississippi—especially Jackson and Vicksburg, the riverside town that inspired him to write the lovely "Vicksburg Blues." Montgomery was a virtuoso who has influenced every other blues pianist since.

Charley Patton, *Founder of the Delta Blues.* Yazoo 1020. To ears accustomed to modern recordings, it will take awhile to get past the surface scratches (yes, even on a CD—these were mastered from worn 78s, since no masters survived) and muddy recording values. But take the time and let your ears adjust and hear the music. Patton was the Delta blues' first star, and still one of the most impassioned artists ever to enter a studio. His songs are varied, intricate, entertaining, and inimitable.

Lonnie Pitchford, *All Around Man*. Rooster Blues 2629. This dazzling 1994 album presents the awesomely talented young bluesman on Robert Johnson–style acoustic numbers, full-band electric blues, one-string romps, introspective piano, and even fake harmonica. Unfortunately Pitchford died (in 1998 at age 43) before he could make a second album—but he sure packs a ton of music into this one.

Jimmie Rodgers, *The Essential Jimmie Rodgers*. RCA 67500. White blues did not begin with Stevie Ray Vaughan or even with Elvis Presley, as this collection proves. This white Mississippian became a huge pop star in the late 1920s and is still credited as the Father of *Country* Music. Yet he was actually singing his own style of the blues, with yodels added.

Bobby Rush, *Best of Bobby Rush*. La Jam 6. There isn't yet a good representation culled from Rush's hundreds of recordings, many of which are no longer in print. This one includes a few of the chittlin' circuit king's suggestive hits—"Sue" and "What's Good for the Goose . . . "—but misses many others. Pick it up to hold you over until you get to see his live show. Featuring booty-shaking dancers, frequent costume changes, hilarious stories and interplay with the audience, a Rush show is something that can never really be captured on a recording, anyway.

Bessie Smith, *Essential Bessie Smith*. Columbia/Legacy 64922. Although she was born in Chattanooga, Tennessee, the Empress of the Blues died in Mississippi and often performed here. This two-CD set is a good introduction to this powerful, sophisticated-yet-downhome singer of sassy, witty songs, who fit into both the blues and jazz worlds.

James "Son" Thomas, *Beefsteak Blues*. Evidence 26095. This high-voiced downhome bluesman was beloved throughout Mississippi and, in the final decade before his 1993 death, to festival-goers throughout the world. Yet there is not much of his work available on commercial recordings. This collection gives a good sample of his electric and acoustic playing, and a glimpse of his eccentric personality.

Mose Vinson, *Piano Man.* Center for Southern Folklore. Born in 1917, this piano man played at countless jooks and parties, sat in on many of the classic Sun recordings of the 1940s and 1950s (he worked at the studio as a janitor but his musical ability was noticed), and in his final years was the house act at Memphis's Center for Southern Folklore. He waited until 1997 to release his first solo album. It is worth the wait.

Muddy Waters, *The Complete Plantation Recordings.* MCA 9344. This fascinating recording captures Waters in 1941–42, before he left Stovall's plantation (outside Clarksdale) to move to Chicago and plug in his guitar. There are solo and group acoustic pieces, and interviews with Waters by Alan Lomax and John Work (Waters, thinking the Library of Congress folklorists were revenuers out to bust him for moonshining, gives brief answers).

Muddy Waters, *His Best: 1947–1955.* Chess/MCA 9370. This one gives you the magnificent music Waters made after his move to Chicago. All of the classics such as "Rollin' and Tumblin'," "I Can't Be Satisfied," "I Just Want to Make Love to You," and "Rollin' Stone" are here. Fellow Mississippians Willie Dixon, Jimmy Rogers, and Otis Spann are part of Waters's Chicago band, along with the exquisite Louisiana-born harpist Little Walter. If you own only one blues album, this should be the one.

Bukka White, *The Complete Bukka White.* Columbia CK–52782. Solo or accompanied by Washboard Sam, White sang his heart out and pounded away at his metal guitar on this collection of personal songs he recorded just after his release from Parchman prison in 1940.

Big Joe Williams, *Shake Your Boogie.* Arhoolie CD–315. Ancient-sounding yet always fresh, Big Joe was a true original who added three extra strings to his guitar and then played it percussively. He also had a wry humor, a knack for writing topical songs, and even a flair for religious material. These recordings from the 1960s capture his essence.

Sonny Boy Williamson II, *King Biscuit Time.* Arhoolie CD–310. This one includes Sonny Boy's early 1950s classics such as "Nine Below Zero," "Eyesight to the Blind," and "Mighty Long Time" (with the amazing Cliff Bivens *singing* the bass part); a piece of a live King Biscuit Time radio broadcast; "Sonny Boy's Christmas Blues"; and a great cover photo.

Howlin' Wolf, *Howlin' Wolf/Moanin' in the Moonlight*. MCA/Chess 5908. Wolf's growling vocals, moans, harp, and killer band-leading make him, along with Muddy Waters, one of the architects of Chicago blues. Most of the songs here have been covered by dozens of blues and rock acts, but there's really no duplicating Wolf's magic. Wolf's lead guitarist, Hubert Sumlin, was Eric Clapton's idol—and this collection shows why.

Various artists, *Blues Masters, Volume 12: Memphis Blues*. Rhino 71129. A terrific intro to Memphis blues and jug-band music from the 1920s through the 1950s. Includes the Beale Street Sheiks' "Mr. Crump Don't Like It," B. B. King's very early "When Your Baby Packs Up and Goes" (before he became a lead-guitar soloist), and great tracks by Furry Lewis, Rufus Thomas, Howlin' Wolf and others.

Various artists, *Masters of the Delta Blues: The Friends of Charlie Patton*. Yazoo 2002. A wonderful collection of the giants of the early Delta blues— Son House, Tommy Johnson, Louise Johnson, Bukka White, Willie Brown, and the mysterious Kid Bailey. With this and a Charley Patton CD, you'll have a good picture of Mississippi blues in the 1920s and early 1930s.

Various artists, *Mississippi Delta Blues "Blow My Blues Away,"* *Vol. 2*. Arhoolie CD 402. This album presents the amazing first recordings of R. L. Burnside, on acoustic guitar at his home in 1967. Joe Callicott, a North Mississippi artist who recorded in 1930 and then again in the sixties, also is included here. And as a bonus, there are a few electric covers of Tommy Johnson songs by the Houston Stackhouse/Robert Nighthawk/Peck Curtis trio.

Various artists, *Sun Records Collection*. Rhino 71780. This three-CD set gives you Elvis Presley's early, bluesy tracks and puts them in context with all the great blues, rockabilly, and country-Western that came out of Sam Phillips's studio. B. B. King, Jerry Lee Lewis, Charlie Rich, Howlin' Wolf, Rufus Thomas, "Doctor" Isaiah Ross, Carl Perkins, Rosco Gordon, Roy Orbison, Little Milton, Carl Mann, Sleepy John Estes, and Johnny Cash are all here.

INDEX

References to illustrations appear in *italics*.